Becoming a Healthy Church

Ten Traits of a Vital Ministry

Foreword by Haddon Robinson

Afterword by Gordon MacDonald

Stephen A. Macchia

BakerBooks
Grand Rapids, Michigan

Published by Baker Books
a division of Baker Publishing Group
P.O. Box 6287, Grand Rapids, MI 49516-6287
www.bakerbooks.com

Paperback edition published 2003

Printed in the United States of America

Library of Congress Cataloging-in-Publication Data is on file at the Library of Congress in Washington, D.C.

ISBN 10: 0-8010-1177-9 (cloth)
ISBN 978-0-8010-1177-1 (cloth)

ISBN 10: 0-8010-6503-8 (pbk.)
ISBN 978-0-8010-6503-3 (pbk.)

Scripture is taken from the HOLY BIBLE, NEW INTERNATIONAL VERSION®. NIV®. Copyright © 1973, 1978, 1984 by International Bible Society. Used by permission of Zondervan. All rights reserved.

The poem "SMART" by Shel Silverstein on p. 203 is copyright © 1974 by Evil Eye Music, Inc. Used by permission of HarperCollins Publishers.

For my family—
Ruth, Nathan, and Rebekah Macchia

and

the Christian community
of New England

For those who forged a vibrant faith into a new
world yet unexplored; to those who live out their faith
in this generation; and for all who carry the torch into
the twenty-first century.
May we be found faithful to the task of being the
people of God serving those who need to hear eternal
words of hope.

Contents

Foreword

Play a word game with me. What comes to your mind when you read the word *church?*

Do you picture a steepled building, dark wooden pews, crosses, offering plates? Do you hear a deep-throated organ, a choir, hearty singing?

Or does *church* trigger childhood memories of wiggling through sermons, playing tag in the church basement, and Sunday school teachers telling stories about Samson and David and Daniel and, of course, Jesus—all of them about as real to you as Superman or Batman or the Lone Ranger?

Or do you experience again the flat taste of the bread and the sweet sting of grape juice or wine at communion? Do you remember a particular Sunday morning when a sermon gripped you as though you were the only one in the crowd, or the day you joined a church?

Or does *church* sketch other pictures on your mind? A baptism, a wedding, funerals, evangelistic services, going forward, confirmation, committee meetings, suppers served in Tupperware dishes, that time at camp when you determined God would have all of you.

When you read the word *church*, do you have good feelings? Like laughter? Warmth? A quietness? Acceptance? Happiness? Awe? Love? Closeness to God?

Or are your feelings negative? Like boredom? Anger? Confusion? Guilt? Rejection? Does *church* remind you of arrogance, hostility, manipulation, anger, or irrelevance? Do you think of it as a poor substitute for a picnic or a ball game on a rainy Sunday morning?

Church dredges up memories and emotions from deep within you, doesn't it? Some are healthy, some painful, most somewhere in between.

Have you noticed that when Christians think negatively about church, they think of "them" not "I"? Church is an institution out there, a group apart from them.

But *we* are the church, aren't we? You and I. We may have a personal faith, but we can't have an individual faith. We can't be Christians by ourselves. Every Christian, to be complete, must be a member of a body of men and women who are followers of Christ. Therefore, whether we are part of a vital, growing, glowing assembly of believers depends in some measure upon us.

Yet if we hope to make a difference in our churches, we need to know what a healthy church looks like. More important, we need to know how sick churches can be made well.

Steve Macchia loves the church and has invested a significant portion of his life asking the perceptive question, What's right with the church? He has studied vibrant, growing congregations in New England—a damaged spiritual environment if there ever was one—and has asked what makes healthy churches healthy. That's wise. If you want to learn to hit a baseball, it is better to study one .300 hitter than three .100 hitters. In the following pages, he tells us what he has found out. In the process, he may describe your church, for better or for worse. But he doesn't stop there. He also offers practical down-to-the-pew advice that you as a pastor, a leader, or a member can follow to make *church* one of the most positive words in your vocabulary.

—Haddon Robinson

Acknowledgments

Special thanks to the entire Vision New England family, who processed this new paradigm in light of timeless biblical principles and who inspire me with their love and faithfulness. Some of their stories are told in detail in this book, and I am grateful for their willingness to be included.

To the godly board of directors and fabulously gifted staff team of Vision New England—I love you all with a deep and profound affection in Christ. This book could never have been completed without the daily assistance of Carole Nason, David McKiel, Don Moberger, Dan White, Andrew Accardy, and the world's best story-finder and in-house editor, Les Stobbe. I am also grateful to the Strategic Planning Team, who masterminded the original ten characteristics of a healthy church with me, and my regional ministry colleagues who live them out in their respective churches. To Baker Book House, thanks for believing in the importance of this project.

Lots of love to my extended family for consistently living out a healthy lifestyle of unconditional love and forgiveness. In addition, four individuals who have since gone home to be with the Lord—my beloved mother, Ruth N. Macchia, as well as Ernie Tavilla, Hugh Corey, and Dick Crowell—tirelessly prayed for me, encouraged me, and believed in my abilities. My pastor, Gordon MacDonald, and my spiritual director, David Vryhof, are to be commended for their ongoing wisdom and prayerful affirmation. And where would I be today without my closest friends in life, who are my emotional mainstays; with specific appreciation to Paul Borthwick, Bob Ludwig, Iain Whitfield, Kevin Parke, Henry TePaske, Dennis Veen, Bob Massie, Rich Plass, Dennis Baril, and David Midwood.

Finally, and most significantly, I owe a mountain of gratitude to my precious wife, Ruth, and my wonderful children, Nathan and Rebekah, for their abiding love and unwavering support—this one's for you!

Preface

Late one September Friday, only eighteen months into my new assignment as president of Vision New England (formerly EANE—the Evangelistic Association of New England), I found myself in an unusual predicament. I had left Boston's Logan International Airport thinking I was headed for St. John, New Brunswick, Canada, to teach an evangelism training seminar in a church the following morning.

After I arrived, I wandered around the airport looking for a Howard Johnson's sign in the baggage claim area. I had been told there would be a courtesy phone near the bright blue and orange sign. I could use it to call for the shuttle to whisk me to the hotel for a comfortable night of sleep. Being a typically stubborn New England man, I was steadfast in my commitment not to ask for help. I could find a bright blue and orange sign all on my own, thank you very much.

When I finally agreed with my hunch that indeed there was no HoJo's sign, I sought the help of an AirCanada official. She politely heard my story and informed me there were no Howard Johnson's in St. John's. I insisted there must be, waving my reservation sheet in her face. She stood there long enough to figure out I was in the wrong airport, in fact in the wrong city, and even more significantly, in the wrong province of Canada! Much to my surprise, I discovered that I had landed in St. John's, Newfoundland, instead! I needed to be in St. John (no *s*)—in another province—the next morning. I humbly swallowed my pride and thanked her for her assistance. She went the extra mile, escorting me to the AirCanada desk to book me on a flight early the next morning.

Earlier that evening, on the plane, I had devoured Stephen Covey's *The Seven Habits of Highly Effective People*. Standing in the airport at St. John's, I realized I was far from being effective—never mind efficient! That irony was coupled with another stark realization. This experience was a picture of my life. I was figuratively hopping on one wrong airplane after another, landing in one wrong town after another. They were all good planes and good locations, but they were the wrong planes and destinations for me. I became desperate to know how God wanted me to respond to this realization.

I spent the next several months realigning my life according to God's principles. Even though I had been in pastoral ministry for nearly a dozen years at that time, I had never gone through such an intensive self-evaluation. For the first time in years I discovered what God's mission looks like for me and the ministry I was called to lead and to serve.

This experience of self-evaluation was the beginning of three strategic planning processes that we have undertaken together at Vision New England. We have been successful in weeding out certain aspects of our ministry, reinvigorating others, and adding new initiatives to move us forward in our shared ministry in the region. The evaluation process has been difficult, sometimes painful, yet it has transformed the team and the ministry.

What emerged in our months of strategic dialogue and discussion was that we needed to ask ourselves some hard questions about the state of the church, God's vehicle for carrying the message of hope to needy people. For Vision New England to be effective in serving the church, we needed to determine the healthiness of the vehicle that would be transporting the message and the people. It was time to take a look at every aspect of the vehicle God had designed to serve in this way—a vehicle that, frankly, needed some serious maintenance.

We asked ourselves what a truly healthy church looks like today. Is it one with strong preaching? A great choir? Lots of wealthy executives in the pews? An effective Sunday school program? A thriving missions program? As we studied what a healthy church looks like, we realized we had identified ten characteristics of a healthy church. This book is the outgrowth of those discussions, several years of field testing, and two major surveys. What will knowing the ten characteristics of a healthy church do for you? They will give you as pastors and church leaders an approach that will revitalize your ministry.

This outline of health, however, is not program-based or prescriptive in any specific manner but is written so that any biblically based congregation can utilize it regardless of local church size, denominational affiliation, ethnic diversity, geographic representation, or type of community. All characteristics are written in language that's universally accepted in most churches, regardless of denomination. They have been field tested in hundreds of churches, taught in seminars and classes, and respected by thousands of pastors and leaders who have requested the brochure and the accompanying evaluation tool created and published by Vision New England.

You will discover that the focus of this book is on principles and stories, not on models. The timeless truths of God's Word inform and instruct every one of the ten principles, and each of the characteristics are presented in story form. We are convinced that when we set up models for churches to follow, they are doomed to fail or at best be successful for a short time. It's time we move away from trying to be carbon copies of our superheroes (and their respective churches). Instead, let's begin to tirelessly pursue God's defined mission and ministry, based on principles that work as they are fashioned and lived out in our unique settings and "for such a time as this." We need the resources, ideas, suggestions, and approaches that our "models" provide without trying to "do church" exactly like they are.

I recognize that our Ten Characteristics of a Healthy Church is not an exhaustive list. In fact, we have said all along that you may want to add characteristics that reflect your church's background, denomination, and theological persuasion. The bottom line for us is that we serve as a catalyst for churchwide evaluation that begins with the pastor and leadership team and works its way outward to the broader church family. The suggested principles in this book are designed as a discussion starter for the development of your ministry—a ministry that only God through his Spirit will be able to construct with you. If we have induced you to pursue this evaluative process, we will trust the Holy Spirit to bring new health and vitality to your church.

Let me suggest that you consider a number of venues for discussing the ten characteristics of a healthy church with your church leaders and members.

1. Take the next three to twelve months to discuss each characteristic with the key lay leaders of your local congregation. Each chapter concludes with questions that will be helpful aids in this process.
2. Use the ten characteristics of a healthy church as the basis for a leadership retreat sometime within the next six to twelve months. Devote large blocks of time to prayerfully studying each characteristic before translating it into the context of your ministry.
3. Urge the adults of your congregation to study the ten characteristics in small groups gathered throughout the week or in an adult class setting.
4. Encourage the youth and children of your congregation to reflect with you on their experiences in each of the characteristics, and listen carefully to their recommendations for the future design of your church's ministry.
5. Ask each major committee of your church to consider in-depth one of the characteristics that is most specifically applicable to their area of responsibility (i.e., the music and worship commit-

tee to discuss God-Exalting Worship; the Christian education committee to discuss Learning and Growing in Community; the deacons to discuss Wise Administration and Accountability, etc.). Invite each subcommittee to share the results of their deliberations with the whole church—in a special meeting, via newsletters, or in small group meetings.

6. Create your own agenda for how you will cover this material in your context, and let me know how it goes. It's amazing what emerges when we are guided and gifted by his Spirit, especially when he tells you how to proceed!

My hope and prayer is that this book will serve as an encouragement to pastors and church leaders. The research we have done was designed as a service to those who are leading the church into the twenty-first century. We have come to recognize that if a church is to be healthy and vital, it needs to be led by a pastor and leadership team who are themselves pursuing health in their personal lives and in their shared leadership capacity. Only then will a local church become the vibrant, healthy entity God intends.

Are you searching your own St. John's airport for the HoJo's sign? If so, then be bold enough to ask for some help. There may be need for realignment, evaluation, and a rediscovery of God's mission for you and your church. It may feel a bit awkward and humbling to start with, but there's hope for your journey. Let's walk together through some exciting principles that are sure to breathe new life into your daily life in Christ and your shared experience as the Body of Christ. Press on, hold fast, buckle up, and enjoy the ride!

Lord, you have searched us and you know us. You discern our needs and desire to walk with us through the peaks and valleys of our life with you. You have given us the responsibility to care for the church, to learn how to love her like you do. You have promised to be faithful, and today we pledge to be faithful in return. Reveal yourself to us as you illumine our hearts with your wisdom and ways. Help us to move forward in faith, believing that you have our very best interests in mind. Do the healing work in us that's needed if we are to serve and lead in the healthiest manner possible. It is only by your grace that this will happen. We put our trust in you today. For Jesus' sake. Amen.

1

Essential Ingredients of a Healthy Ministry

What would you say constitutes the foundation of a healthy church ministry? Many slogans suggest ideas, but wouldn't you agree that the Word of God and prayer are fundamental? They are two of God's greatest gifts to us. In them we find comfort, direction, and hope. In them we discover God through his Spirit. In them we grow in our relationship with our Savior. In them we learn about where we have come from and who we are to become today.

This came home to me with new power when my beloved mother suffered a massive stroke. My father found her collapsed in her small bathroom across the hall from her bedroom. She had just had back surgery five days earlier and was feeling great now that the crippling pain was gone. The surgery was considered a success—until the blood clot that formed in her arteries was thrust to the right hemisphere of her brain.

My mother was admitted into the ICU, fully medicated yet somewhat alert, and my father, my sisters, and I gathered around her bed. Her roaming eyes showed that she knew who was there—the four people she loved the most. Before we had to leave, she made a request that startled all of us—she wanted to recite the Twenty-third Psalm and pray the Lord's Prayer. With glassy eyes, clammy hands, and stammering words, we gave it our best and were able to get out most of the words. While we were struggling to recite Scripture and pray our favorite prayer, my mother, even in her weakened state, was able to move her lips and didn't skip a word. And in the months that followed that infamous day in our lives, her greatest comfort was found in the reading of Scripture and in times of prayer.

Scripture and Prayer Are Essential

Yes, the Scriptures and prayer are the bedrock of our existence as Christ's followers, yesterday, today, and forever. Both the study of, reflection on, and obedience to the Word of God and the cultivation of our relationship with the Almighty One in prayer are to permeate our experience and expression as Christians.

When the Ten Characteristics of a Healthy Church was written, we decided not to give the Scriptures and prayer their own separate categories. We believed it would indicate that the Bible and prayer are distinct aspects of our individual and church experiences, separate from the wider context of our lives. Instead, you will see that the centrality of the Bible and prayer is in every one of the ten characteristics. They are essential ingredients for our personal lives and for our community worship, ministry, and life together.

In our recent survey of 1,899 Christians, most people strongly agreed that local churches should "be prayerful in all aspects of church life and ministry" as well as be "reliant upon God's power and the authority of his Word." With nine points being the highest, prayerfulness got a mean score of 8.71, and God's power and Word got a mean score of 8.84.

Strangely, though Scripture and prayer are highly valued, they are more often promoted than practiced. We not only need to reinvigorate our congregations toward greater biblical literacy, but we must reevaluate our traditional view of prayer meetings and introduce prayer into every context of the ministry.

Immanuel Baptist Church in Chelmsford, Massachusetts, has managed to do both. They see Scripture as the script for worship, and preaching as its main application. They place the highest priority on creatively integrating the Word of God into the morning worship services. Pastor Gary Moore says, "Our morning service is so permeated by the Word of God that it becomes for us a window to heaven. As we encounter the God of Scripture, in his holiness we are reminded of our sinfulness; in his mercy we find forgiveness; in his majesty we find cause for praise and adoration. We are empowered by the Word for life as we sing it, read it, and hear it preached in worship."

This priority of knowing and living the Word of God permeates every ministry of Immanuel Baptist, which offers a multitude of significant programs. Personally, Pastor Moore gives a great amount of time to helping individuals grow in Scripture knowledge and theology. On Wednesday mornings he meets with a small group of men for personal discipling. Every other Wednesday evening, he has been helping another group of men take a historical look at prayer, using a variety of books on the subject.

Scripture and prayer, we found, are at the heart of every truly healthy church.

Lessons from Healthy Churches

In addition to an emphasis on God's Word and prayer, the one hundred churches we visited revealed nine common indicators of health. (For more information on the questionnaire used in these visits and a report on the findings, see VNE's website. The address is listed on the last page of this book.) These churches represent a wide range of theological persuasions, ethnic diversity, congregation sizes, denominational affiliations, and settings.

1. *Love, acceptance, and forgiveness.* In every case, the first theme that surfaced was love, acceptance, and forgiveness. The healthiest churches we visited created an environment of acceptance. People could enter just the way they were, allowing the Holy Spirit to do the refining work within their hearts. No one had to measure up to unwritten codes of ethics. No one was subjected to judgmental attitudes. Instead, the ongoing celebration of the community experience fostered a genuine love for one another that permeated their life together. I found myself drawn in to each church by this one attribute. Such strong, supernatural power is released in churches that exhibit unconditional love—sounds a lot like Jesus, don't you think?

2. *Relational integrity.* The second theme feeds off the first: relational integrity. In the healthy churches we visited, broken people felt safe because these churches exhibited authenticity and transparency in their relationships. They believed firmly that in order for genuine community to be achieved, the attitude and atmosphere of love needed to be modeled first in their life as a family of God before anyone else would ever be drawn to their fellowship. In addition, the pastors and key leaders in these churches made a point of teaching on relational issues like integrity, honesty, communication, conflict resolution, building trust, and learning how to forgive. This teaching was done from the pulpits, in adult education, and in gathering places outside the context of a Sunday morning experience. The variety of small groups in these churches was genuinely staggering: couples' groups, midweek family groups, men's and women's groups, singles Bible studies, missions prayer groups, and more traditional Bible studies. Bottom line—come together on a regular basis for authentic, transparent relationship-building.

3. *Hunger for personal growth.* We discovered a consistent hunger for personal growth in both congregations and individuals. People showed

a strong desire to know God in an intimate manner. In fact, the most commonly mentioned study guide used in many of these churches was the best-selling work by Henry Blackaby, *Experiencing God.* A strong adherence to biblical truth also characterized every setting. The experience of God is outweighing the knowledge of God and his Word in so many ministries that it was refreshing to see a genuine balance in the many churches we interviewed. It's important that we keep a copy of the Scriptures open to refer to along the way while at the same time experiencing his delight in us as his children.

4. *Shift from traditional to contemporary worship.* The fourth theme apparent in healthy churches was the shift in worship from the traditional to the contemporary. Worship teams and bands are being utilized more and more all the time. Church organs and large choirs are being replaced by a wide variety of instruments and up-front soloists and worship leaders. Larger congregations often offer both the traditional and the contemporary expressions of worship to suit the multigenerational style preferences represented in our churches today.

This is not big news; it merely emphasizes the consistent trend of healthy, vibrant congregations not only in our region but all across the country. In the description of God-Exalting Worship in chapter 2, we see that "the healthy church gathers regularly as the local expression of the body of Christ to worship God in ways that engage the heart, mind, soul, and strength of the people." The operative word here is *engage.* Unless we plan worship opportunities that connect our people's hearts with the heart of the Almighty One, we need to evaluate the purpose of our worship. The shift from traditional to contemporary is an attempt to fully engage the worshiper in the experience of worship and in deep love and adoration for the God of the universe who receives the praise of his people.

5. *Prayer.* The fifth theme is prayer. In each healthy church, we were refreshed to observe that prayer is a high priority. The traditional midweek prayer meetings of the past are being replaced by powerful experiences of united prayer throughout the week, such as concerts of prayer, solemn assemblies, pastors in the same city praying together, women and men in prayer within gender-separated groups, worship and prayer celebrations, youth prayer and praise gatherings, prayer retreats, prayer summits, prayer triads, healing prayer, early morning prayer. In many places churches have banded together to pray for every home in their community. In the city of Brockton, Massachusetts, more than a dozen churches have prayed for sixty thousand households in their city.

If there is going to be a revival in our land, it will be because of the quickly-growing movement of prayer that is captivating the hearts of God's people and bringing them to their knees for long, extended times of prayer. I hope I'm alive to see the fruit of this endeavor, which has grown at the grassroots level and is spreading faster than anyone can comprehend. The healthiest ministry settings are the pacesetters, to be sure.

6. *Relationship-centered ministry*. The sixth theme revealed from our healthy church visits is the movement from program-based to relationship-centered ministry planning; in effect, a deprogramming of the church. Although many excellent programs and ministries are still being planned and administered on a weekly basis, the ineffective programs are being consolidated or eliminated. The healthiest churches are free to implement changes and are unencumbered by congregational political systems that discourage shifting and realigning programs according to need.

Healthy churches have switched their focus to relationship building within the local church and to developing relationships in the community they are seeking to reach with the gospel. By carving out those programs that are no longer relevant to the setting, need, calling, and gift mix of the congregation, they are freed to be and do all that God empowers them to accomplish for his glory.

7. *Use of personal stories*. The seventh theme could be described as the celebration of the power of story. Many of the churches we talked with understood the importance of ongoing reminders around the theme of life change. Often, the church would write stories of how people had come to faith within their church or community. On a regular basis they had opportunities for public sharing—giving testimony to what God had done in their lives in the past week or month. They celebrated their young people's accomplishments when they came back from a retreat, missions trip, vbs, or when they graduated high school or college, returned from military duty, or served God in a soup kitchen. Over and over again, stories received their rightful place in the context of the church—how wonderfully like Christ, the greatest storyteller of all.

8. *Service*. The eighth theme is a worthy reminder: volunteerism— serving God with all the talent, time, giftedness, passion, temperament, and energy one can muster. The healthiest ministries of New England emphasize the "priesthood of all believers." Not only are people being trained for select ministries, they are taken through a self-evaluation process to assist them in discovering their spiritual gifts, their temperament and passion, their personal mission, and to deepen their insight into God's will and calling.

As the church defines its focus collectively through writing vision and mission statements that direct their planning, so individuals are also encouraged to define their personal vision and mission. This theme was not apparent in all the churches we visited, but it is definitely worth noting because of the growing trend in this direction. For those who have developed assimilation programs and have a structured approach for networking their congregation into ministry areas, the results are phenomenal. People have a brand-new excitement for service when they know they are working from their God-given and directed strengths.

9. *Networking.* The ninth theme in these congregations is networking. The healthiest churches know that they cannot get the job done in their communities by themselves. The churches we visited understood this and were seeking ways to develop interdependent relationships within their city or county. For some, this means only that the pastor joins a local clergy prayer group. Others, however, share facilities, resources, programs, and even staff.

Does this sound too New Testament-like? Well, maybe we should reconsider whether we are called to be the First Church of Philippi or the whole church in Philippi. My vision is to see more pastors and ministry leaders claim a New Testament view of church ministry—dare I suggest a renewed "parish" mentality that goes beyond our immediate congregations and instead sees the entire community as one's parish? Most communities have a number of different churches, but we can still embrace all of like mind and heart.

Most find this a hard concept to embrace. I am not proposing that we compromise the gospel or the essentials of our faith, but I am suggesting that we build relationships with all congregations within our reach and pray about ways we can serve the same parish together.

Church Attitude Survey Results

Complementing the one hundred church visits was the survey we administered in February 1997 at our annual congress. In a crowd of nearly 8,000 attendees, 1,899 spent upwards of ten minutes taking a computerized, self-administered survey regarding their attitudes about church. (For more information on the survey, see Vision New England's website. The address is listed on the last page of the appendix of this book.) Respondents were queried specifically on their demographics, religiosity, and church involvement. In keeping with our study objectives, respondents also were asked to assess the Ten Characteristics of a Healthy Church. Each of the ten characteristics was grouped into three key elements—an exercise that resulted in thirty attitude statements.

With very few exceptions—and regardless of the race, gender, denomination, age, number of years as a believer, responsibility in the church (pastor, ministry leader, or laity)—the basic rank order of the ten characteristics held constant. Demography, attitudes, behaviors, affiliations, and so forth did not appear to make a difference in how respondents rated these characteristics. They were ranked as follows:

Ten Characteristics of a Healthy Church	Mean Score (nine-point scale)
1. God's Empowering Presence	8.78
2. God-Exalting Worship	8.43
3. Spiritual Disciplines	8.31
4. Learning and Growing in Community	8.21
5. A Commitment to Loving and Caring Relationships	8.19
6. Servant-Leadership Development	8.02
7. An Outward Focus	7.90
8. Wise Administration and Accountability	7.56
9. Networking with the Body of Christ	7.03
10. Stewardship and Generosity	6.94

Even though this order is slightly different from how we originally ranked the ten characteristics, we gained a key insight from the research. The data suggested that respondents—as a whole, within cohorts, and individually—related to the ten characteristics across three basic levels. These levels are unique in their orientation and represent varying degrees of importance and relevance. In order of their relative strength, these levels have been defined as follows:

Level 1: How I Relate with God

God's Empowering Presence

God-Exalting Worship

Spiritual Disciplines

Level 2: How I Relate with My Church Family

Learning and Growing in Community

A Commitment to Loving and Caring Relationships

Servant-Leadership Development

Level 3: How My Church Ministers and Manages

An Outward Focus

Wise Administration and Accountability

Networking with the Body of Christ

Stewardship and Generosity

This interpretation of the data suggests a "higher common denominator" among this particular group of respondents, one that at its core is God centered (level 1). The next level appears to be those varied interactions within a more narrowly defined church community (level 2). Finally, level 3 appears to thrust the church outward in ministry and service while maintaining a high degree of accountability for the management functions of the church.

This research yielded a profound yet simple insight into the life of the church in New England. The fact that in virtually every demographic category and by all forms of religiosity the research affirmed the significance of the ten characteristics of a healthy church should not be undervalued. Further, the research logically ordered the ten characteristics into three basic groupings that should serve to further help focus church leaders across the region and the country.

This research is unique because it was not based on a particular program or model of church ministry, and it was not searching for a programmatic solution for the local church. Also, the research was not based on one particular church or denomination. Consequently, respondents were able to answer more from their imagination or spirit than from a need to support or correct their church. Each value statement began with the phrase "Local churches should . . ." and went on to describe a value that could be accessed within the local church.

This research affirms that the Great Commandment (Matt. 22:37–39) and the Great Commission (Matt. 28:18–20) are the lifeblood and desire of the church. What should not be overlooked are the order and the consistency of that order revealed by the research. I would advise church leaders to develop the life of their church in a manner consistent with the research findings. They could then be assured that they are standing on a solid biblical foundation as a result.

> One of them, an expert in the law, tested him with this question: "Teacher, which is the greatest commandment in the Law?" Jesus replied: "'Love the Lord your God with all your heart and with all your soul and with all your mind.' This is the first and greatest commandment."
>
> Matthew 22:35–38

Our research revealed that those healthy church characteristics which focused on experiencing and relating to God were the most highly valued. On this basis, I encourage leaders to make God, his power, and his presence central in the life of the church.

> "And the second is like it: 'Love your neighbor as yourself.' All the Law and the Prophets hang on these two commandments."
>
> Matthew 22:39–40

"How I relate with my church family" is the phrase used to characterize the study's findings of strong support for relationships within the local church. Local church leaders must secure the bonds of Christian love within the church if they are to attempt to fulfill the Great Commission.

> Then Jesus came to them and said, "All authority in heaven and on earth has been given to me. Therefore go and make disciples of all nations, baptizing them in the name of the Father and of the Son and of the Holy Spirit, and teaching them to obey everything I have commanded you. And surely I am with you always, to the very end of the age."
>
> Matthew 28:18–20

Clearly, the respondents all saw high value in the systems and functions of the local church. The fact that these healthy church characteristics ranked third among some of the most soundly committed Christians in New England should bring insight to all local church leaders. These findings suggest that at the core of everyone's being is a need to first know God, then to love and be loved, before they are willing to risk their relationships or themselves for others.

Visits and Survey Affirm the Ten Characteristics

The one hundred church visits and the 1,899 survey opinions generated over an eighteen-month period highlight the presupposition that Scripture and prayer pervade all of the ten characteristics of a healthy church. The overwhelming unanimity of support for these ten guiding principles will make for vibrant congregations prepared to enter the twenty-first century with renewed energy and power. In order for the ten characteristics to be realized in the context of community life, they must first be owned by each member and leader. These churches will be marked by boldness of heart, conviction of spirit, and determined wills to be and become all that God intends. To him be the glory forever and ever.

Lord of the church, be the Lord of my life and ministry today and always. May the principles of church life be lived out in such a way that you receive the glory through all of our strivings to be healthy, vibrant, alive, and effective. I know that you desire that your church pursue righteousness, wholeness, holiness, purity, and truth. Help us along the way to display the work of your Spirit, and may the fruit of our shared labors of love reflect the image of Jesus. May we be found faithful to the task before us, and may we forever be committed to your priorities for us. May the ministry of your Holy Spirit be manifest in our life of prayer and devotion to your Word. For it is with a heart of glad thanksgiving that I pray, for Jesus' sake and in his precious name. Amen.

2

God's Empowering Presence

Characteristic 1

The healthy church actively seeks the Holy Spirit's direction and empower-
ment for its daily life and ministry.

The Spirit himself testifies with our spirit that we are God's children.

Romans 8:16

Experiencing the empowering presence of God is something we all long
for from the deepest recesses of our spiritual being. We long to know
his Spirit's power in our lives and to live moment by moment in his presence. But how does a church develop a healthy sense of the Holy Spirit's
direction? How do pastors and members experience his empowerment
for daily life and ministry? What can a pastor do to help the congregation develop a healthy reliance on the Holy Spirit rather than depend-
ing on its own ability and strength? Are there approaches that will
increase the focus on the fruit of the Spirit without deemphasizing his
gifts?

Our extensive church attitude survey confirmed that experiencing
God's presence is of utmost importance to the entire church family—
pastors, leaders, and members alike. Those surveyed placed it at the top,
no matter how we sliced the data.

My friend Dennis Baril, senior pastor at Community Covenant Church
in Rehoboth, Massachusetts, coordinated our church attitude research
project. He personally places a high value on this characteristic in his
daily life and in the context of his church. Dennis comments, "If a church
wants to experience the empowering presence of God, it has to become
a high value for all. We have to be attuned to it in all of our culture as a
church. If during a hymn we sense the presence of God in a special way,
we will stop and be quiet in his presence."

At Community Covenant Church, you can sense God's presence each time you enter their new ministry center or go wherever members are together in life and service. When a pizza delivery person entered the building recently, he stopped ten feet into the lobby and asked, "What's going on here? What's this presence?"

Church member Pat Viera says, "Since we need so much love, mercy, and forgiveness, we receive that in his presence in worship and are equipped to give it away freely to others outside the worship setting." She has seen the "floodgates of mercy" opened up throughout the church as a result of experiencing the richness of his empowering presence. They are like deer, stunned by the oncoming headlights of his presence and power, unable and unwilling to move out of the way. Walking in the realization of God's nearness, they sense his love and initiative on their behalf and are empowered to serve him with ever increasing joy.

Not all churches are pursuing this vital course, however. How do we learn to value more deeply dependence on God's empowering presence?

"We are not a microwave church. We are more like a crockpot, where ideas need time to cook and develop savor," says Pastor Kevin Crispell, formerly pastor of Phillips Congregational Church in Watertown, Massachusetts. "Many of our people had never had the Holy Spirit explained to them. Yes, they sang the words in the doxology and in the Gloria Patri, but the idea that the Holy Spirit is a living being is a new and drastic idea. People would say, 'Our former pastor never talked about that.'"

The way to get people in tune with the Spirit is by showing them his role from the Bible, Pastor Crispell says. He taught a course on 1 Corinthians on Wednesday nights, explaining that he was simply presenting "the author's point of view." And the people's response was, "I never knew that was in there."

The fruit of the Spirit also became a theme in the Sunday school classes. The kids sang about it in the church services. Adults were invited into the Sunday school to see the displays the children had made and to take home crafts about the Holy Spirit. "As the more traditional members see the younger couples evidence the fruit of the Spirit-directed life, being willing to roll up their sleeves and get involved, they begin to think seriously about the difference he makes," says Pastor Crispell. "To see an eighty-year-old woman raising her hands in worship at an evening service is truly exciting."

For my friend and colleague Pastor Bob Frederich, Vision New England's coordinator of pastoral mentoring ministries, the most visible evidence of God's empowering presence is joy. And that makes today's healthiest churches attractive to newcomers.

"I saw my life and my presence in the pulpit as an expression of the presence and practice of the Holy Spirit. This was not an artificial putting on of a mask, but a genuine expression of His ministry in my life. Above all, that means that I exude joy," says Pastor Frederich. "How can we bring glory to God other than by being joyful?" Recently Pastor Frederich was engaged in premarital counseling when the young man said, "One of the reasons why I came is because you always look joyful."

For Pastor Frederich, the process starts with preaching and teaching on the subject of the Holy Spirit. "I worked through Acts, Ephesians, John 17, Romans, and Colossians. Then I did a series focusing on the ministry of the Holy Spirit." But it involves more than preaching. "There is an ethos that goes with that—the presence of the Holy Spirit needs to be expressed constantly. That includes corporate prayer in a variety of settings," he says.

For example, during his tenure as pastor at First Baptist Church in Portland, Maine, every Saturday evening half a dozen members would meet with him to pray for him and his ministry and for the congregation's response on Sunday. Each month also began with a Saturday morning gathering for prayer. "I illustrated my dependence on the ministry of the Holy Spirit through prayer by seeing that nothing kept me from those hours," says Pastor Frederich. "That dependence on the Holy Spirit must be caught as we pray in staff meetings, pray before counseling, even as we pray in the New Year." The fruit of this devoted prayer has created one of the healthiest ministries in our region.

Independence Needs to Be Broken

Needing to depend on the Spirit's guidance brings up a crucial issue. If we are to fully understand and experience God's empowering presence in our lives, we need to release our independent spirits into his loving care.

I have found that one of the greatest sins of the Christian church today is an independent spirit. "We'll do it our way or no way, thank you very much" seems to be our attitude. But what concerns me is our lack of reflection on this attitude and what it means to us long term.

In America, we come by this attitude naturally, since our culture fosters an independent spirit. In a land of freedom and democracy we are encouraged to think creatively for ourselves, to go outside the "box" of traditional norms. We are in a staggering growth mode when it comes to technological advances. We thrive in a culture of information, learning, and new tools to better serve whatever cause we are aligned with. The universities influence young adults to bring new ideas into the workforce, family, and community and encourage them to pursue a pioneering spirit for the rest of their lives. Such thinking has many benefits, as the positive advances of our culture show. But this also sets up a serious challenge within a subcultural movement like the church.

Vision New England represents churches and individuals from eighty different Protestant denominations. On the one hand, it's wonderful that we are having a unifying effect on the region by bringing these diverse groups together for learning, resource sharing, networking, and evangelistic outreach ministries. On the other hand, it's unfortunate that over the centuries we have chosen to subdivide ourselves eighty different ways. One person quipped, "At the time of the Reformation, we traded one Pope for a pope in every pulpit." Unfortunately, there's a lot of truth to that statement. Not only does the independent spirit exist in our pulpits today, but it certainly exists in the pews. "Power families" are in many churches, and the lack of submission to authority and the fights for control are the negative implications of the misuse of such power.

Within a few miles of our offices, I know of three churches that have been seriously hindered by this independent spirit. In one, the church asked their pastor to leave because he was introducing too many changes and offending the families that had for generations controlled the direction of the ministry. Today that pastor is not only out of the ministry but, through a series of great discouragements, has abandoned his evangelical faith and is losing his wife and family.

Another church in our community has split because the "power families" did not like what the elders had decided about the music ministry. This led to the release of the organist (who happened to be related to one of the power families) for his uncooperative attitude.

The third church in disarray has had a history of conflicts that have resulted in several pastoral leadership changes, a lack of focus in ministry, and a "majoring on the minor issues" situation, which has created an ongoing decline in attendance and traumatized community witness. These are just a few of the stories, similar to ones you undoubtedly have heard about too, and they are rooted in independent spirits and power-controlling individuals who are wiping out many local fellowships.

As far as I am concerned, our independence needs to be used for enhancing others' lives, most especially the downtrodden and needy. When it gets channeled into self-centeredness and clinging to our own agendas, then it needs to be broken, confessed, and daily left at the cross. A church that's filled with strong, independent-minded people who are unwilling to submit to the Holy Spirit and yield to the needs of others will never become a healthy church. The issue of independence needs to be dealt with openly and honestly within the context of the church on a regular basis. If you recognize yourself in this, stop reading and pause to deal with it. Here's a prayer you may want to consider:

Lord Jesus, I recognize that, at this moment in my life and in the context of my church experience, I may be contributing to an independent spirit which is hindering the work of your Spirit in our midst. For my unwillingness to submit to your authority in my life, I ask your forgiveness. For my unwillingness to submit to others in my family and count them more important than me, I seek your grace. For my unwillingness to submit to others in my church, most specifically those in authority over me, I trust in your mercy. Give me a holy boldness to confess my independent spirit to those I have offended, and lead us onward into the "promised land" of your empowering presence as you refresh and renew us by your Spirit. This prayer of confession is offered to you in the name that is above all names, my Savior Jesus. Amen.

Only when we approach God with open, outstretched hands are we ready to receive from him the work and ministry of the Holy Spirit. As Charles Spurgeon once said, we are merely "beggars helping other beggars find bread"; as such we depend on God to reach out to us with his presence, peace, and power. Once we release our independence and come humbly to receive from God, we can give back to him, receive from others, and give away to others freely. Then, and only then, an environment of health, healing, and hope can emerge under the auspices of the Spirit.

My prayers for God's empowering presence within the churches of our region and beyond are wrapped up in the words of one of my favorite hymns of the church, a wonderful prayer of submission and obedience.

Take My Life, and Let It Be Consecrated

Take my life, and let it be consecrated, Lord, to thee.
Take my moments and my days; let them flow in ceaseless praise.
Take my hands, and let them move at the impulse of thy love.
Take my feet, and let them be swift and beautiful for thee.

Take my voice, and let me sing always, only, for my King.
Take my lips, and let them be filled with messages from thee.
Take my silver and my gold; not a mite would I withhold.
Take my intellect, and use every power as thou shalt choose.

Take my will, and make it thine; it shall be no longer mine.
Take my heart, it is thine own; it shall be thy royal throne.
Take my love; my Lord, I pour at thy feet its treasure store.
Take myself, and I will be ever, only, all for thee. Amen.

Frances R. Havergal

The Fruit of the Spirit

When God helps us release the independent spirit that keeps us from understanding his love and lordship over our lives, then he is free to live through us. When a church is an island of health and vitality, you cannot help but notice the fruit of the Spirit in the lives of the members.

Ever since the highly esteemed British theologian and pastor John Stott became a believer, he has prayed daily that he would display the fruit of the Spirit in his walk with God. That has been a wonderful encouragement to me, and I have been following his lead with that same daily prayer for myself. The apostle Paul's list of the Spirit's fruit serves as a plumb line against which we can all measure ourselves. "The fruit of the Spirit is love, joy, peace, patience, kindness, goodness, faithfulness, gentleness and self-control. Against such things there is no law. Those who belong to Christ Jesus have crucified the sinful nature with its passions and desires [and independent spirits]. Since we live by the Spirit, let us keep in step with the Spirit. Let us not become conceited, provoking and envying each other" (Gal. 5:22–26).

Paul contrasts the nine lovely expressions of the Spirit-empowered life with a life lived in the flesh. When we invite Jesus to reign supreme in our lives as our leader, teacher, sustainer, and friend, we walk away from fleshly desires that feed a life of independence and licentiousness. But for this to happen in the life of a congregation, the values of the Spirit-empowered life must be consistently promoted as a priority for pastors, ministry leaders, and members alike.

One church that displays the fruit of the Spirit in powerful ways is the Boston Chinese Evangelical Church. This church has experienced tremendous growth over thirty-five years of ministry. Currently serving multiple subcultures (first-generation Chinese, Mandarin, Cantonese, Taiwanese, and American-born Chinese), this church has a rich and vital heritage.

Despite the strong distinctives between first- and second-generation Chinese, they have a deep, mutual respect for each other. They effectively minister side by side in both the Chinese and English speaking congregations and affirm each others' strengths. Senior pastor Jacob Fung, who leads the Chinese-speaking congregation, and associate pastor Steve Chin, who leads the English-speaking congregation, have worked as a team for almost twenty years. Pastor Chin said of the church, "When people enter our church, they obviously feel safe and secure to be themselves and from day one are accepted for who they are. And even though our church has high standards for doctrine, and we are considered theologically conservative, we try to practice a genuine spirit of tolerance and patience surrounding the needs of others."

The facility they currently use is much too small for the growing numbers attending each week. And the needs of a large, urban community are staggering. But when I met with the pastoral teams and listened to them discuss these challenges, I noticed how often they honored one another and used such terms as *complementary, interdependent, synergy,* and *appreciation.* Their kind, affirming words for one another made a lasting impression on me.

I noted after my meeting with them how significantly they embodied the fruit of the Spirit. Despite the obstacles they face in ministry today, their Christian graces were a joy to behold. When so many others within our faith communities respond angrily when confronted with a myriad of ministry and relational "inconveniences," it was refreshing to be with such gracious people.

Let's consider the nine fruits of the Spirit one at a time and reflect on the meaning of each for our personal and congregational lives.

Love. The word for love used in this passage is the New Testament word *agape.* It is one of the four common Greek words for the term. *Eros* means the passionate love between a man and a woman. *Philia* is the warm love we feel for those nearest and dearest to us. And *storge* means affection, especially the love parents have for their children. The best definition I have discovered for *agape* is *"unconquerable benevolence.* It means that no matter what people may do to us by way of insult or injury or humiliation we will never seek anything else but their highest good. It is therefore a feeling of the mind as much as of the heart; it describes the deliberate effort—which we can make only with the help of God— never to seek anything but the best even for those who seek the worst for us."[1]

Joy. The Greek word for joy in this passage is *chara,* the kind of joy based in a religious experience, not the kind that comes from our possessions and earthly pleasures. Nor is it the kind of joy we feel when we triumph over someone else in competition. The Spirit's joy has at its foundation our relationship with God. It doesn't need to be vivacious or overpowering; it can be a joy within one's heart that has no outward expression. Such genuine joy comes from the realization that our lives are held securely in the palms of God's hands.

Peace. The third fruit of the Spirit is peace. In the time of the apostle Paul, this word was commonly used to describe the serenity that a country would enjoy under a just and righteous leader. It was also used to describe the kind of law and order that existed in cities or villages because the "keepers of the peace" were doing their jobs correctly. Usually in the New Testament the Greek word *eirene* would stand for the

Hebrew word *shalom* and would mean not just freedom from trouble but everything that contributed to a person's highest good. Here it means the tranquillity of heart and mind that exists in the inner recesses of a Christian's soul—derived from the all-pervading consciousness that our times, lives, and relationships are in the hands of almighty God.

Patience. The Greek word for the fourth fruit, patience, is *makrothumia.* Generally speaking, it is not used to describe the patience we need to handle the events of our lives or the objects we own. No, this kind of patience deals with people. We see it in the person who is slow to anger, even when tempted to fight back. New Testament writers use it to refer to God's attitude toward mankind (see 1 Tim. 1:16). God models for us that which is often our most difficult attribute to reflect—and this makes us all the more dependent on him to live through us in this regard. He has such unlimited patience that he bears with all of our sinning and chooses not to cast us off. That's an awesome truth. In our dealings with one another, especially within the context of the local church, we must reproduce this loving, forbearing, forgiving, patient attitude of God.

Kindness and goodness. The fifth and sixth fruits, kindness and goodness, are like kissing cousins. They are closely related terms that should be considered together; in fact, the Greek word for kindness is *chrestotes,* which can also be translated as goodness. The idea here is goodness that is kind. Kindness can be described as active helpfulness, while goodness can have the aspects of rebuke and discipline added to it. Jesus showed goodness toward the people in the temple when he cleansed it and drove out those who were making it a bazaar instead of a place of holiness and worship. And he showed kindness to the sinful woman who anointed his feet with her tears. In the Christian community, we need that same goodness that expresses both kindness and strength of character.

Faithfulness. The fruit of faithfulness is also considered trustworthiness. The Greek word used here, *pistis,* describes a person who is trustworthy, reliable, true to his or her word. Faithfulness is lived out in the context of Christian community when we are worthy of one another's trust. This takes time, but over the seasons of our life and ministry, when we see each other in our truest forms and work out the bugs of living in community, then we build trust and confidence in one another. There are few things worse about working with or dealing with people than to be in relationship with someone who has breached our trust.

Gentleness. The eighth attribute of the Spirit-empowered life is gentleness. The Greek word is *praotes,* and it has three distinct meanings in the New Testament. First, it means being submissive to the will of God. Second, it means being teachable or not too proud to learn. Third, it means being considerate of others. No matter what the conditions of life may be, no matter how great or unfortunate, gentle people know how to treat others with a tender word, action, or attitude and know how to keep a lid on their anger. A gentle spirit turns away any oncoming wrath and influences the tone of a faith community in a way that is compelling and beautiful. Gentleness is godly, not something to be shunned by the "macho" as a sign of weakness. Instead, it is a sign of inner peace and communion with God.

Self-control. The ninth and final fruit spelled out by the apostle Paul is self-control. He saved the hardest for last! The word in Greek is *egkrateia* and simply means self-mastery. It is used elsewhere to describe the athlete's discipline of his or her body and of the Christian's mastery of sexual temptation. One who is self-controlled knows how to depend on the work of the Spirit to master one's desires, especially for pleasure. And this is truly the virtue that makes a person fit to be the servant of others.

In essence, Paul is saying that for us to truly live out a Spirit-empowered life, we need a healthy self-mastery which is ready at a moment's notice to serve the needs of others. When we are self-absorbed, wanting to meet our needs first, and seeking out the most pleasurable way to do so, then we are not walking with the Spirit or fully prepared to serve and give out of love. Self-control includes the use of our time, our bodies, our minds, our emotions, and our spirits. It affects every aspect of our being. Becoming self-controlled under the lordship of Christ and the leadership of the Spirit is an ongoing process of growth.

If we are to become a healthy church, then our local fellowships need to be filled with people who are willing to abide in Christ and remain empowered by his Spirit. It's the only way we will bear his fruit in our lives individually and corporately. All of us need to assess this need each day. The apostle Paul tells us in Romans 6 that the Christian has died with Christ and risen again to a life, new and clean, in which the evil things of the past are done with and the lovely things of the Spirit are coming to fruition. May this be true in our generation.

The Spiritual Gifts

In addition to cultivating the fruit of the Spirit, pastors and leaders need to foster the discovery and use of the Spirit's gifts in the life of every believer. The Spirit has entrusted into the care of each one of us a unique set of gifts designed to build up the body of Christ. Part of my gift mix includes the gift of teaching. Ever since I first discovered this gift, and it was affirmed by others, I understood why I had such joy every time I taught! New life emerges for people when they can utilize the gifts of the Spirit in the context of ministry, both in the church and in their day-to-day lives.

For my friend Holly Miller, the road to discovering her spiritual gifts has led to some exciting developments. It all began when she was working through her understanding of her temperament, via the Myers-Briggs Temperament Indicator. For Holly, the pressing questions were, "Where do I fit in? What does God want me to be doing? How has he created me as his child?"

This process of self-analysis has led Holly to a deeper understanding of how her spiritual gift of administration works with her temperament in her church, family, and career. Holly says, "There is great freedom knowing who you are and how you have been gifted of the Holy Spirit for daily life and service. It's a lifelong journey, always seeking to know one's place in this world."

This knowledge has helped Holly learn what to say yes to and when to say no, gradually dropping those things out of her life that don't fit her gift mix and temperament. Today Holly is taking time for the important activities of her life, has a renewed focus on serving God within the context of the body, is excited about her roles as a wife, mother, and grandmother, and has started her own consulting business helping people discover what it means to be the kind of person God created them to be. She also helps people in the local church learn about their gifts and use them for God's glory.

The apostle Paul says, "Now about spiritual gifts, brothers, I do not want you to be ignorant" (1 Cor. 12:1). We cannot afford to be oblivious to the gifts God has so freely entrusted to our care. The Bible teaches us that every Christian has received at least one gift (1 Peter 4:10) and that "to each one the manifestation of the Spirit is given for the common good" (1 Cor. 12:7). Nazarene scholar W. T. Purkiser asserts that "every true function of the Body of Christ has a 'member' to perform it, and every member has a function to perform." What an awesome reminder.

What are the spiritual gifts? C. Peter Wagner defines a gift as "a special attribute given by the Holy Spirit to every member of the Body of Christ according to God's grace for use within the context of the Body." A spiritual gift is not the same as a natural talent (i.e., singing). But a spiritual gift can be exercised through the channel of a natural talent, as we so frequently see in the ministry of Christian musicians who impart spiritual enrichment, refreshment, and strength through their talents. A gift may or may not be present before conversion, but it becomes a spiritual gift on use within the context of the body.

Where can we find the gifts in Scripture? Primarily, in Romans 12, 1 Corinthians 12, and Ephesians 4. In 1 Corinthians 7 and 14, 1 Peter 4, and Ephesians 3 we see how the Lord fills us in on other important details related to the gifts. The process of discovering our gifts is vital for the body of Christ to be built up and encouraged, to be equipped for service in ministry, and for loving and caring for the unbelievers in our reach. And using these gifts is how we glorify God, according to 1 Peter 4:10–11: "Each one should use whatever gift he has received to serve others, faithfully administering God's grace in its various forms. If anyone speaks, he should do it as one speaking the very words of God. If anyone serves, he should do it with all the strength God provides, so that in all things God may be praised through Jesus Christ. To him be the glory and the power for ever and ever. Amen." According to the Westminster Confession and the Heidelberg Catechism, glorifying God is the "chief end of man." What greater motivation is there than this?

Pastors and ministry leaders need to help Christians be good stewards of their God-given spiritual gifts. We can start by encouraging people to begin with the gifts they are most drawn to as they study the biblical lists of gifts. Spiritual gifts inventories are helpful tools in this process and require devoted energy and focus. Some I recommend are

BreakThru—A Spiritual Gifts Diagnostic Inventory, by Peopleworks International, Richmond, Virginia

Team Ministry Spiritual Gifts Inventory Questionnaire, by Church Growth Institute, Lynchburg, Virginia

Spiritual Gifts, by Guidance Assistance Programs, Winfield, Illinois

Trenton Spiritual Gifts Analysis or *Wagner-Modified Houts Questionnaire,* both produced by the Charles E. Fuller Institute of Evangelism and Church Growth, Pasadena, California

Networks by Willow Creek Association, Barrington, Illinois

In addition to the Bible study, inventories, and small group discussion, prayer is absolutely essential in the discovery process. If a spiritual gift is to be discovered and utilized, it will be under the auspices of the Spirit of God. As he leads you in this process, watch for development of abilities and the blessings that follow because of your faithfulness. See if others recognize your gifts. Seek training in those areas, evaluate as you go, and deepen your ability to use your gifts for his glory and for the encouragement of the body. There is great joy in this journey!

Thy Kingdom Come

God's empowering presence is clearly seen in healthy churches that advance the cause of God's kingdom here on earth. Now, the kingdom of God does not refer to a geographic territory in which God is King. Instead, it means a condition of the heart and mind and will where God is Lord of all. The Jews of Jesus' day mistakenly thought of old nationalistic dreams of kingly power for the Messiah they longed for. But Jesus was thinking of doing God's will. It was in their hearts and minds that he wished to reign supreme, not on their earthly thrones. Today, a church filled with people of faith who long to do God's will are part of a much wider kingdom on earth.

When we pray, "Thy kingdom come, Thy will be done," are we not in essence asking God to empower us with his kingdom presence every moment of every day? Our churches are filled with people who long to understand their role in building God's kingdom here on earth. Only when we as church leaders commit to unpackaging that concept will we see the hearts, minds, and lifestyles of Christ's followers be transformed. Let's call out to heaven for God's empowering presence so that the work of his Spirit can be released through the lives of his people. *Soli deo gloria!*

Lord, the work of your Spirit is something I long for. You promise your people the gift of your Spirit's presence and power for our daily lives and ministries. So I cry out to you today and ask that you would refresh my life with your presence so that I may know and then do your will. I ask that you would reveal yourself to the church I serve, and I pray that in every aspect of our shared life in you we would together reflect your love and lordship. I know that I need to depend on you for my every breath, and I pray that when I steer off course your hand will be there to gently guide and sustain me. Will you empower me with the fruit of your Spirit this day, and will you reveal your spiritual gifts to me so that I may serve you with joy and full assurance that I am walking a life of obedience? I long to see your Spirit's power and presence released in me and within the fellowship of the body and ask for that today. In the strong name of Jesus, the one who promised the Spirit. Amen.

For Reflection and Renewal

The healthy church actively seeks the Holy Spirit's direction and empowerment for its daily life and ministry.

In seeking to understand and implement God's will, the church:

- articulates a clear understanding of who God is
- teaches the "whole counsel of God" and relates it to the twenty-first century church
- emphasizes a supernatural reliance instead of a self-reliance
- creates enthusiasm about being part of God's kingdom
- prays for God's initiative and anticipates that God will act
- encourages its leaders to be change agents under God's guidance
- desires its members to display the fruit of the Spirit
- seeks the gifts of the Spirit within the body

The Spirit himself testifies with our spirit that we are God's children.

Romans 8:16

1. On a scale of 1 to 10 (1 being not at all important and 10 being most important), rank each of the above statements while answering the questions, "How important is this statement for the health of our church? How highly do we value the characteristic God's Empowering Presence?"

2. On a scale of 1 to 10 (1 being very ineffective and 10 being very effective), rank each of the above statements while answering the question, "How effective are we as a leadership team at instilling these values in our church?"

3. For each of the above statements, ask your team, "Where do we want to be in God's Empowering Presence in this next year or two?"

4. For each of the above statements, ask your team, "How will we get where we want to be in living out God's Empowering Presence in this next year?"

5. Overall, on a scale of 1 to 10 (1 being very low and 10 being very high), rank how well you think your church is doing in living out this first characteristic of a healthy church, God's Empowering Presence.

3

God-Exalting Worship
Characteristic 2

The healthy church gathers regularly as the local expression of the body of Christ to worship God in ways that engage the heart, mind, soul, and strength of the people.

"Yet a time is coming and has now come when the true worshipers will worship the Father in spirit and truth, for they are the kind of worshipers the Father seeks."

John 4:23

"All of creation was created to bring glory to God, but only man was created to do it out of a loving relationship with God as our Father," says Tom Sparling, Vision New England's director of worship renewal and former pastor of worship at Immanuel Baptist Church in Chelmsford, Massachusetts. That insight results in a significant new approach to worship.

Tom continues, "Rather than placing the priority on 'planning worship' at Immanuel, we sought to equip worshipers as our main emphasis. What we have worked at is teaching believers that worship is a way of life rather than primarily a ceremony. Worship needs to become part of the warp and woof of our lives. We want to live in such a way that God is exalted and glorified in all that we do." The Bible indicates that God directs his love to people. This means we have been uniquely created for his love—and our bringing glory to God flows out of our love for him.

"In the Old Testament, worship was associated with the house of God. Yet in the New Testament Christ himself makes the profound statement that God is seeking out worshipers who will worship him in Spirit and truth, who are seeking to accomplish his original purpose," explains

Tom. "After the Gospels, there is a complete absence of the word used both in Hebrew and Greek for ceremonial worship as God's people gather. The word used for ceremonial worship meant to 'prostrate before' as when people prostrated themselves before Jesus when he was on earth. But that word does not appear at all in the epistles, showing up only in the Book of Revelation, where the angels and the redeemed are described as prostrating themselves before God."

What is the significance of this for believers today? "We are the temple of God. The action moves from the temple, or the place of gathering, to the whole of life, as described in Romans 12:1. There the apostle Paul urges us to offer our bodies as 'living sacrifices, holy and pleasing to God—this is your spiritual act of worship.' This means that where we are, everywhere we are, is a place of worship," says Sparling. "I am offering up myself for twenty-four hours a day, seven days a week, as a place of worship."

Once we understand the shift from location to individual, Tom asserts, it changes our whole approach to corporate worship. "At Immanuel, we set our sights on teaching our people that we are to be worshipers by habit and lifestyle. As we focused on that over the years, the majority began to implement that in their life. Now corporate worship becomes an overflow of what has been happening in the lives of believers all week long. When we gather, everything is already in process, people are ready to join in," says Tom.

Shifting Styles of Worship

This approach moves the whole worship debate about style and what people need in worship to what God wants from us in worship. However, we must acknowledge that we are all drawn to certain corporate worship styles more than others. Some churches today try to mix several styles into one service, while others take a variety of approaches and strategically place them throughout the weekend.

At Immanuel Baptist, Tom Sparling blended styles of every generation into both of their Sunday services. That way, all ages could connect with God. However, this is only one way churches are shifting their worship styles to help believers understand their role as worshipers—both in their personal spiritual life and in their congregational worship setting.

Every weekend at Grace Chapel in Lexington, Massachusetts, the worship and music teams lead four subcongregations in God-exalting worship services—in three distinct styles. It begins Saturday evening when the "Congregation of the Good Shepherd" gathers for a liturgical service. The liturgy for one particular service included a quiet prelude, an opening hymn, a call to worship that was read responsively (with the black-robed pastor in the back of the sanctuary), another hymn (pastors processing in from the rear), a collect (prayer), a time to kneel in prayerful repentance, a musical meditation followed by a musical response, the reading of Holy Scripture (Old Testament, New Testament, and Gospel accounts), the pastoral prayer, a sermon, another hymn, giving tithes and offerings, Holy Communion (where the entire congregation gathered around and received the elements at the kneeling rails), and a closing benediction. For an independent church in the suburbs of Boston, the ambiance of worship by candlelight and quiet meditation was in sharp contrast to the remainder of the weekend.

At the Sunday morning services (in the traditional 9:30 and 11:00 slots), the lights were brightly turned on in the sanctuary, the people who gathered were chatting freely with one another up to 9:29 and 59 seconds, and the mood was completely different from the evening before. The choir proceeded to occupy the loft, the pastors walked in from the side doors (this time in business suits), and the service order was much more "traditional" for this evangelical community of Christians. The prelude was upbeat, the welcome and announcements were even livelier, the opening worship chorus was contemporary. What followed were a prayer of invocation, two contemporary worship choruses and the hymn "How Great Thou Art," a reading from Psalms, a choral anthem, a pastoral prayer, an offertory from the pipe organ, another traditional hymn, a ministry moment interview, a sermon complemented by multimedia technology, a closing hymn, and a benediction—all in sixty minutes. It was a good blend of both traditional and contemporary worship forms.

When Sunday evening rolled around, the congregation was primarily young, single adults with a smattering of baby boomer couples and even some young families. The worship was led by a band of musicians—pianist, electronic keyboardist, drummer, bongo player, three guitarists, two soloists (with tambourines and other handheld instruments), and a leader who moved with the beat of the music. He led the congregation in hand-clapping and hand-raising responses to the contemporary selection of worship songs. The pastor who gave the opening welcome wore blue jeans and a sweater, cracked a joke or two, and opened up the service with an informal prayer.

The mood for this entire service was relaxed and free-flowing. Gordon MacDonald, the senior minister, also dressed casually, placed his Bible and notes for his sermon on the bongo drums (his only available pulpit), and delivered a message focused on one verse of Scripture with many practical applications. There was no distributed order of worship, and the only "liturgy" was a prelude by the band, the welcome from the pastor, a worship set of songs, an original offertory written and sung by the pianist, and a message. A total contrast to the robes, candles, liturgy, and quiet reflection of the night before.

The leadership at Grace Chapel has selected three distinct styles of worship to reach the varied groups within their growing congregation. Their goal? "The same in every service—to point people to God," says Grace Chapel's worship pastor, David Bullock. "In essence each of the services are very much alike, whether more cerebral or more celebratory. The blending of diverse styles is more a matter of convenience of time and preference for the individual and must not become the focus of our worship. God is the focus of our worship, and as his people he must remain the ultimate priority in every aspect of our congregational experience. We sing *to* God more than we do *about* God, regardless of the style of music that ushers us into his presence. Every aspect of the worship service is to be a vertical expression of love and adoration—for his glory and to God alone. We vary the styles in order to build a mindset within a diverse people of God—worship is not an event, it is to become a lifestyle."

The Key: Engagement

Through our surveys and dozens of in-church visits, we have discovered that the people of God are hungering today for meaningful worship experiences. Not the kind of worship where they sit passively back in the pews—but the kind that engages and requires their full involvement. The key to effective worship in the healthiest settings is engaging people's hearts, minds, souls, and strength. To be engaged in worship involves varying styles and forms, but is focused on actively drawing in and involving God's people.

If there were such a thing as a Worshipers Anonymous group, I would have to attend the first session and confess to the group that I am a recovering EpiscoBaptiPenteGationalist. You've never heard of a person like me? Well, I think there are many such worshipers in your congregation today. We are the kind of people who are fed and enriched in our love for the Almighty One in a variety of worship settings.

The "Episco" part of me loves to attend Trinity Church in downtown Boston during the Advent and Lenten seasons of the church year. By far one of the most beautiful sanctuaries in New England, Trinity sits prominently at the center of Copley Square in the heart of the city. Its architecture is unparalleled: each wall is graced by fabulous stained glass windows; each pew has individual kneeling stools with hand-sewn, needle-pointed covers; the pulpit area is adorned with exceptional marble and wood carvings graced by statues of biblical and historical figures. The ambiance most assuredly contributes to the worship experience.

At Christmas, Trinity hosts a candlelight carol service rich with Scripture, Christmas carols, readings, prayers, candles, choral anthems of arrangements from old and new composers, and a seasonal homily. All of this is laced with the most remarkable story in human history—the Creator of the universe coming among us as a child in Bethlehem. It's noted in the written order of worship that this great service is "a high point of our life at Trinity Church as we explore the meaning of the Christian faith in our lives throughout the year."

The program notes continue, "An annual part of our Christmas celebration for over seventy-five years, this Candlelight Carol Service proclaims the meaning of Christmas in story and song. It begins quietly with the entrance of the Christ Candle, symbol of the Light of Christ which serves as the focal point for the entire service. The climax of the liturgy is the remembrance of our Savior's birth, which pierced the dark night of human sorrow, just as the procession of lights, led by the Christ Candle, pierces the darkness in the church. We too find our place in that procession as those who are called to take the Light of Christ into the world." Sam Lloyd, the rector of Trinity Church, invites all who are worshiping that night to enter into this worship experience as together we "explore the mysteries of life in Christ."

The "Bapti" side of me worships on a weekly basis at Grace Chapel in Lexington, Massachusetts. My wife and I were formerly on the pastoral staff team of this great church, and we now have the privilege of raising our family there as parishioners. We attend the Sunday morning service at 9:30 A.M. and enjoy this Baptist-style worship experience.

At least once a month, though, I preach at other churches—one of these being the Church of the Open Door in Hampden, Maine, an independent Baptist church. The spiritual fervor of their service was uplifting for me. I was drawn in to their fellowship and sensed God's presence as we sang, prayed, listened to body life announcements, celebrated the Lord's goodness, offered our gifts, and opened God's Word. The theme of the morning was "to continue wholeheartedly" to be the people of God. They certainly embodied his family and lived out his priorities in worship.

One striking symbol of beauty was the stained glass window depicting Jesus with his arms and hands outstretched. Our loving Lord walked this earth in a posture of unconditional love and forgiveness, and this picture appropriately displays his mercy, kindness, grace, and love. From my few days in their midst, I knew that these people were fully prepared to give themselves away—with open, outstretched hands—to the community they were called to serve. Times of worship like that Sunday morning led them to do so . . . in Jesus' name.

The "Pente" side of me comes out in megagatherings of the body, like our annual congress each winter in Boston. Not that this is a typical "charismatic" worship experience, nor is it necessarily designed to be. But when the Spirit of God moves in our midst, we kneel in repentance, raise hands in praise, proclaim in unison that he is Lord, sing choruses with all our might, shout amen and clap our hands when a key point is made or a musician, dramatist, or choir serves us with excellence to the glory of God.

The exuberance of these large worship experiences is inspirational, motivational, and has lasting value for our souls. They are unparalleled in our Christian experience, since in our region there are no other congregations like the ones gathered at congress each year—black, white, Haitian, Hispanic, Asian, hearing impaired, young, old, disabled, rich, poor, urban, suburban, and from multiple denominations and regions.

In addition to the annual congress weekends, we have hosted the pastors prayer summits since 1992. These four days are spent in the presence of God and in rich, God-exalting worship. We come to these events with no agenda except to hear from God. We invite him to do his work in our midst, and it's a joy to see how he refines and renews us for his service. The Spirit of God is apparent in these settings of worship, prayer, confession, relationship building, consecration, and regional interdependence. It's not uncommon to find the pastors prostrate on the floor in prayer, embracing one another after confessing their sins and their need for forgiveness, raising hands in praise and adoration, or sitting quietly around the dimly lit communion table, tearful and penitent before partaking the elements. We belt out with all our might our adoration of God through the great hymns of the church and the contemporary choruses of the day. It's wholesome worship, rich and meaningful, but fully engaging to be sure—no backseats in this crowd!

The "Gationalist" side of me brings me back to my roots as a Congregationalist. The "liturgy" and traditions still mean a lot to me; and each time I return to worship with my extended family in that special place, my memory is flooded with important past worship services. It was in that setting I was baptized as a child, where I made profession of faith and joined the church. It was here where my sister was married and my parents renewed their vows after fifty years of marriage. And it was in this place where friends and family gathered for a final farewell to my beloved mother at her memorial service. Even though I do not consider myself a liberal theologically or practically, I am still refreshed in my soul when I return to this Congregational church of my childhood.

So you see, a variety of worship experiences is engaging for people like me! We can worship in our cars when we sing along with one of our favorite Christian artists. We find ourselves moved by the meaning of the great traditions of the church such as baptisms, weddings, and communion. We enjoy attending Christian concerts and standing on our chairs to see the stage—and reaching out to the heavens as if God himself were reaching down and holding our raised hands. We marvel in awestruck wonder at God's glory in the gorgeous sanctuaries filled with stained glass windows. We are drawn into worship at conferences and retreats by the teams of instrumentalists, psalmists, and worship leaders who give their whole selves in leading us into the throne room of heaven. We reflect on the cross at the front of the sanctuary or a stained glass window depiction of Jesus to capture the serenity of a peaceful moment of worship.

If you see yourself in any of these experiences, you know what I mean when I speak of worship that is engaging. For those who plan worship for a congregation each week, please take seriously the heart cries of the people of God who are gathered in your sanctuary for one purpose—to meet with the Lord. It requires a lot of prayer and energy to prepare for such events. And yes, each worship experience needs to be planned as if it's the last time this side of heaven you will gather to worship the Almighty One. God-exalting worship is not to be taken lightly by any one of us, worshipers or worship leaders, pastors or laypeople, older or newer believers, children, youth, or adults. The Father seeks our worship, and it is to be pure and wholesome, exalting him and giving him the joy that's due his holy name. The style is secondary in importance to the real reason we worship—to glorify God.

Elements of Engagement

If you as pastor and leadership team are merely going through the motions each week in planning your congregational worship, I would suspect that you are not leading a healthy church. Those who prepare effective worship experiences take countless hours to put together every aspect of the worship experience—and this is true even for those who rely more on the spontaneous work of the Spirit.

Since the deepest heart cry of the people of God is for engaging, exalting worship, it's time for churches across this country to prayerfully consider how effective their planning is for these weekly events for the family of God. I would suggest that we work at a zero-based planning model, similar to what business leaders teach about the budgeting process. Start with a clean slate, a white sheet of paper, a wide open heart, and then prayerfully fill in the blanks with God's desire for you and his people.

The leaders at Bethany Congregational Christian Church in Rye, New Hampshire, have been trying to blend a variety of worship styles into three identical weekend services. It has not come without much strain on the system. But the honorable way they are handling all of this is a wonderful testimony.

In a newsletter published for the congregation in November 1997, Chris Matthews, the director of music and worship, wrote the following: "At Bethany we have been creative in:

1. Knowing and practicing scriptural guidelines that lead to excellence in music and worship;
2. Honoring the roots of the universal church, and of Bethany Church in worship;
3. Being aware of the many varieties of musical styles and tastes and utilizing the best in contemporary music;
4. Using the diversity we find in the Bethany community and beyond; and
5. Nurturing an atmosphere where the process of making music is honoring to Christ."

They have chosen to pursue this variety instead of splitting and contributing to the horror stories of other churches that have been devastated by the divisions created because of style differences. They have talked openly and honestly with one another to find the healthiest worship setting for their people. Their focus is on worshiping God and maintaining unity in the body rather than on the style of worship. It's absolutely critical that unity be preserved amid the great diversity that exists in the body today. They have chosen at Bethany to "pioneer a harder but healthier way," says Chris Matthews. "It may take some time to find the right balance with all the variety. But let's be patient with one another, in love, and grow together in providing the fullest expression of worship to the Lord."

Craig Perkins, a music minister in Rehoboth, Massachusetts, reminds us, "Music is really only the vehicle that the message travels on. The message must always be the core truth of God's Word. That's why it is so troubling to see people holding with white-knuckle intensity to the music preferences they had when they were three, ten, or twenty years old."

He continues, "It is not a matter of whether we are using hymns or contemporary choruses, or original music. All have their place in the church. What is most important is that the worshiper is interacting with

God. Those who are writing original music today are heralds of Christ and are producing fruit in the body of Christ through the music they write."

The role of the worship leader is like that of Asaph in the Old Testament, overseeing the delivery of music, organizing the worship team, and seeking to please the heart of God through song. Perkins explains, "A worship leader should be able to hear and interpret the heart of God. It's not just an issue of providing music. It is about seeing into the heart of God, hearing, and then bringing that to the people and helping them respond to that. Our mandate is to please God, not the masses. We must not allow people to make us into the image that is in their mind concerning worship. Churches need not only a song leader but an Asaph who is skilled musically and able to interpret and then convey the heart of God to the people."

Vision New England's director of worship renewal, Tom Sparling, agrees with Perkins' assessment of the role of the worship leader. For Sparling, the focus of our worship is on our great and awesome God—pictured so eloquently by the prophet Isaiah in Isaiah 6:1–4: "I saw the Lord seated on a throne, high and exalted, and the train of his robe filled the temple. . . . 'Holy, holy, holy is the Lord Almighty; the whole earth is full of his glory.'" The worship leader is to point the people to the Lord of hosts.

Then, as we are pointed to the God of the universe, we come to him with a spirit of confession and brokenness. Isaiah continues in verse 5, "'Woe to me!' I cried. 'I am ruined! For I am a man of unclean lips, and I live among a people of unclean lips, and my eyes have seen the King, the Lord Almighty.'" God is there to forgive our sins and restore us to love and service, as the prophet says, "'See, this [live coal from the seraph] has touched your lips; your guilt is taken away and your sin atoned for.' Then I heard the voice of the Lord saying, 'Whom shall I send? And who will go for us?' And I said, 'Here am I. Send me!'" Having met with the Lord, we are empowered to go and serve him all the days of our lives.

In essence, Isaiah presents us with the following outline.

God is seeking God-seekers—his gift to us is his heart, and he longs for us to receive it with joy.

We need to cultivate his heart within us—as we long to "touch the hem of his garment," he will fill us with himself.

We must grow our collective heart for God as his people—drawn together in our worship as his body, the church of Jesus Christ.

We are commissioned to share his heart with others—connecting with others who have traveled this journey before us, joining hands with one another today, and passing on the torch to a new generation of God-seekers.

This simple outline is underscored in Jeremiah 24:6–7: "My eyes will watch over them for their good, and I will bring them back to this land. I will build them up and not tear them down; I will plant them and not uproot them. *I will give them a heart to know me, that I am the Lord.* They will be my people, and I will be their God, for they will return to me with all their heart" (emphasis added). What a powerful promise from the Lord!

These basic priorities are also at the core of the heart song created by Craig Perkins for our ministry in 1997 when we changed the name of our 110-year-old ministry from Evangelistic Association of New England to Vision New England. It reflects the heart cry of God's people for a renewed sense of his exalted presence in our lives:

Call Us Again, Lord

(v. 1)
The voice of God is whispering
Across a darkened land,
Searching for a resting place
In hearts that understand.
He longs to stir the embers
Of a faith once bold and bright,
And call again His people
Unashamed to bear His light.

(chorus)
Call us again, Lord,
To our first love.
Yielding again, Lord,
To Your holy hand above.
Fill New England's rocky shores
And mountains with your grace.
Fulfill your vision with us, Lord,
And let us see your face!

(v. 2)
God's people need to hear again
His certain loving voice,
And shout an answer bold and clear
That we have made the choice
To join our hearts
And leave our sin,
Embracing all His kingdom
And His vision that's within.

(v. 3)
Many hearts are seeking truth,
Weary of their sin,
They know there is a shelter
But not how to enter in.
Prisoners of fear and doubt
Longing for release,
They need to know His loving touch
And comfort of His peace.

(v. 4)
Let those set free from sin arise
And shake the keys of life,
Unlock the chains of those who cry,
Release them from their strife.
Proclaim good news.
Announce His grace.
With mercy and compassion,
Demonstrate His ways. His ways.

Worship is to be seen as the end, not a means to an end. In our passion to know God, we seek him with all our heart as he takes great delight in us, quiets us with his love, and rejoices over us with singing (see Zeph. 3:17). As we come in touch with his heart for us, we grow in our heart to know him. A life of personal and corporate worship results in hearts and lives filled to overflowing with God and God alone.

Practical Issues

God-exalting worship is the missing jewel in our expression as evangelicals today. A. W. Tozer said it so well when he described how God desires to restore to us the missing jewel of worship: "God desires to take us deeper into Himself. He wants to lead us on in our love for Him who first loved us. He wants to cultivate within us the adoration and admiration of which He is worthy. He wants to reveal to each of us the blessed element of spiritual fascination in true worship. He wants to teach us the wonder of being filled with moral excitement in our worship, entranced with the knowledge of who God is. There can be no human substitute for this kind of worship."[1] This is the jewel to be discovered!

As the Westminster Confession puts it, "What is the chief end of man? To glorify God and enjoy him forever." Since all of life is worship, the primary responsibility of the church is to foster worship in the congregational experience so that our members continue to worship genuinely in their daily lives. What, then, are the primary elements to consider?

First of all, *the leader.* The worship leader, in addition to the pastor, needs to have a good understanding of what meaningful, God-exalting worship looks like in the life of his or her church's tradition. And he or she needs to know when and where to make suitable changes in service order, music options, and additional components as needed. This person needs a team around him or her to provide prayer, creative, and logistical support in order to get the job done well each week.

The Leadership Network (headquartered in Dallas, Tex.) offered these essential qualities of effective worship leaders today: quality relationship with the pastor or visionary, an equipper of a team, an example of a genuine worshiper, authenticity, a student of the Scriptures, a coach, a prayer warrior, a program director. These skills need to be honed by all who plan congregational worship so that the people of God are brought into his presence through a credible leader with spiritual integrity. Who are you training in your church to acquire these skills and lead others in God-exalting worship?

Second, *the style.* It's important that churches today not suffer from unnecessary conflict over worship styles. Style of music and worship order should grow out of a church's traditions and be shaped by a church's vision for the future. It should reflect the style of the people, the leaders, the community, and most important, it should grow out of the manifestation of the Spirit of God in your midst. Take the time to listen for God to reveal his intentions for the body in worship—it will ultimately lead you into a fuller expression of his style for you and the people in your care.

Being committed to unity in the body of Christ means that you are open to experiencing different forms and styles of worship. It is healthy for Christians to consider ways in which they can connect with people who are much different from them and reflect their love for God in ways that are often outside their comfort zone. We need to avoid becoming judgmental of the variety of expressions prevalent in the body today; instead, we need to appreciate the colorful ways the Lord directs his people in worship.

One such church where the worship is lively and creative is the Bethel African Methodist Episcopal Church in Boston, where Ray and Gloria Hammond copastor this thriving congregation. Here they deliberately attempt to blend the old with the new in each of their worship celebrations. In the words of Pastor Ray, "It is critical for us to know the anthems of the historical church, where we see ourselves as a part of the stream of Christianity that has flowed for 2000 years. In addition, we must expose our congregation to the more contemporary forms of speaking and singing the gospel message."

This deliberate striving to blend the old with the new has been extremely successful and meaningful to this African-American congregation. Using their full bodies in praise to the living Lord comes naturally to them, so when professional dancers in the congregation develop simple choreography for the songs they sing, it is received with joy and full participation. When they sing out the books of the Bible song that they are learning together, it is full of engaging emotion for all. When it's time for prayer and people are invited to come forward, they come not only individually but often in groups of three to pray with and for one another.

The underlying theme of worship at Bethel AME Church is "to come away strengthened in our fellowship with one another as we direct our praise, prayers, and worship to God," says Ray Hammond. "The lesson of the cross is that God is interested in us reaching up to him vertically while we reach out to one another horizontally."

Ray continues, "It's an absolute tragedy to come to worship and not know one another any better afterward. Our ministry to one another in the context of worship is critical to engaging our congregation in meaningful worship." Gloria agrees wholeheartedly, adding, "Even at the time of offering we all get up and walk forward, singing and praising God for the opportunity to give back to him what he so generously has given to us. Sometimes people in the congregation come forward dancing and singing, giving cheerfully and in a celebratory fashion, all the time fully engaged in the worship of God."

There are no dress code expectations for those who come to worship at Bethel AME Church. Dress is far less important than coming together to meaningfully worship God and connect with each other. In fact, several times throughout the year people come to worship in authentic African dress, a visual reminder of their distinct roots. They are "family," and virtually every aspect of their worship experience is a reminder that they come together out of love for God *and* one another. The traditions, experiences, preaching, singing, and relationships are all blended into a healthy expression of the body of Christ, where everyone is a part of the family, fully engaged in worshiping God together.

The activities of God-exalting, fully engaging worship are nothing new to the church. David MacAdam, pastor of New Life Community Church in Concord, Massachusetts, understands this and shared through his weekly e-mail newsletter to his church,

The following actions are associated with worship: kneeling (Psalm 95:6), bowing down (Psalm 95:6), lifting hands (Psalm 141:2; 1 Tim. 2:8; Psalm 63:4), standing before the Lord in awe (Psalm 4:4 KJV), clapping hands (Psalm 47:1), playing instruments (Psalm 33:2; 92:3; 98:6; 144:9), shaking tambourines and playing percussion instruments (Psalm 150:4), dancing before the Lord (Psalm 150:4), bowing our heads (Gen. 24), lifting our heads and eyes (Psalm 3:3; Psalm 123:1), plus praying, praising, singing and shouting for joy (Psalm 32:11; 47:6; 59:16; 66:8; 69:30; 98:1; 100:1–2; 132:9). Worship is a total exercise—we worship with our regenerated spirits (Romans 1:9), renewed minds (Phil. 2:3–5), and revived emotions (Romans 12:11–15). Intelligent worship is to present our whole bodies to God as a living sacrifice (Romans 12:1), exercising ourselves unto godliness (1 Tim. 4:7–8).

This creative Bible study on the actions called for in worship is a wonderful example of the variety of styles open to us as God's people. Despite the chosen style of the congregation or the individual, however, God's priority is not style but substance.

Third, *the substance.* In our brochure *Ten Characteristics of a Healthy Church,* we list the following elements in God-exalting worship:

- prayer—adoration, praise, thanksgiving, confession, and petition
- reading the Scripture
- preaching from God's Word for instruction, guidance, encouragement, comfort, challenge, and rebuke
- baptism and communion
- singing songs and hymns that praise God and encourage believers
- affirmations of those truths we believe
- dedication to the service of God in our lives and throughout the world

In addition to this abbreviated listing, where you fill in all of the blanks each week, I would suggest that the following issues be overlaid on top of these essential elements:

Celebration: taking time to offer our praise to God for all that he is, all that he has done in creation, his Word, and all that he means to us today through his Son.

Continuity: entering into worship that reflects a thematic flow for the entire time you are gathered, attuned to his voice and ready to respond to his initiatives.

Confession of sin: coming clean individually and corporately before God through prayer, in brokenness and need for cleansing and forgiveness. This may involve corporate reading of confession from Scripture.

Communion with God: having been restored to newness of life in him, we commemorate our belonging to him through baptism and the Lord's Supper.

Community: being united as one in him, the body of Christ relates in a new way with one another, expressing compassionate, unconditional love freely and generously.

Consecration: choosing to serve him through the living out of the Great Commandment and the Great Commission, rehearsed in and through the acts of worship.

Children: passing on from one generation to the next the stories of our faith, the expressions of our love for God, and the joy we have throughout this journey of life in Christ.

The substance of our worship plants us firmly in the divine encounter with God through the spoken Word, the songs of our faith, the traditions that bind us together, the ceremonies that reflect our convictions, and the relationships that last a lifetime. Form without substance is shallowness, to say the least. Substantive experiences in worship drive down stakes that hold us in communion with God and keep us united as his people.

God-exalting worship has stood the test of time and is being redefined for this generation too. It's time for the church to rise to the challenge of being sensitive to the new and renewing work of the Spirit and fully engage the people of God—in styles that fit the generation, under gifted leaders who are called to renewing worship, with a substance that holds fast to the Word of God and his appointed priorities for his people.

Worship—is it your missing jewel? It doesn't have to be. Once discovered, it will be your prize possession. Mining for it is definitely worth the effort!

Loving Father, you are the object of my worship this day. I long to know you more intimately and follow you more sincerely. I recognize today that in order for my heart to grow in your direction, I need to submit to your love and lordship. I must be in your Word more and communicate more regularly through prayer in my daily life. As a result of being filled to overflowing with you, I can then contribute positively to the worshiping community of faith each week. May I be open to the work of your Spirit in our midst so that the worship we enjoy together will reflect your love, grace, and tender mercy. Restore within me a priority for holiness in all its fullness. Lead me nearer to your heart, I pray, and build within me a longing to worship you every waking moment of my life. Give me the freedom I long for in my worship in congregational settings, both the familiar and the new. May I be a positive example of unity amidst our diversity. For I ask all of this in the strong name of Jesus, the one who tenderly leads me into God-exalting worship. Amen.

◼ FOR REFLECTION AND RENEWAL ◼

The healthy church gathers regularly as the local expression of the body of Christ to worship God in ways that engage the heart, mind, soul, and strength of the people.

Corporate worship is the ongoing reminder of:

- the lordship of Christ
- the power of the Holy Spirit
- the redemptive work of God the Father among us
- the truths of God's Word
- our need to share the gospel
- our mandate to serve others in need

Worship includes such elements as:

- prayer—adoration, praise, thanksgiving, confession, and petition
- reading of Scripture
- preaching from God's Word for instruction, guidance, encouragement, comfort, challenge, and rebuke
- baptism and communion
- singing songs and hymns that praise God and encourage believers
- affirmation of those truths we believe
- dedication to the service of God in our lives

Yet a time is coming and has now come when the true worshipers will worship the Father in spirit and truth, for they are the kind of worshipers the Father seeks.

John 4:23

1. On a scale of 1 to 10 (1 being not at all important and 10 being most important), rank each of the above statements while answering the question, "How important is this statement for the health of our church; how highly do we value God-exalting worship?"

2. On a scale of 1 to 10 (1 being very ineffective and 10 being very effective), rank each of the above statements while answering the question, "How effective are we as a leadership team at instilling these values in our church?"

3. For each of the above statements, ask your team, "Where do we want to be in the characteristic God-Exalting Worship in this next year or two?"

4. For each of the above statements, ask your team, "How will we get where we want to be in living out God-Exalting Worship in this next year?"

5. Overall, on a scale of 1 to 10 (1 being very low and 10 being very high), rank how well you think your church is doing in living out this second characteristic of a healthy church, God-Exalting Worship.

4

Spiritual Disciplines
Characteristic 3

The healthy church provides training, models, and resources for members of all ages to develop their daily spiritual disciplines.

But the wisdom that comes from heaven is first of all pure, then peace-loving, considerate, submissive, full of mercy and good fruit, impartial and sincere.

James 3:17

The late Peter Marshall, an eloquent speaker and for several years the chaplain of the United States Senate, used to love to tell the story of the Keeper of the Spring.

The Keeper of the Spring was a quiet forest dweller who lived high above an Austrian village along the eastern slopes of the Alps. The old gentleman had been hired many years ago by a young Town Council to clear away the debris from the pools of water up in the mountain crevices that fed the lovely spring flowing through their town. With faithful, silent regularity, he patrolled the hills, removed the leaves and branches, and wiped away the silt that would otherwise choke and contaminate the fresh flow of water.

By and by, the village became a popular attraction for vacationers. Graceful swans floated along the crystal clear spring, the mill wheels of various businesses located near the water turned day and night, farmlands were naturally irrigated, and the view from restaurants was picturesque beyond description.

Years passed. One evening the Town Council met for its semi-annual meeting. As they reviewed the budget, one man's eye caught the salary figure being paid the obscure Keeper of the Spring. Said the Keeper of the Purse, "Who is this old man? Why do we keep him on year after year? No one ever sees him. For all we know the strange ranger of the hills is doing us no good. He isn't necessary any longer!" By unanimous vote, they dispensed with the old man's services.

For several weeks nothing changed. By early autumn the trees began to shed their leaves. Small branches snapped off and fell into the pools, hindering the rushing flow of sparkling water. One afternoon someone noticed a slight yellowish-brown tint in the spring. A couple of days later the water was much darker. Within another week, a slimy film covered sections of the water along the banks and a foul odor was soon detected. The mill wheels moved slower, some finally ground to a halt. Swans left as did the tourists. Clammy fingers of disease and sickness reached deeply into the village.

Quickly, the embarrassed Council called a special meeting. Realizing their gross error in judgment, they hired back the old Keeper of the Spring . . . and within a few weeks the veritable river of life began to clear up. The wheels started to turn, and new life returned to the hamlet in the Alps once again.[1]

Ever wonder what's happened to the "veritable river of life" that's supposed to be flowing out of you today? What about the "hamlet," the faith community you are called to serve? Is your local church hamlet filled with people who know the value of the Keeper of the Spring? Or are there "foul odors" in the attitudes and lifestyles of the people of God within your jurisdiction?

This profound story has meant more to me than any other story as I consider the rhythms of my personal spiritual disciplines. Each new day I need to "rehire" the Keeper of my inner spring, my soul, and invite him to clear away the debris that settles within me so that what flows out is lovely spring water. I need him to do his cleansing work in me, faithfully, silently, regularly patrolling the depths of my heart, removing any leaves or branches that have fallen in and threaten to choke or contaminate the fresh flow of his Spirit within me. If I don't take that time to prayerfully ask him to do his work in me, then inevitably a foul odor will be detected in my words, attitude, mind-set, and lifestyle. It may not be apparent immediately, but eventually it will spill out and foster clammy disease and sickness in others.

Inviting the Keeper of our soul to do his faithful work within us is the crux of the matter when we dive into a subject such as spiritual disciplines. Our relationship with God has a direct impact on our relationships with others, our decision-making ability, our understanding of our mission, our vision for service in ministry. Each member of a healthy church must understand the value of a vital walk with Christ, be taught how to foster a personal devotional life, and urge one another on to growth in this area of our spiritual journey. What transpires in this inner circle of concern will impact each of the remaining characteristics of a healthy church. As pastors and leaders drink deeply at the clear spring, they will motivate and inspire others.

At First Church of Christ in Wethersfield, Connecticut, the pastoral staff realized the importance of showing the congregation they were serious about such a commitment. What transpired was a voluntarily accepted covenant.

"At the annual retreat for the pastoral and program staff in the spring, our senior pastor, Dr. Jey Deifell Jr., introduced the idea of a program staff covenant. We discussed it, wrote it, and agreed to hold each other accountable," says Cindy McDowell, director of caring ministries. "At the weekly meeting of our program staff we each turn in a written report on where we have been, where we are now, and where we want to go, based on the covenant. Then we each report verbally to the whole group."

At each fall weekly meeting, one of the staff presents a meditation on one of the disciplines in the covenant. After implementing the covenant in the fall of 1996, the pastoral staff got up in front of the congregation in December and shared the covenant with them. It was designed as a display of unity, but the congregation was also asked to pray for the staff as they sought to be God's men and women while in leadership.

"We wanted to say to the congregation that we are trying to live out the disciplines of the Christian life and ask for their prayer support," says Cindy. After the presentation before the congregation, the chairman of the church board prayed for the staff as they held hands.

"The response was most gratifying. We had some businessmen say that this covenant definitely had application in corporate offices," says Cindy.

The covenant is set up under three key principles:

1. *Seek godliness through faithful living.* This stresses daily study of the Bible, doing everything in love, maintaining a life of intercessory prayer, displaying the fruit of the Spirit.
2. *Support one another in relationship.* This includes always speaking well of other staff and leaders, expecting the best of one another, being available for prayer with each other, truly listening with the heart, maintaining confidentiality, rejoicing in each other's successes and sharing in each other's sorrows, and taking problems first to the person involved.
3. *Work together as body parts of the whole.* This means being aware of each other's gifts, learning styles, and personality; committing to attend all staff meetings; maintaining the freedom to express differing opinions; working through philosophical worship and clergy issues; being sensitive to how worship and program deci-

sions affect all; clearing all new or canceled programs at staff meetings; getting permission from parishioners to alert a colleague to a personal need, and being part of annual constructive staff reviews.

Cindy, who also doubles as director of women's ministries, says that this focus on personal spiritual disciplines suffuses all aspects of women's ministry. "My goal is to equip, empower, and mentor my leaders. We emphasize Bible study, memorizing Scripture, intercessory prayer on a consistent basis," she says. The same is true in her focus on the caring ministry teams in the church. "I try to model what a daily life of discipleship is like. We have many coming to Christ as adults who have little background in the Bible and the lordship of Jesus Christ. So I put my energies into equipping the leaders of the twenty-three care teams for which I am responsible to meet the needs of these people," says Cindy.

In a larger church like First Church of Wethersfield, where Cindy's husband, Mike, is associate minister for adult education, there are many programs for all ages. The pastoral staff's focus on spiritual disciplines has a tremendously positive ripple effect throughout all the ministries of this local church.

The subject of discipline is not always a popular one, especially within the context of ministry today where people's lives are often spinning out of control because of a rampant lack of discipline. As disciples of Christ, however, we have answered the call to follow Jesus into a life that is redirected in obedience to him. Having heard the call and heeded his loving voice to come and follow, we are to live a life of imitation and discipleship. When we are grasped by Christ and his unending love for us, we undergo a transformation that blossoms under his lordship and grace.

The Tension between Being and Doing

To be a disciple of Christ requires that we be disciplined in our life of faith, which comes alive and becomes fruitful in love. It means that we exercise self-control, engaging only in activities that enhance our walk with the Lord, while at the same time resisting the demon of busyness and finding a healthy balance between the doing and being sides of our lives.

The tension that exists between doing and being is real. We cannot outweigh one over the other, or we will find ourselves in trouble in both the short and long term. Both sides of ourselves need to be fed and nurtured daily. Reuben Job, in his *Guide to Retreat for All God's Shepherds*, says, "Consider it a gift when you keenly feel the tension between doing and being. It is a positive sign of your awareness of God's call, a sign of your maturity in Christ, and one of the places where every Christian minister may experience significant growth and renewal."[2]

It is God's priority that we understand our "being," for it is there that we discover him more intimately. Being in Christ requires that my soul first listens to his still, small voice out of my love and obedience to his Word, his lordship, his revealed truth and will. The Great Commandment (Matt. 22:34–40) begins with words that focus on our being, "Love the Lord your God with all your heart and with all your soul and with all your mind," before issuing the command to "love your neighbor as yourself." Mary, sitting at Jesus' feet (Luke 10:38–42), chose what is better, and her heart and soul were refreshed as a result. In John 6:22–40 we are reminded that Jesus is the Bread of Life, and if we come to him we will never hunger or thirst—he will be our all-sufficiency. Sitting at his feet and listening to his gentle voice is a must for all disciples.

My spiritual director once reminded me that the Latin root for the word *obedience* means "to listen." Only after we have first taken time to listen for God's voice will we be able to fully respond to his love and Word. We must tune our ears to hear his voice. It's like the child who was told by his father during a symphony orchestra concert, "Listen for the flutes in this song, don't they sound beautiful?" The child, unable to distinguish the flutes, looks up at his father with a puzzled look, "What flutes, father?" The child first needs to learn what flutes sound like on their own, separate from the whole orchestra, before he is able to hear them in a symphony. So it is with us as children of God. Unless we take the time to hear his voice in the quiet moments of life, we will not be able to hear him in the symphony sounds of life. As he reminds us, "Be still, and know that I am God" (Ps. 46:10).

"Doing" for Christ means that, out of the inner core of my being in him, I walk and talk and serve and love and live for him. I do for Christ what he beckons me to do, and I do it by the power he gives me, for his greater glory, for the edification of his created ones, for the building up and expansion of his kingdom. What I am to do for him is lived out in Jesus' words in Matthew 25:35–36, 40: "For I was hungry and you gave me something to eat, I was thirsty and you gave me something to drink, I was a stranger and you invited me in, I needed clothes and you clothed me, I was sick and you looked after me, I was in prison and you came to visit me. . . . Whatever you did for one of the least of these brothers of mine, you did for me."

A life lived for Christ is a pathway of healthy balances between intimacy and action, between prayer and compassion. The being and doing sides of us go hand in glove, both needing proper nurturing along the way. We learn the rhythms of our spirituality, compassion, and action through the disciplines of prayer, study, and practice. If we truly believe that the quality of our relationship with God determines the quality of our vision and ministry, then attending to our souls is a must.

Reuben Job, in his *Guide to Retreat*, quotes from Henry Simmons's book *In the Footsteps of the Mystics* a simple outline summarizing the tension that exists for all serious disciples of Jesus between being and doing:

1. This tension is normal and the place where God meets us;
2. It is possible to live with this wound of tension and still be faithful and fruitful in ministry;
3. Many have been able to fashion a healthy rhythm of prayer, action, and reflection that has led to effective, joyful, and faithful ministry;
4. Our doing can be an occasion for our formation in Christ, for our becoming more fully what we have been created to be;
5. Our being, who we are as Christians, inevitably leads us into action in the world.[3]

It becomes crucial, then, that we begin each day with a structure of prayer and reflection. Only then will we see all of life's activities as an opportunity for companionship with God. When we invite the Shepherd of our souls to lead and nurture us, we seek to be fully formed in Christ. As our lifelong companion, the Lord desires to commune with us, share the vast resources of his love and grace, and lead us in fulfilling his will. When local church members come to a deep appreciation of this truth, the atmosphere of health and vitality is significantly improved.

Center of Quiet

Dallas Willard, a leading voice in the area of spiritual disciplines, says, "There is nothing that requires more energy for the typical American Christian than the discipline of doing nothing. The hardest thing you can get anyone to do is to do [and say] nothing. We are addicted to our world, addicted to talk. . . . The goal of Christian spirituality is conformity to Christ—not togetherness, or meditation, or acceptance. The issue is discipleship. Discipleship is learning from Jesus Christ how to live my life as He would live it if He were me."[4]

Our discipleship must be lived out in a life of quiet submission to God. The late Henri Nouwen, in his book *Making All Things New*, reminds us that, "We do not take the spiritual life seriously if we do not set aside some time to be with God and listen to him. . . . The amount of time will vary for each person according to temperament, age, job, lifestyle, and maturity. . . . The more we train ourselves to spend time with God and him alone, the more we will discover that God is with us at all times and in all places. Then we will be able to recognize him even in the midst of a busy and active life. . . . The discipline of solitude enables us to live active lives in the world, while remaining always in the presence of the living God."[5]

Enjoying a center of quiet, cultivating the disciplines of silence and solitude, needs to be pursued by all believers in your local church. It's a must for health, healing, and wholeness in any congregation.

When the prophet Elijah, zealous for the Lord, was sent to the mountain to wait for God to pass by (1 Kings 19:9–13), was God in a powerful wind? No. In an earthquake? No. A fire? No. Surprisingly, the Lord made his presence known through a gentle whisper. So often we come to God and want to be "zapped," tingling with his presence, when all the while he wants us to rest in him, be comforted by his love for us, and listen carefully for his gentle whisper. Are you able to distinguish his voice today?

For ElizaBeth Emery, chaplain at Endicott College in Beverly, Massachusetts, part of her growing hunger for hearing God's voice has been the result of setting aside blocks of time for silence. "Silence was incredibly difficult for me, but it created a hunger for God that I could not let go of. Silence before God is a very powerful time. It is very confrontive, but it is also very encouraging," she says.

ElizaBeth's spiritual disciplines of silence and solitude include several elements:

- meditating on and contemplating a passage of Scripture;
- journaling, which helps her reflect on what God has been doing in her life;
- spiritual reading of devotional writers like Henri Nouwen, Richard Foster, Brennan Manning, Max Lucado, and the classics;
- silent retreats, where the hunger for being alone with God is satisfied on a regular basis.

Facing Our Distractions Head-On

More often than not, we are unable to discern God's voice because we are far too busy. In fact, many of us are addicted to our busyness, thinking that we are significant only if we are overwhelmed with daily activity. Janet Ruffing, in her article "Resisting the Demon of Busyness," writes, "I am convinced that this love of busyness is profoundly destructive to self-intimacy, intimacy with the Divine, interrelationships, reflective thought, the social fabric of our society, our care for the planet, and our own psychological and physical health. For many, the feeling of busyness is exhilarating, almost like an altered state of consciousness. A burst of adrenaline carries us from one activity to another. As a result, we avoid making time for leisure, for play, for relationships, for reflection."[6]

In reality, we force out any hope for a spiritual life when we are too full of engagements, talks, tasks, and every other escalating demand on our time, attention, and care. It's no wonder we are so stressed out today! We are having a love-hate relationship with our very existence. All islands of solitude have been invaded, and we have become resentful and anxious. It's time we hop off our treadmills of activity and take time out to be quiet before the Lord.

That's easier said than done, I am afraid. We have complicated our lives with multiple distractions. One of the greatest is the multiplied ways we are communicating with one another. We not only carry the burden of our snail mail (general delivery), but we also have overnight mail, voice mail, interoffice and external e-mail, answering machines, cell phones, fax machines, memos, checklists, and hundreds of unnecessary pieces of junk mail. We are cluttered to the maximum capacity, and finding the time to dig down to the bottom of our paper piles before coming to the Lord is oftentimes overwhelming.

With God, the way we communicate with him is the same yesterday, today, and forever. He is not available by phone, fax, snail mail, or e-mail. He will not be sending out any junk mail, nor will he be developing his own web page. The way to get in touch with him is the same as it always has been: "'Call to me and I will answer you and tell you great and unsearchable things you do not know'" (Jer. 33:3). Too many of us in the local church have forgotten how to communicate with him and, as a result, have lost sight of his vision and mission for us.

He longs for us to hop up in his lap and hang out with him for hours on end. But most of us are with him more like minutes or seconds when we are on the run to "do" something for him—or more accurately, for ourselves.

Beyond our busyness and our lack of communication with God, what are some of the other distractions we face? The occupations and preoccupations that get us off course from the direction we should be heading as Christ-followers?

The lure of the evil one. Satan's activity level is heightened when he thinks we are vulnerable to his attacks and his cunning nature. We need to be fully aware of his sly movements that seek to destroy and devour God's people.

Messed-up priorities. Too often, we are not wise in the use of our time and energies, and the tyranny of the urgent far outweighs what's truly important. It may be time to reassess your priorities and realign your schedule so you can spend time developing your heart for God and his Word.

Our desire to climb the ladder of success. When our hearts and minds are fixated on adding wealth to our portfolios, we are distracted from spiritual formation and pulled away from a sacrificial lifestyle of love and generosity. The needs of others tend to wait until it's more convenient for us to give. But Jesus calls us to a life of sacrifice, service, and surrender.

We hunger and thirst for things that don't feed our souls. A carryover to the success syndrome is the accumulation of things and experiences that thrill us, often to the neglect of the spiritual life. We have computers, laptops, handheld gadgets, boats, skimobiles, golf sets, summer homes, winter homes, fancy cars, expensive vacations, and a ton of other "stuff" that gets accumulated over the years. The more we have, the more we want; all the while our excitement for being alone with God and his Word wanes. I am convinced that the judgment on our generation will be focused on the almighty dollar and how we spent it so luxuriously on ourselves, often to the neglect of the poor and needy.

Skepticism. In many respects, we don't take seriously the role of the Keeper of our soul, mostly because we are skeptical if he's really necessary. We are an independent people who like to make it on our own. This works for a while, but eventually our attitudes and speech reveal the state of our souls. If we fully believe in the fruit of ongoing spiritual disciplines, though, our skepticism will be reversed and heartfelt commitment will return.

A lack of models. We are human "doings" much more than human "beings," so creating a quiet center is generally more difficult. But we need to be modeling for each other what a healthy spiritual life looks like. I long to see the day when local church leaders hold one another accountable for their personal spiritual life and see this role as more significant than the work they are called to accomplish together.

We are more self-reliant than God-dependent. We are very confident in our own abilities, so we don't depend on God for our day-to-day needs. In crisis moments we cry out for mercy and strength because of our desperate need. But in the mundane aspects of our life in him, we tend to walk the walk how we see fit.

We are far more reactive than proactive. Instead of reacting to the issues of life all around us, we need to proactively choose to step off our treadmills and find a place and time to be alone with God. It takes focused discipline, but it's absolutely essential.

We have lost our first love. This is the most difficult possibility to raise and sometimes the most difficult to discern if it's true. If you sense that you are falling out of love with God, remember that he is still faithful. He has always been by your side, available and aware of your heart cries. He has always longed for your love and is waiting with open arms to receive you once again. If you are a prodigal child and need to return home, he will be there to greet you. Don't let your feelings of love lost for God hinder your return to him today.

Overcoming the many distractions that keep us from living a disciplined spiritual life will take time. It will take a patterned intentionality for a minimum of one month straight. The distractions will keep presenting themselves, as Henri Nouwen notes, but "as they receive less and less attention, they slowly withdraw." Nouwen adds this illustration: "One of the early Christian writers describes the first stage of solitary prayer as the experience of a man who, after years of living with open doors, suddenly decides to shut them. The visitors who used to come and enter his home start pounding on his doors, wondering why they are not allowed to enter. Only when they realize that they are not welcome do they gradually stop coming. This is the experience of anyone who decides to enter into solitude without much spiritual discipline."[7]

The Lord refers to his people in Isaiah 61:3 as "oaks of righteousness, a planting of the Lord for the display of his splendor." God chose a wonderful analogy for us. He has done the planting and will actively participate in the growth process if we let him. He has provided the nutrients and longs for us to be nourished by them for our daily sustenance. Hold fast to his Word, and cling to his promises as you pray each day. The deeper the roots, the stronger the tree.

Attentiveness to God's Voice

Richard Foster once wrote, "We must understand the connection between inner solitude and inner silence. We must come to understand and experience the transforming power of silence if we are to know solitude. There is an old proverb to the effect that 'the man who opens his mouth, closes his eyes!' The purpose of silence and solitude is to be able to see and hear."[8]

Developing attentiveness to God's voice is a life-changing exercise. Henri Nouwen puts it this way, "Jesus in no way wants us to leave our many-faceted world. Rather, he wants us to live in it, our lives firmly rooted in the center of all things. Jesus does not speak about a change of activities, a change in contacts, or even a change of pace. He speaks about a change of heart."[9]

What matters most is where our hearts are. So the first reason we develop attentiveness to God is so that we may *listen for the heart of God*. Often our deepest feelings are difficult to express adequately in words. Even with those with whom we are most intimate there are times when silence is the most comfortable alternative. Sharing tears or a warm embrace can even be better than words. And so it is with God. There are times when we are simply awed into silence before him, needing to be in his presence, warmed by his loving embrace, listening to his voice of comfort and grace.

Many of us lack the skill of listening. We far prefer talking or having the answers, rather than asking the question and listening for the response. To become good listeners we need to find space for quietness, cleared of all the clutter and distractions. It requires that we spend time alone with God, unhindered by the demands of others. It demands that we pray and wait on God in silence and solitude, trusting that he has our best interests in mind regardless of how he answers our prayers. The psalmist reminds us in Psalm 62:5, "Find rest, O my soul, in God alone." God gave us two ears and one mouth—maybe because he wants us to do twice the amount of listening!

Second, we develop attentiveness so that we may *learn about the heart of God*. In chapter 20 of *The Imitation of Christ*, Thomas à Kempis writes, "In silence and quiet the devout soul goeth forth and *learneth* the hidden things of the Scriptures. Therein findeth he a fountain of tears, wherein to wash and cleanse himself each night, that he may grow the more dear to his Maker as he dwelleth the further from all worldly distraction. To him who withdraweth himself from his acquaintance and friends, God with his holy angels will draw nigh."[10] Coming away to listen to God teaches us to fear him and to walk in all wisdom and truth.

The psalmist continues this thought in Psalm 25:4–5: "*Show me* your ways, O Lord, *teach me* your paths; *guide me* in your truth and teach me, for you are God my Savior, and my hope is in you all day long" (emphases added). The psalmist is in a learning posture throughout these few verses, the action of showing, teaching, and guiding underscores the significance of learning about the heart of God. God is willing to reveal his will and his heart, and he has done so through the Scriptures and most specifically through his Son, Jesus Christ. When we approach our center of quiet with joyful expectancy, he will not disappoint us.

Ask yourself the following questions: What have I learned from God or about God in this past week? Month? Year? How has God spoken, taught, and groomed me to fulfill his purposes? What in my life needs to be changed in order for me to be more open and receptive to learning from God in this next week?

Be open to grow and change and become more like him—it's a life-long process for all of us. Who we are and what we do need to reflect what we learn from God, most intimately from our times alone with him in prayer, study, and reflection.

Third, we develop attentiveness so that *we may live out the heart of God*. All of our love and service grows out of the center of quiet within us. Inner strength and peace arise out of silence, solitude, prayer, and study of God's Word—power from on high to face the challenges of life. Our words should edify all who hear them; our hearts should be filled with encouragement; our minds should be enriched by godly thoughts; and our service should be energized with his joy. Developing attentiveness to God's heart will enhance every aspect of our life in him.

A Few How-Tos

Serving in a local church for eleven of more than twenty years of ministry, I found myself on several occasions teaching on this important subject. I encouraged our staff to be diligent in pursuing this aspect of their daily disciplines. I suggested many alternatives for developing one's spiritual disciplines, until one day I hit a wall.

During one of my monthly retreat days alone with the Lord, I added up all of the spiritual "should dos" that I had been seeking for myself and teaching others to aspire after. When I listed them, I was shocked—I had more than a dozen such disciplines. Fasting, praying, reading the Bible, memorizing the Bible, being well read in good Christian books, memorizing great hymns of our faith, stewarding all of our resources effectively, sharing our faith with nonbelievers, visiting the poor and needy through local and international missions, praying for all the nations of the world, daily and weekly worship, attending meetings, participating in conferences, listening to Christian radio and audio tapes, serving in the local church, counseling and mentoring others, etc., etc.

I realized at that moment in my spiritual pilgrimage that I was feeling the brunt of my own teaching, stressed to the maximum with a mountain of expectations that I and others had heaped on the body of Christ. How can we possibly accomplish all of these should-dos daily, weekly, monthly, or even annually—never mind in a lifetime!

The reality is that few of us can accomplish all of the above and still have a life in the world he has called us to redeem. We should be people of life, love, and freedom in Christ. Our role as leaders in the church is to point people to Jesus, the author and finisher of our faith, the joy set before us, the object of our daily worship. He wants us to find his joy for the journey, not be crippled with guilt for falling short of all the expectations accumulated over a lifetime in the faith.

All of the should-dos are valuable in and of themselves, and we should pursue them in the various seasons of life in him. But to consider them a must-do list for each day or even each week sets up the impossible for the average Christ-follower today. Instead, we need to highlight the absolutely essential ingredients of a spiritual life and reinforce a few simple priorities on a regular basis.

I would suggest that at the heart of the matter are the simple musts of prayer, study, and reflection. These need to become our primary disciplines for each new day.

Prayerfulness is listening to that still, small voice. It's going into our prayer closets and spending time alone with God. It includes our quiet listening, our silent praying, our audible requests, our prayers of praise and adoration, confession, thanksgiving, and supplication. It can lead us into prayers of dedication, songs of prayer, psalms of prayer, the recitation of the Lord's Prayer, or assorted prayers for healing, restoration, and renewal.

The unique elements of each person's prayer life are achieved in the stillness and openness by which you approach the presence of your Creator God. He is there to meet you in every time of prayerful meditation. Taking the time to pray is the discipline; what you do when you pray is the delight of one's heart in communion with him.

Often, those practicing the discipline of prayer will be led to fast for a season. Many will fast for one meal, one day, one week, or for more extended periods of time. Fasting is a discipline for those who feel led of the Lord to give up what the body craves in order to secure what the heart longs for.

Mention prayer, says Pastor Brian Simmons of Gateway Christian Fellowship in West Haven, Connecticut, and most pastors cringe. They all know they ought to do more. "Mention fasting, and we feel even more guilty," says Pastor Simmons.

"I knew there was virtue in fasting, and I had done a ten-day fast in 1989, but it took Bill Bright's call to fasting to win me over." Pastor Simmons began his first forty-day fast the day after Thanksgiving in 1996, and it proved to be a breakthrough in several exciting ways. Pastor Simmons found that the longer the fast, the deeper the spiritual effect on him. But the impact of a fast, in his experience, comes only after the fast is over.

"Fasting alone can make you very self-righteous, and a lot of older writing I have seen on fasting has that spirit. It's only the hunger for God that keeps one humble," Pastor Simmons concluded.

Study is the discipline of purposeful Bible reading. The resources for personal Bible study are countless, available at any local Christian bookstore. But the only required text is a copy of the Scriptures. What we aim for in study is to see the Bible come alive in relation to our understanding of the original context as well as for us today. Opening his Word each day is the discipline; what one studies and the resources utilized to enhance the study are supplemental to his Word.

Pastor Bill Boylan of Byfield Parish Church in Georgetown, Massachusetts, is committed to enhancing the personal Bible study skills of his congregation while at the same time enriching the impact of his preaching and teaching ministry. Each Sunday he publishes a weekly devotional guide designed to prepare the members of the church for the next week's worship service. On the cover of the devotional are the following words, "This devotional guide is designed to help you hear each Sunday's sermon better. Faith comes from hearing. Hearing is the key to a living faith. When we come to worship prepared to hear from the Lord and primed to listen to Scripture, our faith is strengthened." The Scriptures, combined with exceptional scholarship and practical instruction, come alive for the student of the Word throughout the week and especially during the weekly worship experience.

Meditative Bible study includes such options as reading through the Bible in one year or taking one book, chapter, or verse at a time. It is enhanced by other authors' treatments of the passage or in the words and music of hymn writers and contemporary musicians. The focus must remain on the Word, and any additional resources utilized in one's personal devotional life are to underscore the central role of the Bible. It is in his Word that God reveals himself and points us to the redemptive story of Jesus.

The third aspect of the must-do list is *reflection*. The mystics of old tell us, "Action without reflection is meaningless action." That truth has stung my conscience and remained with me for many years. I find that in the Christian life we tend to avoid or neglect this discipline. Reflection requires that we probe, ask questions, and listen carefully. It necessitates that we not jump from one activity to the next without first reflecting on the reasons why. The evangelical community at large is quite poor at the discipline of reflection, and that is a most unfortunate reality for us to consider when we are trying to instill within our people the priority of a spiritually disciplined lifestyle.

The discipline of reflection forces us to stop what we are doing long enough to analyze where we have come from, what we have learned, and why we are pursuing the direction we are forging for the future. It includes periods of silence and meditation, thinking through and even journaling the events of our days so that we can look back and evaluate the words we have spoken, the actions we have performed, and the attitudes we have displayed. Not to spend time in reflection is to stunt our growth in Christ.

Reflection is akin to looking in the mirror of our lives and seeing ourselves for who we really are. It defines for us our realities and sets our feet on course to fulfill the direction ordained for us by God. We need to be open to seeing the true picture of who we are in light of what God intends for us to become. We need to hear his voice of affirmation and love, and we need to listen to how others see us. It all begins with taking time to stop our activities long enough to look back, draw strength from God's guiding hand, and look forward to growing in faithfulness to his desires for us.

An option to consider is journaling. For my wife, Ruth, it's her most significant growth aid and an "oasis of peace." Daily she spends time with God in the pages of her journal, where she records her activities, feelings, and reflections in this safe confidential environment.

Writing out our prayers can also enhance our reflection. It is here that we pour out our hearts to God in an attitude of submission and love. Studying and praying through others' prayers also strengthens the Christian. Reading the biographies of saints of old can also enhance this renewing activity, reflecting on the lives of faithful ones who have paved the way for our generation.

Retreats can offer large blocks of time for reflection. My monthly times alone with God, as well as the times I connect with my spiritual director, have been the most significant renewal activities of my spiritual life. When I carve out this time to feed my soul, the Lord opens vistas of understanding and growth. Since I am an introvert, personal retreats are something I long for each month. Others with more of an extrovert nature will find the extended time alone with God somewhat overwhelming and possibly frightening. However, under the proper guidance of a spiritual leader, it can be the most memorable and life-changing time of one's life.

Another key way to foster attentiveness to God through developing spiritual disciplines is mentoring. We desperately need to reclaim the priority of mentoring, also known as discipleship or spiritual direction, in the church today. Regardless of the term you choose, there is a crying need for men and women of God to "take on" a younger believer, investing time and wisdom into the lives of those who are growing in their faith. When my colleague Les Stobbe's daughter introduced a young man to him after a couple of dates, he had no idea the twists and turns this relationship would take. Instead of gaining a son-in-law, he gained a mentoring relationship that has lasted more than fifteen years.

"When we first met in San Bernardino, California, Peter was struggling with God's plan for his life. A relatively new convert, he believed God had called him to the ministry, but he had no preparation. So while he worked with a landscape architectural firm, as draftsman at a construction firm, as shoe salesman in a department store, I encouraged him to finish college and consider seminary training," says Les. "He would come to our house on Saturdays and help me cut grass, seed winter rye in fall, put together a computer hutch, just so he could talk about life, about theology, about how churches operate, why he wasn't being used more in his church. When he studied at a local Bible college, we would go over my library shelves for books to supplement his courses, since he was hungry for a lot more than he was being offered at the school. We watched sports events on television together, attended hockey and baseball games together."

Having grown up in a single parent home in the Pittsburgh area, Peter quickly began calling Les "my California Dad." He shared with Les about an on-again, off-again relationship with a young woman who had entered his life about the time of his conversion. Many discussions later they were engaged and eventually married. Les and his wife, Rita, attended both Peter's wedding and his graduation from Bible college.

When Peter moved his California wife and first child back into his home area near Pittsburgh, the telephone became the mentoring vehicle through a really tough transition and job search. He needed to be constantly reminded that even though he dreamed of being a pastor, his wife and children were his first "congregation." After two years— and several jobs—a pastoral position opened up for Peter in New York State.

A year later Peter joined a denomination that provided not only a new pastoral opportunity but also the pastoral support a young pastor needs. The telephone calls became fewer and fewer, but when he did call the topics of conversation centered around marriage, parenting, personal, and pastoral issues. "Being available was more important than providing answers, no matter how well I had tested them in my own life," says Les. "Ultimately, it's the Holy Spirit that holds any of us accountable, and any attempt to take over his role will fail or alienate the person I am mentoring."

We need to help others grow in their relationship with Christ. The development of our personal spiritual disciplines is not accomplished in isolation, even though the amount of time we spend alone with God is growing all the time. Being held accountable to our spiritual formation is vital to all of us. Are you willing to invest in the life of one of your members and believe God for their maturity in Christ? I guarantee there are people in your congregation who would welcome your mentorship and grow in Christ as a result.

Richard Foster, in his classic *Celebration of Discipline*, says, "Superficiality is the curse of our age. The doctrine of instant satisfaction is a primary spiritual problem. The desperate need today is not for a greater number of intelligent people, or gifted people, but for deep people."[11] I could not agree more wholeheartedly. The path to depth in the spiritual life is a path of prayer, study, and reflection. These need to become our daily habits of health, life, and vitality. When this occurs, we maintain the rhythms of rest and renewal in balance with our busy lives.

If we want to give to others out of the overflow of our lives, then time spent cultivating our center of quiet is a must for every believer. We will realize the goal of healthy churches only when the people in our congregations are filled to overflowing with the joy of the Lord, spilling out over all who are in our care. Maybe it's time to rehire the Keeper of the Spring.

Lord, I confess today that at times I have lost my first love for you. I have followed after the ways of this world and pursued many more objects of affection. I am tired of playing the game and acting out the part of what it looks like to be a Christian. I know all the right words to say, and I know how to please the people around me with actions that show that I am a Christian. I need your forgiveness and cleansing from walking hypocritically, in my own strength, and aloof from your power and grace. I need a touch of your unfailing love today, and I am desperate for your kindness and mercy. Draw me close to your heart, I pray. Instill within me a yearning for righteousness that extends beyond my ability to muster up good works to please the eyes of my brothers and sisters. I am passionate for you today, and I long to be in your presence, profoundly touched by your love and affirmation. May my center of quiet be refined and renewed this day and in the weeks to come, and may the habits of my heart be a reflection of your desire for an intimate relationship with me. I love you, Lord, and I submit my life into your tender care. I am responsive to your work in me and prayerful that in all of my ways I may reflect your joy in this world. Empower me with your Spirit, and give me a heart like Jesus. For I pray all of this in your Son's precious and holy name. Amen.

■■■■■ FOR REFLECTION AND RENEWAL ■■■■■

The healthy church provides training, models, and resources for members of all ages to develop their daily spiritual disciplines.
These disciplines include such things as:

- Bible study
- personal worship
- confession
- petition for one's self and others
- journaling
- recognizing and utilizing one's spiritual gifts
- fasting
- listening to God's voice through prayer
- pursuing God's will
- growing to Christlike maturity
- instilling a strong sense of integrity
- growing as a person in body, mind, and spirit

> But the wisdom that comes from heaven is first of all pure; then peace-loving, considerate, submissive, full of mercy and good fruit, impartial and sincere.
>
> James 3:17

1. On a scale of 1 to 10 (1 being not at all important and 10 being most important), rank each of the above statements while answering the question, "How important is this statement for the health of our church; how highly do we value spiritual disciplines?"

2. On a scale of 1 to 10 (1 being very ineffective and 10 being very effective), rank each of the above statements while answering the question, "How effective are we as a leadership team at instilling these values in our church?"

3. For each of the above statements, ask your team, "Where do we want to be in the characteristic Spiritual Disciplines in this next year or two?"

4. For each of the above statements, ask your team, "How will we get where we want to be in living out Spiritual Disciplines in this next year?"

5. Overall, on a scale of 1 to 10 (1 being very low and 10 being very high), rank how well you think your church is doing in living out this third characteristic of a healthy church, Spiritual Disciplines.

5

Learning and Growing in Community
Characteristic 4

The healthy church encourages believers to grow in their walks with God and with one another in the context of a safe, affirming environment.

Let us therefore make every effort to do what leads to peace and to mutual edification.

Romans 14:19

When Jeff and Cindy Poor began praying for revival in their hearts, their home, and their church in the fall of 1996, they had no idea the course God would take to answer their prayer, nor the growth that would result from it. Even when Jeff was being treated for a highly aggressive cancer, he looked back and said, "The joy I have is indescribable." Why? Because of the glory Jeff's illness has brought to Christ—and because of the people who have begun to truly worship and serve God because of his testimony.

Jeff and Cindy were active members of West Congregational Church in Haverhill, Massachusetts, for eighteen years. Despite Jeff's serving as chairperson of the diaconate, as coordinator for short-term missionary service, and as point man for Promise Keepers trips, Jeff and Cindy felt dissatisfied. They felt that God had more for them, and Cindy began fasting and praying for a fresh touch from God. And God used Vision New England's Congress '97 to jump-start the process.

"We had been attending Congress for fifteen years," said Jeff and Cindy. "But Congress '97 was different. When Bruce Wilkinson issued a call for boldness in witnessing to our faith and for repentance in our lives, God spoke to us." Jeff shot out of his seat, determined to go forward in response to the invitation for repentance. "God's Spirit said to me, 'You can't be a Christian of compromise any longer. You need to be a Christian with boldness,'" said Jeff. And Cindy added, "God had been speaking to me as well, and I knew I needed to repent."

Jeff and Cindy were among the more than three hundred who surged forward after Wilkinson's invitation, kneeling before God and crying. During the next days, they read Bruce's book *Firsthand Faith*, which God used to deepen their resolve to live boldly for Christ. "After Congress we personally decided to be bold as witnesses. We wanted our non-Christian friends to know we were different because we have Jesus in our heart. At the same time God was preparing us for an even greater opportunity," said Jeff.

As a first step, they asked their church if they could lead an adult class in a study of *Firsthand Faith*. Given a group, they determined to pray on their knees for each class member individually every week. And they turned the leadership of this group over to the Lord more than they had ever done before. "We have always been overprepared as teachers. This time we determined to let God teach the class, which was radical. We opened it up for sharing, and there were many tears as people shared from their heart," said Cindy. Little did they know how the Holy Spirit would take over the teaching in the classroom.

For Jeff, the ten-week class meant taking another step in commitment. He reported, "There were areas of my life that God told me I needed to surrender. I told the class that I wanted to stop smoking, and I want you to hold me accountable, which they did." Also throughout these months God seemed to create opportunities for both of them to share their faith. A cook in a restaurant where Cindy was doing the accounting seemed open, so Cindy began to witness to her. She now regularly attends church.

That summer Jeff and Cindy taught another class, this time using Henry Blackaby's best-selling book, *Experiencing God*. This was a smaller group, a little more like a covenant group, according to Cindy. In the fall, they asked if they could teach the fourth and fifth graders in Sunday school, recognizing that nine and ten were critical decision-making ages. Then in October Jeff had a cough he could not get rid of. Thinking it was bronchitis, he visited his doctor. X rays showed abnormal nodes in one lung. After more tests, the fateful news came—Jeff had an aggressive form of cancer, with possibly one year to live. The chemotherapy did not touch the nodes.

"Just after I started chemotherapy I asked a barber friend in our church to give me a buzz cut. He tipped off my friends and pastor, David Midwood, so when I got to the barber shop there were ten men there to get a buzz as a symbol of them standing with me during chemotherapy," said Jeff. "One of them had alerted a reporter of the local daily, and she interviewed every man there. That article and picture of all of us with buzz cuts appeared not only in the local newspaper but has been reprinted all over the country. I'm getting calls from all over the U.S. from guys who have seen it on bulletin boards in factories and offices."

One of the women who cut some of the men's hair was not attending any church at the time. She has been at West Congregational Church every Sunday since that event. The other men who got a buzz have had many opportunities to share their faith in response to questions as well.

On the Sunday before Thanksgiving, the church was celebrating the completion of fund-raising for their new sanctuary. Although Jeff was already in the hospital, he asked to be released so he could give his testimony at the morning service.

"That testimony had an incredible impact on the congregation, with many tears evident. Jeff emphasized that we needed to strive for relational healing, that we needed to have a sense of eternity awaiting us— and that his illness was a weakening of the chains of earth. 'If I had the strength, I would run to this,' he said. Even though we don't have altar calls, I decided to invite people to come forward if they felt they needed to make a new commitment to Christ," reports Pastor David Midwood. "An ex-marine literally shot forward, gripping the pulpit so hard I thought he'd knock it over, weeping as he encountered God. Another guy who had been in the church for fifteen years went forward. I'm told that half of the congregation ended up in front, crying out to God. It was definitely a breakthrough event, with the testimonies of people whose lives have been changed an ongoing event."

Jeff then gave his testimony in the church he grew up in, as well as in the church his wife grew up in and in which they were married. In each case the impact was tremendous. And what about that class of fourth and fifth graders? Jeff said, "They have been walking through this with us. My hope is that when the day comes when I die, they will be able to come and see the celebration, to recognize that death is not something to be feared but to look forward to."

"We now have a literal prayer closet in our home. There we have had to repent from things we have never repented of before. As a result, things have been happening that only God could do," said Cindy, as she described another facet of lifestyle worship and spiritual growth. Jeff's deterioration was a physical and emotional struggle. Jeff Poor went home to be with the Lord on February 14, 1998. Two weeks before he died, he said, "I would not trade one day of my cancer. On my own I could never have had this effect on the lives of people." And on his own, he could not have survived the trauma without the help of almighty God and the strong support of his healthy faith community in Haverhill.

The story of Jeff and Cindy Poor is multiplied in congregations all over this region and throughout the country. Faith communities learning and growing together. Loving and serving God and each other in safe, affirming environments. Recommitting themselves to the example and teachings of Jesus, the awesome creator of community and the model of how we grow and learn side by side in daily life and ministry.

Jesus and Community

What Jesus developed with his disciples is embodied in the word *community*. When the disciples first encountered Jesus, they responded to his call, "Follow me . . . ," and their lives were transformed. Living in community with Jesus, the disciples followed his teachings and example.

Jesus and his disciples often huddled together, and then he would send them out continually to perform his will in the hearts and lives of needy people. In Matthew 10 we see a wonderful picture of such a huddle, in which Jesus taught his disciples, "'A student is not above his teacher, nor a servant above his master. It is enough for the student to be like his teacher, and the servant like his master'" (Matt. 10:24–25). Jesus' desire was that his disciples would become like him as they grew together and learned within the environment he created. Then he said to them, "'What I tell you in the dark, speak in the daylight; what is whispered in your ear, proclaim from the roofs,'" (v. 27). His teachings, given in the context of community, were to be shared with others.

These words, and hundreds of other such instructions, were given to the disciples so they could grow and discover what it means to be a Christ-follower. He taught in parables, gave specific examples of his teachings, expected discipline and obedience, and put up with a lot of immature behavior. Jesus continually strove to build community with his disciples and to encourage them to pursue this among themselves. The cycle of bringing the disciples into community and then mobilizing them for new experiences was repeated throughout the years he spent with them. For Jesus was preparing them for his earthly departure, when they would be establishing the Christian church.

He built community by teaching people in groups both large and small. He even fed them in community (Luke 9:14). Robert Coleman, in his classic book *Master Plan of Evangelism*, describes in-depth the community building tactics of Jesus. Coleman summarizes the example of Jesus in eight key concepts:

1. *Selection*—Jesus called a few men to follow him who could bear witness to his life and carry on his work after he returned to the Father;

2. *Association*—he stayed with them, making it a practice to be with them, drawing them close to himself;
3. *Consecration*—he required obedience, so that they would willingly deny themselves for others;
4. *Impartation*—he gave himself away to his disciples, giving all that he had, withholding nothing, not even his own life;
5. *Demonstration*—he showed them how to live, practicing prayer, turning to the Scriptures, teaching, serving, and sharing the gospel naturally and freely;
6. *Delegation*—he assigned them meaningful work, keeping his vision before them and calling them to fulfill his will;
7. *Supervision*—he kept check on them through his questions, illustrations, warnings, and admonitions in order to keep them on course to know and fulfill his work through them;
8. *Reproduction*—he expected them to reproduce themselves in the lives of others through witness and mission.[1]

Hindrances to Community

Unfortunately, we have far too few examples of community similar to what Jesus and his disciples experienced. But that should not prohibit our pursuit of meaningful community within our churches today. First, however, we need to consider some of the hindrances to effective community-building in our churches. Then, we'll discover ways to work around these hindrances and create learning and growth in our Christian walk within the context of our faith communities.

By far the greatest contributor to the challenge of community building is the fast-paced society we live in. Many families have both parents working outside the home. Our work weeks have grown beyond the standard forty hours, and even when people have full-time employment, many are seeking additional income as well. If you have a family, the stresses of homework, soccer practices, dance classes, after-school activities, and countless other areas of involvement all compete for a limited amount of hours available in an average week. Even those without a family are overbooked in their involvement with scores of interesting yet time-consuming activities. We are enmeshed in a driven society, and leisurely moments of building community with friends and family are fewer than ever.

In addition to our fast-paced society, another community blocker is the constant pulling away from the central thrust of the faith community into countless causes that occupy our time and energies. We Christians strive to make a difference in our world, often pursuing the re-Christianization of our land more than pursuing the God of our universe.

The Christian causes and issues are multiplying in number and significance each month. In and of themselves, they are worthwhile causes, such as pro-life and pro-family ministries. But when you add up the growing number of parachurch ministries clamoring for our time, talent, and resources, you can see that they leave little for building a community. When a cause or an issue puts the local church on the periphery instead of front and center, then we are walking on dangerous turf. The church is the central force for Christian action and service, and the local church is the place where issues and causes must be hashed out so that the living church, mobilized effectively in each community, is in the limelight.

Another hindrance to building community is the multiplicity of needs represented within the varying subcongregations of each local church. The fact is, we have several generations seeking to coexist. The needs of the young children are very different from the single adults, needless to say. The focus of the youth is in juxtaposition to the elderly. The baby boomers are often in conflict with the gen Xers. The couples with young children face different issues than those with an empty nest.

However, when has there been a time when we all need each other more than today? This potential hindrance to building community can and should be flipped upside down so that each generation within the local church can learn from the next and grow together in our shared faith in Christ. We need generational continuity and cross-generational interaction to achieve genuine community in our churches.

A lack of transparency and shallowness in relationships are two other hindrances, and they are often due to the transience of our culture. In our relatively small ministry of thirty-five staff members, we have seen almost one hundred staff come and go in less than ten years. That's a lot of change to cope with, and the local church experiences similar kinds of change in personnel both on the leadership level and within the congregation. It is tiresome to those who stay put over the years to constantly build new friendships. It is also difficult for those in transit to discover a sense of community for themselves when moving to a new area. As a result of this hindrance, we find it difficult to open up to others, and trust in relationships can take much longer to develop.

Other hindrances to be added include our newly formed addiction to the internet, our compulsion to overwork and underplay our lives away, and our own checklist of individual needs that surpass this extensive roster of community-killers in our generation.

Overcoming Obstacles

The list of hindrances to developing community within the local church could stretch on and on, and it would certainly be a worthwhile investment for the leaders of your local church to identify which obstacles are most relevant in your setting. Suffice it to say that despite the specifics for your church, this is an area of challenge for most churches pursuing health.

If our goal is constructing faith-based communities that grow in the knowledge of God in preparation for the fulfillment of his will, then radical change in programs may be required. What would happen if your church suspended all of its programs for a season in order to focus on hearing from God and building relationships with one another? What would you do if faced with the challenge of only coming together to worship God, teach the children his Word, and create small groups of adults to discuss the Scriptures and pray together? What would your church look like if after such a season you decided to suspend certain programs that were no longer relevant?

Sounds too radical for your church to consider? I would suggest that each church should entertain such an idea or something similar. We need to hop off the treadmills of our highly activity- and program-based ministries for a time in order to reflect on who we are and who we've become and what we're seeking to accomplish together. Such a "retreat" from programs and activities will help us see what's most important to reinstate as ministry foci for the future.

When I was a Christian education minister in a local church, one of my top priorities was to free up our teachers from worrying about any of the administrative and programmatic details of teaching so that they could focus on the creative presentation of God's Word. They were to hold the Scriptures paramount in each lesson they were teaching. I was not on their back, looking over their shoulders, badgering them about smaller, detail-oriented issues. Instead, I wanted them to focus on their own learning and growth and multiply that in the lives of their students.

My training of these teachers emphasized involving their learners in the discovery of God's truth spelled out in his Word. They as teachers needed to have absorbed the central truth of each lesson so they were teaching from the heart and in the context of real life application of the Bible. I wanted them to so love the Scriptures and the God of the Scriptures that they could not wait to share that love with their students.

In order for this lofty goal to be accomplished—regardless of the age they were teaching—I determined early on that the teachers did not need to concern themselves with whether they would have enough chairs for their students, what the condition of the classroom would be, whether the supplies they needed would be on hand, or whether the heat would be turned on in time for their class. The growth and learning we sought to encourage was to be unhindered by the incidentals that surrounded the precious moments spent in study, worship, and relationship building. So we provided department leaders and others to serve the teaching staff so that we could accomplish the joyful learning we intended to produce.

It was not a perfect system, but the goal was clear: *support the teaching staff with the training and resources they need to create a sense of community inside and outside the classroom that will enhance the learning and growth of each student.*

In essence, what we were trying to do as a leadership team was to maintain our mission of life-change through prayer and the power of the Word of God and not overprogram ourselves in the process. Relationships were of highest value, and when antiquated programs needed to be eliminated, we did not hesitate to do so. We were guided all the while by our objective of building safe environments for people to grow to Christlike maturity.

I am convinced that virtually everything we accomplish in ministry is the direct result of the quality of our relationships. Without true community there is limited growth and learning. Without first creating a safe environment for each person in the faith community to be himself or herself, their growth in Christ will be hampered. Therefore, as leaders in the local church, we must consider the needs of the disciple and all who are in the disciple-making process and determine ways to facilitate their development, whether in a classroom setting or in a small group, a ministry context or on the mission field.

Test Your Zeal

A trustworthy benchmark for evaluating your church's effectiveness in building a community of growth and learning is to ask yourselves as leaders, What are we most excited to accomplish together as Christ-followers? What are the top three issues we want to tackle together in this next season of ministry, as well as over the long run? I would suspect that issues of relationships and community and growth in Christ would be somewhere on your list if you are truly pursuing health and vitality.

Even though so much of our time as leaders is absorbed by the mundane details of administrative concern, we must regularly rise above those issues and dream about the results we are hoping for. In building community, there are seven big issues to address in assessing our zeal for expansion and maturity in Christ.

1. *Care for our children.* I start here because in so many ways we neglect the next generation due to the overwhelming needs of today's dysfunctional adults. When you compare how much of our time and resources are expended on adult-focused ministries versus children's ministries, the discrepancy is immense. I am concerned about how today's adult population will be judged in comparison with previous generations as it relates to passing the torch of our faith to our children. Or what condition the torch will be in when it is finally passed on.

What the culture is doing to and for our children impacts the church. Take a look around your corner of the culture and list all of the services provided for children in the media, the schools, towns, and cities across our land. How many of them are proactively building up our children? How many are systematically destroying their innocence? How many are devoted to fixing the problems created by their adult role models? What is your analysis of the positive effects our culture contributes to our children? Come up with a specific list of such services in each category.

Now, ask these same questions in relationship to your local church. How many of our ministries are proactively building up our children? How many of our programs are systematically destroying their innocence? How many hours are devoted to fixing the problems our children and youth face due to the stresses our adults are facing? What positive effects on our children do our churches contribute to? Make a list, and compare it with the multiple ministries offered to the adults in your church. What do you discover?

It takes more than a basic Sunday school program, an occasional children's pageant, and a vacation Bible school to deliver the goods for our children. They need a lot of time and attention for their growth and development to occur in a healthy fashion. Whatever you do in this area, please, for the sake of the children, make wise choices on their behalf and consider their needs as *far* more important than your own!

2. *Consistency of contact with "significant others."* My son, Nathan, is virtually alone in his public middle school. There are plenty of children in this particular school, but in many respects he is all alone as a Christian. We live in an unchurched corner of the country, and the population of evangelical believers is similar to the unreached people groups of nations around the world. Approximately 6 to 8 percent of New Englanders are evangelical Christians, so it doesn't take a rocket scientist to figure out that this translates into many children like my son who feel isolated as believers. In fact, many adult believers also feel the same sense of isolation.

Therefore, for families like ours, our children and youth need to have significant others in their lives who reinforce Christian values. We cannot raise Nathan on our own, so it is vitally important that we have partners in the church who assist and encourage us along the way. Nathan's youth pastor, Jim Petipas (known affectionately as J. P.), plays a crucial role in Nate's life. Without people like J. P., and many close family friends in the church, we would feel very alone in raising our son and daughter, given the fact that for now we have chosen to keep our children in the public school system.

Our family story is multiplied a thousandfold in towns and cities across our region and beyond. The need for building Christ-honoring communities in which all of us are being taught, nurtured, mentored, and led by "significant others" in the faith is growing faster than we can keep up with. The "significant others" who are identifiable within our churches are few in number, and many of them are overcommitted already. I am continually approached by pastors and leaders who are searching for mentors and disciplers who can invest time and energy into their lives. Those who are not as aggressive in the search for a mentor need it just as much, if not more. The need is staggering and the resources are gradually on the decline, unless we do something about it in our local church settings.

When Larry and Ellen Bishop first signed up to teach toddlers in our church, little did they know they would fall in love with these children. So much so that they followed these toddlers to the two-year-old class the next year, the threes and fours the following year, all the way up to junior high Sunday school and youth group several years later. Larry and Ellen have made a sizable investment in these young lives, and over the years they have tracked with them in their personal lives, with their families, and in their school, social, and church lives. Their faithfulness and consistency have produced lasting fruit in the hearts of several young people who today consider Larry and Ellen an intricate part of their lives.

Consistency of commitment is a lost art. The Larry and Ellen Bishops of the world are hard to find. No longer are people willing to commit to anything beyond a few weeks, never mind asking people to serve for a few months or a year. When I was serving as a pastor in a local church, we required all of our teaching and ministry staff to commit to at least a year with summers off. Now, in that same church, it's challenging to maintain this objective, and there always seem to be unfulfilled needs. I am beginning to wonder if this trend will change by my generation or by my children's—the ones who are needing it the most and who most likely will offer it to their own sons and daughters.

3. *Covenant groups.* Who among us doesn't need a group of people with whom to share our lives? If we are going to experience healthy growth and learning in the context of community, then we need to be a part of a small covenant group. This need is for all ages, from the youngest to the oldest believer. Our eight-year-old daughter, Rebekah, needs a covenant group as much as my eighty-three-year-old father does. All of us crave relationships with people we trust and can share our lives with through thick and thin.

When we enter into a covenantal relationship, we make an unusual commitment to one another. We say in essence, "I want to grow up in Christ with you. I want to play with you, laugh with you, cry with you, pray with you, share with you, study with you, grow with you, and I hope you want the same." We are committing to each other with the willingness to live out all of the "one anothers" of the Scriptures:

- love one another (John 13:34–35; Rom. 13:8; 1 Peter 1:22; 1 John 3:11, 23; 4:7, 11–12)
- confess your sins and pray for one another (James 5:16)
- care for one another (1 Cor. 12:24–25)
- greet one another (1 Peter 5:14)
- bear one another's burdens (Gal. 6:2)
- encourage and build up one another (1 Thess. 5:11; Heb. 3:13; 10:25)
- submit to one another (Eph. 5:21)
- bear with each other and forgive (Eph. 4:2; Col. 3:13)
- admonish one another (Col. 3:16)
- serve one another in love (Gal. 5:13)
- spur one another on toward love and good deeds (Heb. 10:24)

When we are in covenantal fellowship with a small group of like-minded and like-hearted believers, we will discover that when the hard times come our way, we are not left to stand alone. In crisis moments, when it feels like our worlds are spinning out of control or the bottom is dropping out, we can cling to one another and find hope and joy for the journey. That is what the Christian community is supposed to look like—is that your experience in your local church?

4. *Curriculum for growth and learning.* The substance of the teaching and small group experiences that reinforce the preaching need careful consideration by church leaders. Similar to the "curriculum" of the preached Word that pastors must prepare is the "curriculum" of the taught Word that teachers and other leaders must consider. As a Chris-

tian education major in college, I was taught the importance of considering the scope and sequence of what each age level was being taught. All of us, for example, need a balanced understanding of the Old and New Testaments, the story of Creation and the life of Christ, the writings of the apostle Paul, and a synopsis of the early church. When we emphasize one part of the Bible over another, we are not receiving the whole counsel of God.

Our own family struggled with this issue several months ago. We realized that even though we are part of a great church, our children were not covering some of the basics of Scripture. So we determined to write our own family Bible memory book. Both of our children have their own copies, which include a list of the books of the Bible, the seven days of creation, the Ten Commandments, the Beatitudes, the twelve disciples, the Twenty-third Psalm, Psalm 121 (a family favorite), and other selected passages. We have created our own family curriculum, which we want to pass on to our children. This is our starting point, and we're excited to see what will develop over the coming years.

I would love to see churches by the thousands take seriously the notion that each believer needs to cover a basic curriculum over the course of several years of study. I have suggested to a local church and a seminary in our area the idea of producing a wallet-sized card with a core curriculum of courses listed on it that would be distributed to each of their members. (Different cards would be needed for children, youth, and adults.) Next to each area of core curriculum would be a place to write the date of when such a class was taken. For example, one card could list one or more of the following subjects:

- Old Testament Survey
- Genesis (or other book studies)
- Prophetic Books
- Psalms and Proverbs
- New Testament Survey
- Life of Jesus/Synoptic Gospels; Gospel of John
- Early Church/Acts Study
- Pauline Epistles
- Peter, James, and John
- Revelation
- Church History
- Personal Spiritual Disciplines
- World Missions

Those who are charged with leading this area of ministry should then provide learning opportunities that pick up on each of these subjects so that each member has the opportunity to take such a class. In addition, wherever possible, make other long-distance learning and internet courses available to members of the congregation who are motivated to participate. And for the small covenant groups already in existence, provide resources for teaching this material in their context.

The goal here is to grow well-balanced members who have a clear sense of God's whole Word. And we want them to understand God's work in the history of the church over the ages. Also, we want our members to have a handle on developing their personal spiritual disciplines and discover where they fit into the worldwide missionary endeavors of the church. Hopefully, they will be equipped to apply these truths to their everyday lives and share them with others along the way.

5. *Continual improvement of teachers.* If we are going to learn and grow in community, those nurturing this process need to be trained to do so. One Sunday school teacher told me several years ago that he didn't need to attend our training days. I recall him saying something like, "I've been teaching this age level for years. I know everything I need to know and don't have any room in my head for newfangled ideas about teaching the Bible."

I put to him this question, "If you needed to go to a dentist for a root canal or even a simple toothache, would you go to the dentist who hadn't attended a single refresher course in twenty years or the one who was up to date on the latest technology and the best equipment to care for your hurting tooth?"

"Very funny, Steve," he replied. "Well," I said, "Isn't it far more important to care for a broken heart than it is a hurting tooth? Please try to join us for the next teacher training event so our children have the best Bible teachers possible." Much to my amazement, he showed up for the next meeting and over time became a positive contributor to the teaching ministry of that church.

Take advantage of every possible opportunity to instill new skills, ideas, methods, and principles for effective teaching into those who are charged with this responsibility. Teacher training is critical to the success of any learning environment within the local church. You cannot assume just because people have a heart for teaching, are willing to give it their best shot, or even feel gifted in this area that they will be effective communicators of God's Word.

Some of the issues to cover include: age level characteristics of the learner, methods of effective classroom discipline, listening skills, creative Bible learning activities, how to lead a discussion, dealing with problem students, writing and completing learning objectives, caring for learners outside the classroom or covenant group setting, the use of media, creating environments that teach, the use of stories and illustrations, basic Bible study skills for teachers, team building, the role of the Holy Spirit, methods of evangelism in the context of a small group, relationship building, etc.

Countless resources are available in your local Christian bookstore for help in creating meaningful training sessions. Or you can design them on your own, according to the need of the moment. Often the use of a case study that brings out several issues at once is helpful to discuss in a training session. It's vitally important that leaders come together to share their experiences and grow together in this process. Whatever you do, don't assume that teachers and covenant group leaders have the skills to effectively serve in these capacities. Spend the time and allocate the resources necessary to equip them for these roles. It will certainly pay off in the long run.

6. *Communication within the family.* With the family in crisis today—with the enormous pressures on marriages, between parents and children, and within the single adult population—we desperately need loving communication. The local church community has an unprecedented opportunity to take the lead in this area within their learning and growing environments.

Communication skills, learning how to resolve conflicts, expressing love tangibly and intangibly, listening carefully, asking good questions, spending quantities of quality time together, and other relational skills can be modeled in these settings. The Sunday school classes, covenant groups, and various informal settings are wonderful occasions to reinforce the most competent ways of relating to one another within the family.

I trust that you will agree that the family is the bedrock of our society. What happens in the home is translated into all of our lives. When we bless one another with love and affirmation, reinforce the work of Christ within one another, and prayerfully support the growth and development of each member of the family, then we positively impact the church of Jesus Christ. What greater testimony to the world at large than to have a church filled with healthy family relationships at every stage of development.

Resources like Family Builders Ministries, Marriage Savers, Focus on the Family, PREPARE, Family Life Conferences, Promise Keepers, Women Aglow, Women's Ministries, various national singles ministries, and countless other pro-family ministries scattered across the country are available to the local church. These excellent services define and reinforce what the Scriptures teach about relationships. They need to be incorporated into the learning and growing environments of the local church.

Out of the context of meaningful relationships will flow effective service to the communities of this world that God has called us to impact for his glory.

7. *Community impact.* The visible statement of the body of Christ to the world is the reason we gather in settings designed for learning and growth. Why are we studying the Scriptures together, growing in Christ together, urging one another on to love and good works, building meaningful relationships? To let the world know of our love for Christ and our desire to share his love with a lost and needy world. Only then will they truly know the love of God for themselves.

After thirty-four years of effective ministry in an urban African American church, the Reverend Nellie Yarborough determined that group Bible study and fellowship would take the church to a new level of spiritual health. "People are coming to the Lord as a result of our 'Touch Teams,'" reports Rev. Yarborough. "Our goal is to reach sinners, backsliders and people of the street—I tell people who come from other churches to get things straightened out and serve there. We are here to impact our community for Christ, and the study of the Scriptures has opened up a door we could not ignore." She decided on the name Touch Teams to make it clear this was a "high touch" ministry of the church despite its Bible-teaching objective. They are currently working through a curriculum study of *Through the Bible in One Year* with Dr. Hensley.

What began as a nine-month training class for potential leaders in the church has blossomed to become one of the hallmarks of Mt. Calvary Holy Church, where Rev. Yarborough has served all these years. God has honored the choices of his people in this church as they hold high the standard of learning and growing in community. And their neighborhood and city has been impacted as a result of their faithfulness.

The process of growth to Christlike maturity is one we need to patiently walk through in the context of community. We need one another in order to grow and become all that God intends for us, for it is impossible to experience any kind of significant growth on our own. Robert Fulghum says it so beautifully in his book *All I Really Need to Know I Learned in Kindergarten:*

> All I really need to know about how to live and what to do and how to be I learned in kindergarten. Wisdom was not at the top of the graduate school mountain, but there in the sandpile at Sunday school. These are the things I learned: Share everything. Play fair. Don't hit people. Put things back where you found them. Clean up your own mess. Don't take things that aren't yours. Say you're sorry when you hurt somebody. Wash your hands before you eat. Flush. Warm cookies and cold milk are good for you. Live a balanced life—learn some and think some and draw and paint and sing

and dance and play and work each day some. Take a nap every afternoon. When you go out into the world, watch out for traffic, hold hands, and stick together."[2]

Let's walk through the maze of life together, learning and growing up in Christian community.

Lord, you know that so often my inclination is to go it alone in life. I think that I can make it without help from anyone, even you. Or at times I lean too much on others to the neglect of your presence. Please forgive me for my self-sufficient ways. I know that I need to hold on to my brothers' and sisters' hands, even when at times they have not been secure. I need to become more transparent, more trusting, more open with my feelings, more encouraging and affirming, and more willing to receive the honest love of others. In many respects I need to recommit to the community of faith you have placed me in so that I will be a positive influence of learning and growing in the lives of others. Restore within me a renewed desire to build community in my marriage, family, church, ministry, and friends. May my lamp be filled with your love and my little light shine ever so brightly for your glory. I love you. Amen.

FOR REFLECTION AND RENEWAL

The healthy church encourages believers to grow in their walks with God and with one another in the context of a safe, affirming environment. To accomplish this objective, the healthy church:

- enables people to see Jesus clearly
- helps them to know his will for them
- equips them to follow him in all of life
- helps each person to find his or her calling—either at home or abroad, either clergy or layperson
- encourages people to discover and use their God-given gifts and trains them accordingly

- provides settings for members to come together for teaching, prayer, sharing, and service

It does these things through:

- individual mentors
- small group Bible studies and discipleship groups
- a variety of training and learning opportunities

Let us therefore make every effort to do what leads to peace and to mutual edification.

Romans 14:19

1. On a scale of 1 to 10 (1 being not at all important and 10 being most important), rank each of the above statements while answering the question, "How important is this statement for the health of our church; how highly do we value learning and growing in community?"

2. On a scale of 1 to 10 (1 being very ineffective and 10 being very effective), rank each of the above statements while answering the question, "How effective are we as a leadership team at instilling these values in our church?"

3. For each of the above statements, ask your team, "Where do we want to be in the characteristic Learning and Growing in Community in this next year or two?"

4. For each of the above statements, ask your team, "How will we get where we want to be in living out Learning and Growing in Community in this next year?"

5. Overall, on a scale of 1 to 10 (1 being very low and 10 being very high), rank how well you think your church is doing in living out this fourth characteristic of a healthy church, Learning and Growing in Community.

6

A Commitment to Loving and Caring Relationships
Characteristic 5

The healthy church is intentional in its efforts to build loving, caring relationships within families, between members, and within the community they serve.

This is how we know what love is: Jesus Christ laid down his life for us. And we ought to lay down our lives for our brothers.

1 John 3:16

In early 1998 four men beat a cab driver to death in Lawrence, Massachusetts, while all around people looked out of windows and saw the beating in process. No one bothered to call 911.

In a New England church the leader of a class on counseling sent a class member to the kitchen for coffee. She returned in tears, "She would not give me coffee because she says our class did not return the cups last time."

A pastor couple who were leaving the ministry visited six churches in the area. Not one person in those churches said hello or welcomed them. They were not surprised that none of these churches were growing.

Even in the church, we live in a narcissistic age, a period of history marked by self-centeredness and relational challenges. The world around us promotes values that pull us further into ourselves and farther apart from one another. The church of Jesus Christ must counter this phenomenon, presenting an alternative that breathes life and hope into the hearts of lonely, confused, disenfranchised, hurting people.

I am intrigued by the subject of narcissism and only recently have really dug into the meaning of this term. Narcissism is described this way: "The essential feature of this disorder is a pervasive pattern of *grandiosity* (in fantasy or behavior), *hypersensitivity* to the evaluation of others, and *lack of empathy* that begins by early adulthood and is present in a variety of contexts."[1] The self-esteem in the narcissistic personality is extremely fragile, and as a result, interpersonal relationships are inevitably disrupted.

The roots of such a personality disorder are found in early childhood, when basic needs of individuals were short-changed. Many people in our churches today can highlight the pain of their childhood, often recounting with horror the memories of their earliest years of life. It pains me to think of the countless stories I have heard from individuals who have crossed my path in over twenty years of ministry. The hurt is real, and it manifests itself in adult dysfunction of mammoth proportion.

Narcissistic personality traits are evident in many who sit in our congregations crying out for loving, caring relationships. In many respects, the need for such relationships is so strong that unless we meet this demand today, we may suffer the heart cries of yet another generation in desperate need of unconditional love and acceptance.

The narcissistic personality described below is evident in the lives of people within your reach—does any of this ring true for you or members of your congregation?

The picture of the narcissistic personality can be described as

> having an exaggerated or grandiose sense of self-importance; as having a remarkable absence of interest in and empathy for other persons; as eager to obtain admiration and approval of others; as entertaining fantasies of unrealistic goals; as lacking emotional depth, and unwilling or unable to understand the complex emotions of other people; as angry and resentful, but often concealing such resentment beneath depressive moods; as deficient in genuine feelings of sadness and compassion; as cold and indifferent, icy and unresponsive; as manipulative, exploitive, and unprincipled; as having strong feelings of insecurity and inferiority, alternating, but in no predictable pattern, with feelings of greatness and omnipotent fantasies; and as lacking enthusiasm and joy in the pursuit of goals, but reflecting, instead, a driven, pleasureless approach to goals, which are fueled by an insatiable ambition. Interpersonal relationships are extremely unstable due to a tendency either to overidealize or to devalue a relationship on an alternating basis. The other is expected to respond to one's desires and wants, but has no right to expect similar treatment in return.[2]

When I was introduced to this material by my mentor and friend Rich Plass, I was alarmed by the significance of this disorder for church leaders. I do not expect that we will become experts in narcissism, but we certainly must be alert to the characteristics evidenced by this personality disorder since it is so rampant in our society today. It has undoubtedly infected the pews; and from my experience with people and the issues they carry, these descriptions are right on. Self is of greater importance than others, and if the church is to be relevant in our world today, this trend must be supernaturally reversed.

The antidote to the narcissistic personality is a healthy sense of who we are as unique creations of God and beloved children of the King. We all have basic needs in common with one another. When those needs are fulfilled throughout our life, then a healthy sense of self is created, and healthy relationships are developed. If those needs are left unfulfilled, we will be left with a serious vacuum within us, and our interpersonal relationships with one another are hampered significantly.

Simply put, our needs are threefold:

1. the need to be loved, affirmed, and accepted by significant others in our lives, most specifically our parents;
2. the need for authority figures to guide and direct us appropriately through life, most importantly by our parents, grandparents, and other significant leaders;
3. and the need to belong to a group, attached by birth or adoption, most significantly evidenced in the family system.

Overlay our Christian experience on top of these basic needs, and it's readily apparent that we need to be loved and accepted by God; we need to be led by the authority of the Scriptures and the lordship of Christ; and we need to belong to one another within the fellowship of believers in the context of the church.

Since we internalize from others the formation of who we are as individuals, we must realize the significance of healthy relationships if our local fellowships are to become vibrant places of worship, love, and service. We need to get to know one another and deepen our loving and caring relationships so that true wholeness will emerge from within our people.

Knowing Your Community

Who are we seeking to reach and bring into environments of loving acceptance and caring response? How well do you know the people in your congregation and community? When is the last time you stopped to look around, listen, and catalogue your findings about the characteristics of those you are serving? How many have you sat with and listened to as they interacted with others?

Because of an alarming rate of burnout and ministry frustrations among young pastors in our region, Vision New England and the Ockenga Institute of Gordon-Conwell Theological Seminary recently embarked on research to discover the common traits of persons within our region. We were convinced that by knowing more about our region and the people who live here, our ministry relationships can be enhanced. We devoted over a year to this endeavor and unpackaged several traits that are distinctive to our region. The generalizations of people in New England often lacked factual verification. It was fascinating to find data that supported many of our assumptions while pointing us in new directions. After much sorting, sifting, testing, and verifying, eight distinctive traits of New Englanders were identified:

1. New Englanders tend to resist change.
2. New Englanders tend to value tradition.
3. New Englanders tend to be Roman Catholic.
4. New Englanders tend to have a secular mind-set.
5. New Englanders tend to be self-reliant.
6. New Englanders tend to be reserved.
7. New Englanders tend to favor insiders.
8. New Englanders tend to operate locally.[3]

When we took this information to church leaders throughout the region, there was unanimous fascination and agreement with our findings. We discovered that no matter the size of the church, the ethnicity of the people, the setting of the ministry, or the ages of the people being served, the data was helpful to pastors and leaders alike. The more we know about the people we seek to develop in Christ, the better off we will be in utilizing such data to shape our ministry priorities and relationships. How well do you know your community?

Building Loving, Caring Relationships

Once we know the community to whom we are ministering, how do we go about building loving and caring relationships? Seven directives are essential.

1. Express Unconditional Love and Acceptance

For Pastor David Malone and The Eliot Church (Presbyterian) in Lowell, Massachusetts, relationships are of prime importance. Since the community they serve is 50 percent white and 50 percent ethnic (mostly Cambodian, with some African), and since they do not have the advantage of sharing a common language, the love and care they exhibit to one another is the glue that holds this church together. In their worship services, before the Scripture is read in Cambodian, the reader says, "Good morning," and the whole congregation responds. Before the same passage is read in English, the reader presses palms together and says, "Chim riap sua," and the whole congregation responds. New members must learn appropriate common greetings in both English and Cambodian as a necessary relationship builder within this ethnically mixed fellowship. Even their annual ham and bean supper now includes egg rolls and rice! In every way possible, they act to show concern for people and the difficulties they have in their daily lives.

The people of Eliot Church reach out to the youth gangs in their neighborhood with loving and caring relationships. They recognize the dilemmas these kids on the street face with so many of their basic human needs neglected during their formative years. Pastor Malone has taken this ministry seriously and has even accompanied many of these troubled teens to the Lowell District Court and stands with them and their parents during these difficult moments.

In addition to the youth gang ministry, they have reached out to a mentally disabled veteran administration patient who lives in a halfway house next to the church. Their ministry to this man has resulted in his desire to tend to the front door of the church each Sunday morning. "We may be the only church in New England with a government certified paranoid schizophrenic as our every Sunday greeter," says Pastor Malone. "No one is offended by his bizarre dress and behavior. Or if they are offended by him or the rest of this strange mix, they go elsewhere. Our norm is to welcome everyone—and we are literal about that!"

In their efforts to literally reach out and welcome everyone in Jesus' name, they offer our society a countercultural approach to a narcissistic age. They live out the scriptural principles of loving and caring relationships that Jesus revealed so long ago.

> "Blessed are the poor in spirit,
> for theirs is the kingdom of heaven.
> Blessed are those who mourn,
> for they will be comforted.
> Blessed are the meek,
> for they will inherit the earth.
> Blessed are those who hunger and thirst for righteousness,
> for they will be filled.
> Blessed are the merciful,

for they will be shown mercy.
Blessed are the pure in heart,
for they will see God.
Blessed are the peacemakers,
for they will be called sons of God.
Blessed are those who are persecuted because of righteousness,
for theirs is the kingdom of heaven."

Matthew 5:3–10

Blessed are the people of Eliot Church who love and care for others less fortunate than they are, for theirs is truly the kingdom of heaven!

In all of our visits to healthy churches, the most consistent quality of vitality focused on this issue of unconditional love and acceptance. When we queried church leaders about what attracted new people to their congregations, it was the reputation their church had in the community regarding the basic relational dynamic of love and acceptance. There were no hoops to jump through or entry requirements for coming to church. When the people of God express unconditional love to a person new to the fellowship, that gift has lasting value.

That gift was given to me as a seeker. Even though I was attending a church at the time, I had not come into a personal relationship with Jesus as my Lord and Savior until I was a junior in high school. My friend Rich Plass invested in my life despite some of my bad habits. For example, even though he disapproved of my smoking, he did not alienate me from hearing the gospel and being loved into the kingdom. In fact, I accepted Jesus as my Savior in November of my junior year and did not kick the smoking habit until I was a sophomore in college! Did that stop Rich and other spiritually wise mentors and teachers of mine from withholding love and acceptance? Certainly not. They prayed for me, urged me to quit, and counseled me with strong biblical teaching. It finally took the urging of a roommate at college to encourage me to discard that bad habit forever. I "saw the light" and quit smoking, not because I was ridiculed or humiliated, but because I was encouraged to do so out of love and caring concern.

Far too many churches would prefer to withhold love and acceptance because of the visible bad habits of others. I recall with vivid clarity the time I was teaching on this subject at a church in north central Maine, where there were people in my presence who were vehemently opposed to any outreach to "those lousy drunks" in their community. I could not resist the temptation to refute their logic. I told them, "If we are unable to get close to those in our community who have great needs, how will we ever reach them with the life-changing, love-infested gospel of Christ?" They had a turnaround that day—not because of my words but because of the conviction of the Spirit of God. They subsequently started an effective recovery ministry to reach "those lousy drunks."

Since we have been unconditionally loved and accepted by God, forgiven, restored, and ushered into a new relationship with him, the church is to exhibit those same Christ-honoring graces to the world he has called us to reach.

2. Encourage Authenticity, Transparency, Honesty, Integrity

To be authentic (real), transparent (open), honest (truthful), and full of integrity (trustworthy) in all of our relationships means we willingly show ourselves to others without any pretense or pride. Few of us are willing and able to be real, open, truthful, and trustworthy to all who cross our path. It is a huge risk.

Because we are so filled with empty clichés toward one another—"Hi, how are you?" "Oh, just fine, and you?" "Isn't it a nice day?" "Yes, it really is"—we find it difficult to penetrate with words that take us beneath the surface. It's not possible, practical, or necessary to go deeper with many acquaintances whom we see for brief encounters. However, each of us needs to know what it feels like to be real, open, truthful, and trustworthy to those we know on a more intimate basis.

When we begin to plumb the depths of relationships with those we love and trust, the essence of our personhood can be enriched. Yet, these relational values are not the highest priorities in our world. The church, then, needs to be the safe place for people of faith to show their true colors and reveal the hurts, needs, and anxieties that plague so many of us. If we dare not share the true elements of who we are with others who can pray for us and speak to our personal issues with biblical insight, then we are left out in the cold to fend for ourselves.

One of the relational truisms that I hold dear is, "I will love you enough to be honest with you, and I will expect the same from you." Since I am an "all cards on the table" kind of guy, I am comfortable with myself and able to handle (most of the time) the honest feedback I receive from others. The greatest gifts I have received from others is their openness and vulnerability, even when they are guiding those qualities in my direction for my edification and growth. Sometimes the honest truth hurts, but often when it does, I can be assured that the fruit it will bear will be the greatest gift of all.

My wife and I try to live out this principle in our marriage, and we seek to empower our children with the same freedom. It does not mean that our home is free from conflict—far from it—but it does mean that we are seeking to build a safe environment where truth can be spoken and received in love.

In addition to my family, I meet weekly with my very good friend Paul Borthwick for conversation, accountability, and prayer. We have been meeting on Monday mornings for several years and have both found this venue to be a safe place to be ourselves and share with one another openly, honestly, and vulnerably. The transparency of our times together have been enlightening and enriching. We have been able to say hard things to one another, rejoice in the accomplishments of one another, pray for each other's needs, listen to and counsel each other surrounding life-shaping decisions. This long-standing relationship has been a gift from God that I treasure, and I pray that all who read these words will discover a similar gift of friendship from which to draw upon and learn from as you share your life with another.

The relational health of a church emanates from the relational core of family and friends. When we know what relational health looks like within the context of our key contacts, we can translate that into the life of the church. On the other hand, when our families and friendships are in disarray, it's difficult to contribute positively to the health of the body of Christ. Our goal as church leaders is to instill health into families and friendships so that the extended family of God can become a healthier, more vibrant example of Christlike love and unity . . . and they'll know we are Christians by our love.

3. Exhibit Grace, Mercy, Forgiveness

Micah 6:8 tells us: "He has showed you, O man, what is good. And what does the Lord require of you? To act justly and to love mercy and to walk humbly with your God." When I asked myself the questions, "What is mercy? How am I to love it? How am I to reflect this love and live out mercy in my daily life?" I began to ponder anew the meaning of this biblical concept. It is a powerful mandate fully deserving our in-depth consideration.

Webster's dictionary defines *mercy* as "compassionate or kindly forbearance shown toward an offender, an enemy, or other person in one's power; compassion, pity, or benevolence." The Lord embodies mercy and expresses it generously to his people.

Our family was faced with a serious dilemma when my mother was coming to the end of her life, having suffered for several months following her stroke. Her insurance coverage was running dry after staying her allotted days in the nursing center. We wanted to take her home, but we knew that my father was unable to care for her. Where would we turn for help? Hiring a full-time nurse seemed impossible to us. But God, through his miraculous love and mercy, sent us a dear woman of faith, to move into our parents' home and care for my mother through her final weeks of life. Irene Vincent was an angel of mercy, given to our family for a specific season, and remained a precious gift to all of us during a terribly difficult time. I will never forget Irene Vincent, nor will I forget to thank God for the miracle he performed in sending her to us when we needed a touch of his mercy. Irene's faith in God and her willingness to respond to his leading was a wonderful reflection of what mercy looks like in real life.

Finding the end of God's mercy is like finding the end of a ring. It is impossible! His mercy is unfailing and eternal (Ps. 103:17). It is boundless (Ps. 108:4). It prolongs life (Lam. 3:22–23). It forgives our sin (Mic. 7:18). It makes our salvation possible (Titus 3:5).

Where are God's angels of mercy in this day and age? Unfortunately, we are too often quick to judge, swift to convict of sin, anxious to find fault in others. How low will we sink in such a miry pit of dismay? The church is struggling with the sin of pettiness today. We are all over one another because of small issues of inconvenience. We don't like how the ushers take the offering or how the kids get the fellowship hall dirty. We cringe when the soprano misses a high note or when a baby's cry disturbs our worship. We nitpick the budget of the church line by line and critique the pastor's best effort in preaching God's Word. We don't like the design of the new choir robes or the hair color of the women's Bible study leader. The list could go on and on, but it's demoralizing writing and reading such a list because it points out how true our smallness really is.

Mercy, however, overlooks the petty concerns of life and focuses on the main issues of people in need. A church where love and caring exists is a church where lots of tender mercy is shared with "one of the least of these." Jesus put it this way (Matt. 25:34–36, 40): "Come, you who are blessed by my Father; take your inheritance, the kingdom prepared for you since the creation of the world. For I was hungry and you gave me something to eat, I was thirsty and you gave me something to drink, I was a stranger and you invited me in, I needed clothes and you clothed me, I was sick and you looked after me, I was in prison and you came to visit me. . . . Whatever you did for one of the least of these brothers of mine, you did for me."

It's time for us to become a church that embodies mercy and grace so that others will be ministered to in ways that delight the heart of God.

Then what does it look like to love mercy? To love mercy is

- to love God and hunger after him each new day (Matt. 5:6; 6:33);
- to be repentant, coming clean with our sins, and expressing daily our dependence on God's forgiveness and tender mercies (Ps. 51);

- to be obedient to the God of mercy; faithful to his love and lordship (Exod. 20:1–17—the Ten Commandments; Matt. 22:37–40—the Great Commandment; and Matt. 28:18–20—the Great Commission);
- to be compassionate, empathetic toward the needs of others (Luke 10:30–37—the good Samaritan; Matt. 18:23–35—parable of unmerciful servant; Matt. 15:29–39—Jesus' compassion on the four thousand; Matt. 9:36—compassion on the shepherdless sheep; and Matt. 20:29–34—compassion on the blind men);
- to be forgiving (Luke 15:11–32—the prodigal son);
- to share the gift of life with others (Eph. 2:4–9; Titus 3:5);
- to be wise and truthful (James 3:17; Ps. 85:10 kjv);
- to be prayerful (1 Tim. 2:1–8);
- to be a healer and a peacemaker (2 Cor. 5:16–21);
- to receive mercy in return for giving it (Matt. 5:7; 2 Tim. 1:16–18);
- to care for those less fortunate (Matt. 9:13; 25:34–40);
- to not be judgmental (Matt. 7:1–5; Luke 6:37–38; John 8:7; James 2:12–13).

My mercy-giving secretary, Carole Nason, captured the essence of mercy in a wonderful poem she wrote titled "Your Mercy, Lord."

Your mercy, Lord . . . your mercy, Lord,
Extends to the highest heaven;
Yet it reaches down to my hopelessness
And makes me your child—forgiven.

And it flows
From the veins of Jesus,
Looking beyond all the faults in me.
You deal with me, Lord,
According to your mercy, Lord,
And not my iniquity.

Your mercy, Lord . . . your mercy, Lord,
Is fresh and new every morning.
You surround me, Lord,
With your truth and your mercy, Lord.
Your mercy is my crown adorning.

And it flows
From the veins of Jesus,
Looking beyond all the faults in me.
For as the heavens are high

Above the earth, O Lord,
So great is your mercy to me.

So great is his mercy to me . . . and to you . . . so give it away freely to others!

4. *Communicate and Resolve Conflicts*

In Dolores Curran's book *Traits of a Healthy Family*, she begins with the number one characteristic, "The healthy family communicates and listens."[4] In my own study of relationships within the family, community, church, and world at large, I would agree with her. The number one relational need is the ability to effectively communicate. A tandem thought to communication is the willingness and ability to listen. Listening is the Achilles' heel of church people today because we have such a strong desire to be "right" all the time. We don't take time to listen to opposing points of view; instead, we insist on asserting our position and alienate the audience we are seeking to reach. In addition, when we refuse to listen to the other side of an issue, we can become terribly wrong about the other person's position or background and miss that person's heart for God.

Communication is "a process (either verbal or nonverbal) of sharing information with another person in such a way that he understands what you are saying. Talking and listening and understanding are all involved in the communication process."[5] Norm Wright, marriage and family expert, also reminds us that communication is hard work, especially when "I know you believe you understand what you think I said, but I'm not sure you realize that what you heard is not what I meant." The goal in all communication is to say what you mean and mean what you say—and to say what we mean in an ever deepening fashion. John Powell, in his book *Why Am I Afraid to Tell You Who I Am?* describes the five communication levels of increasingly effective communication: cliché (non-sharing), fact (sharing what you know), opinion (sharing what you think), emotion (sharing what you feel), and transparency (sharing who you are).[6] The deeper you go in the communication process, the deeper you enhance the level of trust, the commitment in relationship, and the ever-deepening friendship with the one with whom you communicate.

However, because our communication is 10 percent words, 40 percent tone of voice, and 50 percent body language (give or take a few percentage points), the message we seek to convey often gets muddled. Because everything that is spoken either helps or hinders, heals or scars, builds up or tears down, we all need some work at taming the old tongue. James 3 offers helpful metaphors for the tongue (a rudder and a fire) and describes how difficult it is to tame it. And yet, if our communication is to be effective, we must become disciplined in the taming process. Otherwise relationships quickly get out of hand.

With communication serving as the number one relationship issue, why are we not emphasizing its importance in the church? I would suspect that most churches need to develop some sort of creative tongue-taming program for their members, wouldn't you agree? Then, when the communication cycle breaks down, we need the skills to resolve the inevitable conflicts that plague our relational existence. All too often, families and churches lack the skill of conflict resolution. Thus the people of God are left with a basic inability to handle relational challenges as they emerge.

Conflict is nothing new. It has been with us since the dawn of time. Even the Scriptures are filled with relational conflicts. Consider Cain and Abel (Genesis 4), when the hatred of one brother turned deadly. Or how about Joseph and his jealous, vindictive brothers (Genesis 37)? Even Paul got into a spat with Barnabas over John Mark, and they went off in two different directions (Acts 15). The Book of Acts is filled with case studies in relational ills, like the unfair treatment of the widows in chapter 6, the resistance to allow Paul to minister in chapter 9, and the doctrinal disagreement that ensued in chapter 15. Whether it was Jesus' disciples jockeying for position in Matthew 20 or the spiritual warfare recorded by Peter in 1 Peter 4:12, conflict has been a part of God's people's lives for generations.

Conflict is cancerous to relationships if left unattended. Resolving our conflicts begins with an honest assessment of our heart in line with Scripture. We need to meditate on passages like Romans 12:9–18, 1 Corinthians 13:4–8a, Ephesians 4:22–32, Colossians 3:12–17, Hebrews 12:1–3, and James 3:13–18. Then our hearts will be prepared to address lovingly the conflict at hand.

A story is told of two unmarried sisters who had so bitter a ruckus they stopped speaking to each other. Unable or unwilling to leave their small home, they continued to use the same rooms and sleep in the same bedroom. A chalk line divided the sleeping area into two halves, separating doorway and fireplace, so that each could come and go and get her own meals without trespassing on her sister's domain. In the black of night each could hear the breathing of the foe. For years they coexisted in grinding silence. Neither was willing to take the first step to reconciliation.[7]

All over America "chalk lines" divide households—and yes, even churches, marketplaces, neighborhoods, and ethnic groups—and it's time for them to be erased. Materials are available for teaching on this subject, written by experts like David Augsburger, Norm Wright, Lewis Smedes, and Larry Crabb.

Resolving conflicts is not a complicated science to teach to people in our churches. But it is a life-changing skill to master in order for our church families to become healthier in their relationships and service together. It cannot be ignored or neglected any longer.

5. Establish Means for Bearing Each Other's Burdens

What did the apostles do when the widows were being overlooked in the daily distribution of food in Acts 6? They appointed seven deacons who were known to be full of the Holy Spirit and wisdom, and they turned the responsibility over to them. What do you do in a local church when a need is brought to the attention of the pastor and church leadership team? How do you engage the services of others in bearing the burdens of those within your care?

"Our church's slogan is 'A Loving Church in a Hurting World,' so we developed a system that would avoid overlooking anyone in our congregation who had a particular need to be addressed," reports Brian Fleming, senior associate pastor at Maranatha Christian Church in Williston, Vermont. "We developed a dot system and started getting together as a pastoral staff every weekday morning at 8:55. We touch base on what we have heard during the previous twenty-four hours and with what has come in on the answering machine." Today at least one pastor is at every funeral or memorial service and visits every family with a new baby.

Not that the church of about eight hundred hadn't already established a caring mechanism. After all, they had cell groups of all kinds. And they had a leadership team of about seventy, including the cell group leaders. But only 60 to 65 percent of the congregation participated in the cell groups—and the 35 to 40 percent who did not could easily fall through the cracks. The dot system now prevents that from happening.

The Maranatha dot system is based on the signal lights at intersections. On a large chart in a room off Pastor Fleming's office, they have listed every family, including every member of the family, on one line. And every family's status is identified by colored dots. Pastor Fleming also has all families on a database in his computer and enters family information every day, since the chart is updated only every three or four weeks.

"A green dot means a family is doing well. A yellow dot is a caution signal indicating that the family needs special attention—and a member of the leadership team is assigned to that family. A red dot indicates a family in crisis, and a pastor and possibly an elder will be assigned to that family. A black dot indicates a family that is in the process of leaving or has left—they are the one sheep that has gone astray, in biblical terms," explains Pastor Fleming.

The dot system includes families of those in leadership positions too. "Even leadership families can experience crises like loss of a job, illness, or death, so they are very much a part of the dot system of caring follow-up," says Pastor Fleming. Every time a new person shows up at Maranatha, that person is assigned to someone in leadership for personal contact and follow-up. They become part of the dot system as soon as their family needs can be identified.

Those in leadership positions meet every six weeks on Sunday evening for prayer, sharing, and training. In addition, some of the training is provided by letters from Pastor Fleming. Occasionally that will include exhortation to improve an area of caring. A response rate of 70 percent on reports jumped to 90 percent when leadership was reminded of the importance of turning in reports on their contacts.

"We have experienced some genuine breakthroughs since we initiated the dot system of caring at Maranatha. For example, a family that had been attending the church for some time went into red dot crisis when the husband disappeared, taking the family car. He had developed gambling debt pressures and slipped back into alcohol and drug use," reports Pastor Fleming. "A pastor and an elder began to work with the man's wife, who had a job but no transportation. His parents and a sister were also in the church, so we worked with them to provide baby-sitting and transportation, as well as child care for their little girl when the mother was at work. We found the husband, helped him get back together with his wife and into rehabilitation. Meanwhile, his wife and little girl are staying in fellowship at the church and benefiting from the support provided."

The best system for caring is still in the small groups, says Pastor Fleming, but since they do not include everyone in the church, the dot system provides a well-received supplementary caring program.

"It's really a matter of attitude, not merely a system like our dot system," adds Pastor Fleming. "We have to take care of the little things, even though it takes a lot of effort, if we want to be true to our church's slogan, 'A Loving Church in a Hurting World.'"

6. Welcome Diversity into Your Fellowship

When Osterville Baptist Church first presented plans for expansion of their facilities to the town fathers, a concerned village official asked, "You're not leaving Osterville, are you? We need you here." They received approval from both the local planning commission and the state's historical commission—nothing short of a miracle when you are dealing with Cape Cod town planners and the State of Massachusetts Historical Commission.

Relationships with the village and its residents were not always this amicable. "Ten years ago we were known as a fundamentalist church that did not participate at all in community life. As a result, we were not listened to or appreciated," confesses Pastor Mike Rowe. "We had a lot of relationship building to do."

How did Osterville Baptist Church do it?

"Each year our community has a Village Day in the summer. It's one big party for the community. Five or six years ago we decided to get involved, so we put on a children's fair as part of Village Day activities—and everything was free: crafts, games, face-painting, even hot dogs. We actually give away about a thousand hot dogs—and no one does that!" says Pastor Rowe. "Each year twelve hundred to thirteen hundred kids participate—and forty to fifty show up at vacation Bible school because of the love we showed them at Village Day. And we have gained several families at the church as a result."

Another advertised community event is the church's "1835 Thanksgiving," memorializing the year the church was organized. At church services Wednesday night ("We are packed out") and Thursday morning, the church re-creates how Thanksgiving was celebrated 160-plus years ago. "I had a suit from the period made for me, including a hat and sconce. Maggie [Mike's wife] is dressed in a hoop skirt from the period. Our lighting is period, the piano is played without a pedal, singing is a cappella or with a period instrument. The only difference, I tell the audience, is that I preach only twenty minutes instead of an hour," says Pastor Rowe. "Since the Catholic church has no services at that time, we always get a number of Catholics who really want to celebrate Thanksgiving."

During Fall Festival Days, the church makes its parking lot available to a local academy for their fund-raising car wash. At Christmas, they have a Christmas program on the front steps in cooperation with other churches, and they become a stop on a Christmas tour. Pastor Rowe has also joined the Osterville Business and Professional Association and has been active on the subcommittee for village events. And his wife, Maggie, has taken her dramatic portrayal of Mary, the mother of Jesus, "on the road." As a result of giving that portrayal on local cable, she has been invited into Catholic churches, where the message of Christ as Savior is clearly presented through Mary's discussion of her son's mission.

Looking ahead, the church is planning to open its expanded fellowship hall to seniors in the community. "We want to make it a gathering place for the approximately two hundred seniors in this area who would, for example, be afraid to go out in the dark during the Christmas walk," relates Pastor Rowe. "The message we have been trying to get across to people of all denominations is that this is a safe place. As a result, when we presented our plans for expansion to the village, they were enthusiastically received."

The example of Osterville Baptist is a wonderful reflection of this characteristic of a healthy church. The staff and people of this congregation have aggressively targeted their village on Cape Cod for the gospel, and they are reaching out to others with loving and caring relationships that go outside their normal boundaries into new areas of relationship and service. By including all of the people of their community into their ministry programming, they are spreading the Good News through the intentional building of quality relationships. A healthy church recognizes its need for diversity—ethnically and communitywide—and strives to build this diversity through creative efforts of outreach and service to others within its reach.

7. Equip Families through Intentional Ministries

The family unit is the fundamental place of learning about loving and caring relationships. And the local church is the family's greatest ally and partner in raising up new generations of Christ-followers. The family and the church need each other in order to properly and effectively function, for both learn from the other about how to relate in this hurting world.

"The best school of discipleship is the family. We are only a substitute, so our priority is the parent," says Senior Pastor Jay Abramson of Valley Community Baptist Church in Avon, Connecticut. "We are intentionally family-oriented in all areas of church activity. For example, we have the children with their parents for the first part of every worship service, and we plan the worship to intentionally include all ages in the family."

This means that members of the family are not only present—they are actively involved, with both the minister to children and families and the youth pastor part of the planning process in the worship team. "We plan for some visual presentation every Sunday. For example, we have a puppet presentation every five or six weeks. Some of our young people learned how to use clowns in drama on a YWAM (Youth with a Mission) trip, so that became part of the introduction to worship. We also use specially prepared banners, readers' theater, video productions, and Scripture dramatizations," says Pastor Abramson.

In addition to these inclusive worship services, the church gives the family priority in a wide range of activities. "We have an annual family-oriented winter retreat, where everything is done as a family. Even the discussion groups bring together families. But in terms of bringing families to Christ, our divorce recovery workshops have been the most productive. We have many families as part of our congregation who have come to the Lord during this ministry," reveals Pastor Abramson. With the influx of parents coming to faith in Christ through the divorce recovery program, in addition to other relationally based evangelistic outreaches, the potential for deepening the health and vitality of this congregation is great.

Intentionally Relational

When a church chooses to be intentional about building loving, caring relationships within families, between members, and within the community they serve, God blesses their shared work in beautiful ways. When we lay down our lives for our brothers and sisters, then we are making it clear to the world around us that we know what love for Jesus looks like. He has laid down his life for us, so we must do the same.

"We should love one another. . . . This is how we know what love is: Jesus Christ laid down his life for us. And we ought to lay down our lives for our brothers. If anyone has material possessions and sees his brother in need but has no pity on him, how can the love of God be in him? Dear children, let us not love with words or tongue but with actions and in truth" (1 John 3:11, 16–18).

Lord, I acknowledge that my love of others is often predicated on how they have treated me. I am conditional in my love so often, and I confess it to you today. Restore in me a hearty love for the people you love, which includes all who cross my path each day. May I have the heart of Jesus for the downtrodden of soul, may I be filled with the Spirit of love and care for the needs of others, and may I walk in the footsteps of my heavenly Father in administering grace and mercy to those who are heavy laden today. If I am to recommit myself to loving and caring relationships within the context of my family, my church, and my community, I recognize the need for your supernatural love to guide and sustain me. Fill me to overflowing with the tender, unconditional love that only you can supply. May I find great joy in giving that away to others even today. For the glory of the Lord Jesus, I pray with a heart of gratitude. Amen.

████████ FOR REFLECTION AND RENEWAL ████████

The healthy church is intentional in its efforts to build loving, caring relationships within families, between members, and within the community they serve.

The healthy church understands, models, teaches, and affirms the essential elements of quality relationships and recognizes the needs of those who come from dysfunctional families. The body serves as an affirming place for marriage and family life, including single adults, senior adults, and all phases of family development. It builds relationships within the body of Christ through:

- modeling authenticity and affirming it in others
- sharing lives with one another
- caring for one another
- open communication
- conflict resolution
- forgiveness
- healing
- bearing one another's burdens

The church acknowledges and encourages great diversity within the body of Christ and teaches its members how to work together, disagree with love and respect, and creatively resolve conflicts.

It includes people of different ages, races, ethnic groups, socioeconomic groups, previous church affiliations (or no affiliation), and stages of spiritual maturity.

> This is how we know what love is: Jesus Christ laid down his life for us. And we ought to lay down our lives for our brothers.
>
> 1 John 3:16

1. On a scale of 1 to 10 (1 being not at all important and 10 being most important), rank each of the above statements while answering the question, "How important is this statement for the health of our church; how highly do we value loving, caring relationships?"

2. On a scale of 1 to 10 (1 being very ineffective and 10 being very effective), rank each of the above statements while answering the question, "How effective are we as a leadership team at instilling these values in our church?"

3. For each of the above statements, ask your team, "Where do we want to be in the characteristic Loving, Caring Relationships in this next year or two?"

4. For each of the above statements, ask your team, "How will we get where we want to be in living out Loving, Caring Relationships in this next year?"

5. Overall, on a scale of 1 to 10 (1 being very low and 10 being very high), rank how well you think your church is doing in living out this fifth characteristic of a healthy church, A Commitment to Loving, Caring Relationships.

7

Servant-Leadership Development
Characteristic 6

The healthy church identifies and develops individuals whom God has called and given the gift of leadership and challenges them to become servant-leaders.

From him the whole body, joined and held together by every supporting ligament, grows and builds itself up in love, as each part does its work.

Ephesians 4:16

If you were to ask Paul Bertolino about investments, he would say that the best investments he has ever made are in believers willing to be trained for servant leadership. "From the beginning, we took 2 Timothy 2:2 very seriously. We determined we were going to invest in believers who would become reliable in ministry," says Bertolino, pastor of Calvary Bible Church in Meredith, New Hampshire. Pastor Bertolino's first experience of this principle was at his first church, when he was still a mail carrier and part-time pastor.

"I began calling others into ministry assignments several years ago when I called Gary Havener away from a fishing boat in Maine as my full-time associate, even though I was only part-time," recalls Pastor Bertolino. "He would accompany me on my mail route. We'd stop for lunch at Papa Gino's so we could really talk about his ministry at the church. He then began calling others into servant leadership positions. Today he is pastoring his own church in Springfield, Massachusetts."

Pastor Bertolino believes in following Jesus' example another way. "Everywhere Jesus and his disciples went, they ate. So we have a luncheon staff meeting every week. On the last Friday of the month all the people in leadership meet for lunch as well," he adds. So much can be accomplished relationally in building a team through such informal gatherings. Paul Bertolino's jovial spirit and gift of hospitality makes these times enjoyable for all who participate.

How does he identify those in whom he wants to invest his time and effort? "I believe in the principle that ministry precedes office. I look for those who are already showing an interest in the Word, who are already involved in ministry at some level. In addition to my personal mentoring of one of our leaders, I'll encourage these people to attend Vision New England training events like Congress and the Equip Convention (for Christian education and church ministry leaders). I'll suggest training they can get at nearby schools like Gordon-Conwell Theological Seminary. Only as they become genuinely active in ministry will we give them positions of leadership," he says. Using this approach, Pastor Bertolino has seen few dropouts.

He is also heavily involved in training interns from area colleges and seminaries. One of the women studying with the Conservative Baptist Seminary of the East and on the staff at Calvary Bible Church was an intern involved in visitation and counseling. She meets on a regular basis with one of the deaconesses in the church and an associate pastor whose expertise is in counseling. Servant-leaders are long-term investments that pay off in people won to Christ and the church being served. Pastor Bertolino knows the biblical pattern works—he is already seeing third generation servant-leaders at work in various churches of New England and across the nation.

Biblical Models of Servant Leadership

Where do pastors and church leaders like Paul Bertolino develop their understanding of servant leadership? The Scriptures are replete with examples from the life of Christ and others who modeled effective leadership—Moses, Joshua, the prophets, and the apostle Paul, to name a few. All had their own unique styles, but all were effective leaders.

Jesus exemplified the life of a servant while offering strong leadership and vision. His investment in the lives of his disciples was the focus of his entire being—in fact, his investment cost him his life. He demonstrates his commitment to them in John 13:1–17 in his washing of their feet. This is how he "showed them the full extent of his love," (v. 1). With a towel, some water, a basin, and a heart of loving servanthood, he washed each of his disciples' feet. "When he had finished washing their feet, he put on his clothes and returned to his place. 'Do you understand what I have done for you?' he asked them. 'You call me "Teacher"and

"Lord," and rightly so, for that is what I am. Now that I, your Lord and Teacher, have washed your feet, you also should wash one another's feet. I have set you an example that you should do as I have done for you. I tell you the truth, no servant is greater than his master, nor is a messenger greater than the one who sent him. Now that you know these things, *you will be blessed if you do them*'" (vv. 12–17, emphasis added).

When I consider the full extent of Jesus' love for his disciples and compare it to the full extent of my love for those I am called to lead, the gap is overwhelming. I say that I am committed to the team, willing to serve at all cost, open to doing the lowliest of tasks, free to share the glory of success, but does my talk really translate into servanthood? Each new day must begin with the prayer,

Lord, teach me how to love and serve and lead as you have modeled and taught me. Help me to focus on the needs of those on the team who are working diligently at the tasks at hand. May my agenda be subservient to the agenda of others. May my words, attitudes, and actions convey my sincere love and appreciation for those who tirelessly serve by my side. Give me the strength and wisdom to lead as you would lead through me. Express your unfailing love through a vessel that often fails others, not because I always choose to but because of my sinfulness that keeps the focus on me rather than on them. May my ministry to the team today be likened to a towel, some water, a basin, and a heart of loving servanthood, willingly and cheerfully giving myself away so that they may know and love and serve you more dearly. For Jesus' sake and in his name I pray. Amen.

When James and John, the disciples of Jesus, were clamoring for the opportunity to sit at Jesus' right and left hand in glory, Jesus used this opportunity to teach them a critical principle. "You know that those who are regarded as rulers of the Gentiles lord it over them, and their high officials exercise authority over them. Not so with you. Instead, whoever wants to become great among you must be your servant, and whoever wants to be first must be slave of all. For even the Son of Man did not come to be served, but to serve, and to give his life as a ransom for many" (Mark 10:42–45).

What James and John were asking for was terribly inappropriate, and the Lord graciously rebuked them. His investment in them at that time would be remembered not only by the two who asked for such placement but by generations of Christians who have reflected such an attitude in their attempts to serve others.

We are not called to "lord it over" others! Instead, we are called to serve others and imitate Jesus' example. The apostle Paul captures these thoughts for us in several key passages that define the roles of a servant leader. First, Philippians 2:3–8 calls us to imitate Christ's humility:

> Do nothing out of selfish ambition or vain conceit, but in humility consider others better than yourselves. Each of you should look not only to your own interests, but also to the interests of others.
> Your attitude should be the same as that of Christ Jesus:
>
> Who, being in very nature God,
> did not consider equality with God something to be grasped,
> but made himself nothing,
> taking the very nature of a servant,
> being made in human likeness.
> And being found in appearance as a man,
> he humbled himself
> and became obedient to death—
> even death on a cross!

The apostle Paul reinforces this challenge to live out Christ's humility in his own servanthood to the church in Thessalonica.

> As apostles of Christ we could have been a burden to you, but we were gentle among you, like a mother caring for her little children. We loved you so much that we were delighted to share with you not only the gospel of God but our lives as well, because you had become so dear to us. Surely you remember, brothers, our toil and hardship; we worked night and day in order not to be a burden to anyone while we preached the gospel of God to you.
> You are witnesses, and so is God, of how holy, righteous and blameless we were among you who believed. For you know that we dealt with each of you as a father deals with his own children, encouraging, comforting and urging you to live lives worthy of God, who calls you into his kingdom and glory.
>
> 1 Thessalonians 2:6–12

The apostle Peter picks up on this same theme in 1 Peter 5:2–4: "Be shepherds of God's flock that is under your care, serving as overseers—not because you must, but because you are willing, as God wants you to be; not greedy for money, but eager to serve; not lording it over those entrusted to you, but being examples to the flock. And when the Chief Shepherd appears, you will receive the crown of glory that will never fade away."

Humility, servanthood, shepherding—three essential principles of servant leadership. The ultimate goals of effective servant leadership are summed up by the apostle Paul in Ephesians 4:11–13, for it was Christ who gave us servant-leaders, "some to be apostles, some to be prophets, some to be evangelists, and some to be pastors and teachers, to prepare God's people for works of service, so that the body of Christ may be built up until we all reach unity in the faith and in the knowledge of the Son of God and become mature, attaining to the whole measure of the fullness of Christ."

Paul defines for us four major reasons why we are to serve others:

1. To prepare God's people for works of service;
2. To build up the body of Christ;
3. To reach unity in the faith; and
4. To become mature, attaining to the whole measure of the fullness of Christ.

The Results of Leadership Training

When churches pursuing health take the mandate of servant leadership seriously, developing leaders takes on new fortitude. For my friend and senior pastor at Wintonbury Baptist Church in Bloomfield, Connecticut, Rich Ainsworth, the Ephesians 4 passage took on a dramatic role in the life of his church.

A few years ago a regionwide recession in the Bloomfield area forced the church to reduce their pastoral staff to one member. However, decisions made and actions taken as a result of this crisis have resulted in a 30 percent growth during a two-year period. "That turning point created a whole new role for me," Rich says. "I announced to the congregation that 'I need to be equipping leaders who will equip the saints for works of service.' We took Ephesians 4:11–12 seriously in order to do ministry together." The first step was to rewrite the vision of the church.

"We decided we wanted to be a church where small groups are central. We see the small groups as the caregivers," says Rich. But how do you get enough small groups going for them to become caregivers? How do you train the leaders?

"I'm the kind of guy who says, 'Let's start tomorrow.' But I had a former Navigator staff member in my church who said, 'No, it's important to train them.' I accepted his advice and set out to train sixteen couples as small group leaders," Rich reveals. "Initially we met every week as two groups of sixteen each to gain the small group experience during the training. After four months we moved to meeting every other week, and in the summer we met once per month. By this time they were beginning to form small groups for the fall."

Eleven of the sixteen actually gave leadership to small groups as the fall church season started. The leaders met in monthly "huddles" to receive new skills and study more principles of small group leadership. During the year they enlisted others as assistants so they could begin on-the-job training for future leadership. At the end of the year, Rich says thanks to the leaders with a picnic at his home.

"We have just completed our fourth year. We are seeing our goal of multiplying leaders being reached. And this leadership is now impacting other areas of our church's ministry," says Rich. "I would not attribute our growth of 30 percent over a twenty-four-month period totally to this leadership training and the small group ministry, but that effort is helping to fulfill the vision of our church—and that has to be at least part of the reason for the growth."

Yet another facet of servant leadership development at Wintonbury Baptist Church is on-the-job training of part-time ministry personnel. That involves mentoring those still gaining experience. Like Paul Bertolino, Rich Ainsworth is investing in future leaders for the local church in Bloomfield and for the mission field beyond their community.

"The other day one of our part-time staff members came into my office discouraged. He felt he was not making any difference and wondered, 'What's the use?' I simply asked him, 'Are you being faithful? If you know you are being faithful, God will give the increase. That's up to him.' Now that kind of leadership perspective comes only through the process of ministering. Mentoring can provide that perspective," says Rich.

At the same time Rich is keenly aware that he and the church need to learn a lot more about the process of leadership development. Rich sums it up best: "After twenty-four years of ministry at the church, the past few years have been the most productive and personally rewarding. Seeing leadership multiplied and people growing is a great joy. We have never been closer to accomplishing our mission of 'connecting people to God and each other.'"

Leadership Defined

Jesus personified leadership. He directed thinking, guided people, aimed them toward truth, and showed the way to love, forgiveness, and eternal life. The best place to start in defining leadership is with Jesus.

J. W. McLean and William Weitzel, in their book *Leadership: Magic, Myth or Method*, define leadership as:

1. A person
2. involved in a process
3. of influencing and developing a group of people

4. in order to accomplish a purpose
5. by means of supernatural power.

This definition has become my favorite because of its simplicity and because in it I see the example of Christ at work. Leadership always begins with a person. Howard Hendricks said at a leadership conference, "A leader is a person with a magnet in his heart and a compass in his head." Many of us have the skills to lead, but when one is called on to marshal those abilities in a leadership setting, it is imperative that we respond affirmatively to God's call. The more leaders understand themselves, the better off the group and the mission being served.

Next, a leader is involved in a process of growth and development. Leadership is distinct from management. We manage things, we lead people. Leading people is a process accomplished over a stretch of time, through the seasons of life, in the good times and the hard times. In many respects, the process takes a lifetime. There are very few "finished products" in the work of leadership. It proceeds along a journey of development with many turns, ruts, detours, and climbs along the way.

Third, there is no leadership without a group of people to influence and develop, and the size of the group is immaterial. Effective leadership occurs when those served feel loved, admired, appreciated, and accepted by the leader. When these relational dynamics are absent from the group, the leader and the leadership process suffer. Unless the leader takes time to invest in the people, there will be no true leadership. Leadership is a gift that's earned over time, granted out of trustworthy acclaim by the people being served.

Building trust became job number one the first couple of years at Essex Alliance Church in Essex Junction, Vermont.

"I did not announce what my vision was for the church," said Senior Pastor Scott Slocum. "I first set about developing the trust of the elders by being open and transparent with them. My goal was to make them my friends and colleagues. I believe you have to consciously ask the leaders of the church to trust you—and then ask the Lord to give you such good ministry judgment that they can trust you. I exercised bad judgment in one situation, and when I told the elders that, they responded that compared to the number of times I had shown good judgment, this was easily forgiven."

Some of the elders found the new openness uncomfortable and were unwilling to change. But Pastor Slocum found a core group of people who were authentic and relevant.

"When I came I found people who did not want to do church as usual. They did not know what they really wanted, but they knew what they didn't want—doing church as usual. Thus there was an immediate match. I came looking for people ready to follow me as a leader with new ideas—and they needed a leader," says Slocum. While developing trust and collegiality among the leaders was one focus of Pastor Slocum's approach, the other was to help the congregation develop the freedom to be open with each other about what God wanted for them in their church and community. God's purposes for them needed to be discovered, and Scott's role in this process was key.

Fourth, there are always purposes for leadership. The purposes can be stated or implied. When I lead my children to faith or in spiritual growth, the purposes unfold according to the needs and seasons of their lives. When I lead a ministry team, then I must also clearly state the purposes from the outset. Understanding and unpacking the purposes of a group require astute insight that stems from research, mission definition, goals, plans, implementation, monitoring, and evaluating effectiveness. In addition to group purposes, we also forge out individual purposes that are defined by relationship and need.

Fifth, and most important for Christian leaders, is the fact that the leadership process is supernaturally empowered. We cannot perform our leadership responsibilities in our own strength, power, or wisdom. Leadership means that we know how to follow *the* Leader and rely fully on *his* power to guide and direct our every step. Our most significant resource for becoming an effective church leader is the Holy Spirit's influence on our daily life and service. Servant leadership is impossible without a life in full submission to the love and lordship of Christ. It's folly to proceed without the leadership of our heavenly Father guiding, upholding, and gifting us for service.

Are the Sheep Flourishing?

The fine art of leadership is something to be learned over time, and it is measured by one's followers. For the focus of leadership is on those being served rather than the one leading. Jesus said, "'I am the good shepherd; I know my sheep and my sheep know me—just as the Father knows me and I know the Father—and I lay down my life for the sheep'" (John 10:14–15).

Michael Youssef, in his wonderful book *The Leadership Style of Jesus*, answers the question, What makes a good shepherd?

> For the shepherd, the reward comes in seeing that his sheep are contented, well fed, safe, and *flourishing*. His energies are spent not just to make a reputation for himself, but rather to supply the sheep with the finest graz-

ing in the lushest pasture, to store winter feed, to find clear water. Good shepherds spare no effort in providing a shelter from the storm. They constantly watch for ruthless enemies, diseases, and parasites to which sheep are so susceptible. From dawn to dusk these good shepherds selflessly dedicate their days to the welfare of their woolly followers. They do not even rest during the night; they sleep with one eye and both ears open, ready to leap and protect their own at the slightest sound of trouble.[1]

The signs of outstanding leadership appear primarily among the followers. Are the followers reaching their potential? Are they learning? Serving? Do they achieve the required results? Do they change with grace? Manage conflict?[2] In other words, are the sheep flourishing?

In order for the sheep to flourish, we who are called to shepherd need to consider ways of leading the sheep that are worthy of following. The following principles of shepherdlike leadership create church leaders who are followed with dignity, honor, and respect.

Be a Leader Who Is Led

After having asked Peter three times if he loved him more than the others, and after having commissioned him three times to be a shepherd, Jesus said emphatically, "I tell you the truth, when you were younger you dressed yourself and went where you wanted; but when you are old you will stretch out your hands, and someone else will dress you and lead you where you do not want to go" (John 21:18). Jesus confronts Peter with the hard truth that the servant-leader is the leader who is being led to unknown, sometimes undesirable and painful places. The way of the Christian leader is not the way of upward mobility, in which our world has invested so much, but the way of downward mobility ending on the cross.[3] This kind of leadership is powerless and humble, and it's the place where the suffering servant, Jesus, is made manifest in our ministries.

What does it mean to be led as a leader? It means first of all that an effective leader is primarily a follower of Jesus, the Good Shepherd. An effective servant-leader honors the lordship of Christ first and foremost. He or she has a vital prayer life, maintaining constant communion with the Lord, confessing sin, seeking forgiveness and cleansing, finding restoration and renewal alone with the Savior. As a follower of Christ, the leader engages in theological study and reflection, modeling the life of a follower to the followers, doing all for the glory of God.

Second, being a follower means responding to the leadership of all who are in authority over you. As leaders, we all must have a system of accountability in place so that we are not left to our own devices and ultimately our own deviations from the central purposes of God. We are called to honor and respect the wisdom offered by those in authority over us. We need to trust their motives, communicate with them openly and honestly, accept any constructive criticism offered to us, and be willing to serve them and give to them graciously and freely. So often our character development occurs when we submit to the authority of others who love us and want the best for us as leaders. The healthiest settings of ministry have this in place and work diligently to maintain the quality of such relationships.

Third, being led means being a follower of those you lead. This seems confusing at first, but when you think about it, if we are effective as leaders it is because we follow closely the needs, hurts, joys, and desires of our followers. When we pay attention to the lives of our followers, then over time they will offer us the freedom to lead them because trust has been built. Leaders need to recognize this trust as a gift and lead with faithfulness and love. We want to serve with our followers' blessing.

Ted Engstrom and Ed Dayton offer nine "followership" qualities that are worthy of our reflection.

1. *Commitment*—first to who we work for, second to fellow workers, third to the organization we serve.
2. *Understanding*—of our task, role, relationships, others' style and goals.
3. *Loyalty*—protecting one another's reputation.
4. *Communication*—always with complete information provided.
5. *Competence*—and willing to keep growing and learning.
6. *Promise keeping*—doing what you say you'll do.
7. *Participation*—understanding where you fit into the whole.
8. *Getting along*—"how" one participates with others.
9. *Sacrifice*—the cost of followership, the payment made for the good of others and the bigger picture.[4]

It may be worth your while to stop here and reflect individually or with your leadership team about how these qualities are being lived out in your midst. In what areas do you need to grow?

Be a Leader Who Loves

My secretary, Carole Nason, is a superb assistant. She handles every task given to her with Christian grace. She deals with the public we serve with excellence. She tirelessly types and processes mountains of dictation, organizes our files, manages a myriad of daily and weekly tasks with consistency and regularity. I cannot recall the time she ever refused performing a necessary task. She provides hospitality to individuals who come and meet with me, as well as groups that I host for breakfast or lunch meetings. She offers wise counsel on sticky personnel issues. She prays for me and every member of the team with a faithful and generous spirit. She loves my wife and children and encourages each member of my family with a special affection. She is the envy of many other executives who currently have a fraction of what we have at Vision New England because of her.

If all you knew about Carole was in the above information, you would probably be satisfied and somewhat overwhelmed by her competencies. But there is more than meets the eye in what Carole does on the job. She happens to be an only child who lives next door to her delightful parents in a community near Boston. She is married to a great guy, Al, and has three terrific children and three adorable grandchildren. She is a worship leader in her church and is also a professional photographer.

If Carole were not on our staff, she would probably be working in a business with her husband or serving as a nanny to her grandchildren or taking photos for *National Geographic*. She is much more than my secretary; she is a friend, a trusted confidante, a photographer, worship leader, daughter, mother, and grandmother. She is loved as a sister and trusted as a team member.

I tell you all of this to make one point. If all we know about the people we work with is wrapped up in the tasks they perform in church, we do a disservice to the body and to them as individuals. We are not to treat those who serve with us in a robotic sense—paying attention to them only in the functional roles they play in the ministry. Our people, the ones God has called us to lead and serve, are multifaceted individuals with full lives outside the context of our connections with them each week. They need to be treated lovingly and carefully by their leaders and not taken for granted in whatever area they serve with you. It takes time and effort to instill this value, but it's worth every ounce of energy. The quality of our team-based service is enhanced as a result.

How well do you know and love those you are called to serve? Get to know them as people, love them where they are today, and nudge them forward in their growth and maturity. Accept and understand their diversity, and learn to make adjustments in your leadership style accordingly. Empathize with their hurts, pray together, encourage their personal growth, give them the gifts of grace, mercy, and forgiveness. Affirm them, build them up, and challenge them to grow. There's no better way!

Be a Leader Who Learns

Robert Clinton writes in *The Making of a Leader:* "One of the striking characteristics seen in effective leaders is their desire to learn. They learn from all kinds of sources. They learn from Scripture. They are pressed by their situation to see new truth in the Scriptures and in the situations themselves. They learn about their own uniqueness. They build on the natural abilities they have. They acquire skills needed by the challenges of the situations they face. They learn to use their spiritual gifts. Effective leaders, at all levels of leadership, maintain a learning posture throughout life."[5]

What is your learning posture? How are you being fed? What are you reading? How are you growing? The making of an effective leader means that we are constantly learning and discovering new ideas and opportunities to improve our service for Christ. Leaders need to personally model the disciplines of growth—spiritually, professionally, and relationally.

When we have a posture of lifelong learning, then we will not grow stale in our thinking or ineffective in our methods of ministry. Leadership that breathes life and hope into the lives of others is forever adding insight to the issues that surround us in ministry. Healthy leaders are learning and growing all the time.

Be a Leader Who Listens

Two essential skills are wrapped up in this point—the facility to ask good questions and the art of listening. Too many leaders present themselves as people who have all the answers. We are often fearful of saying the dreaded words, "I don't know." We want to be up on every issue, capable of handling every question, offering the sagest advice for every concern that comes down the pike. I am trying to get away from that rhetoric and give myself the freedom to not always have the best and last word on any given subject. I have to admit, I must discipline myself to do this because I am greatly tempted to try to offer the keenest insight and the authoritative word, when my opinion may not actually be the best.

Instead of having all the answers, healthy leaders need to facilitate a group discussion that will surface the best alternatives. Asking good questions, though, is a skill I do not find in many church settings. When we get into meetings we often seek answers to questions that were never asked.

For example, when a church board is dealing with an issue surrounding a drop in giving, the discussion will focus on where expenses can be cut in order not to go into the red. A better question to wrestle with may be, Why are the people not giving? And if such a question is raised, it would be far better to listen to the concerns of the congregation than to try to answer it among a small group of potentially out-of-touch-with-the-grassroots leaders. When we ask questions first, before expressing our own opinions, we allow others to participate in decisions.

During a consultation with a church in our region, we explored the strengths, weaknesses, opportunities, and challenges of their overall ministry. I invited each member present to take sticky notes and write separate answers on each note. We then heard from all group members as they shared their answers, placing their sticky notes on the board. After everyone was finished, we rearranged the notes into major groupings and discovered some patterns that were insightful to the vision and mission development process. The group commented to me later that evening that this was the first time they had been asked their opinion about such matters!

The art of listening as leaders begins with our tenacity to listen to God. When we take time to hear from him through our own centers of quiet, he reveals his will to us. The ability to hear from the Lord through his "still small voice" is a discipline worthy of acquiring and discussing among leaders in the local church. Unless we are able to discern his voice through prayer, Scripture study, and healthy dialogue with one another, we will not fully discern his will for us individually and collectively as his people.

Listening to one another is a statement of love, especially when we look into each other's eyes while we listen. I have found that women especially find it disconcerting when the one they are talking to is constantly looking around, down, or working on something. When we take the time to hear each other's heart (that involves more than words alone), then we give each other a priceless gift. Who among us doesn't want to be heard when we "just need to talk to a friend"? Confidentiality in listening to a brother or sister in Christ is also essential, as is empathy. It's important that in our listening, we do so fully, not halfheartedly, not merely to the words spoken but to the meaning behind the words.

In situations where people are in conflict with one another, the skill of listening becomes all the more essential. In our listening and processing of information, we set out to bring peace to those parties involved. Listening to all sides of the story helps a leader discern directions for resolution. The goal of resolution expresses to all who are involved in a conflict that you value both the issue at hand and the relationships in jeopardy. Anything less than full resolution means that either the relationship, the issue, or both will be compromised. A leader who listens first will gain respect from followers who are struggling for appropriate alternatives in resolving their issues with each other. All parties must be heard so that lopsided judgments are avoided.

Be a Leader Who Lightens the Load of Others

When is the last time you asked your followers what you could do to lighten their load? Have you ever asked them how you could help them accomplish their responsibilities? Are there ways that the roles others are carrying could be simplified or shared by others? How often do you laugh as a team and build happy memories together? What about the expectations you have for those you are leading: are they unnecessarily high and unachievable, desperately needing adjustment? Healthy leaders ask these kinds of questions of themselves and the teams they are called to serve.

The business principle called MBWA (managing by walking around) forces a leader to be present to the team, being available to both observe what is happening on the job and to participate in the life of the ministry at hand. When we see firsthand what pressures the team members face daily, we can follow up our observations with penetrating questions. Being present shows that you are interested in a given ministry and are making yourself available to serve and to offer support where needed.

Leaders who lighten others' loads are willing to make the changes necessary to enhance the ministry. If this entails making environmental or structural changes, they tend to them as quickly as possible. If it's related to resources, supplies, and equipment, they make them available. If it concerns personnel, they tend to the relationships and responsibilities within a reasonable time frame. Change is the one constant you can rely on in ministry—so be open to change, not for change's sake, but for the purpose of lightening the load of your team members and making their ministry environments more conducive to effective service.

Another way you can lighten the load of others is to create special memories for the team. When I served as a minister of Christian education, our team decided to do something completely different for our annual Christian education weekend. We decided to focus on appreciating all who served on the team in a creative way. Saturday morning we rented out a local bowling alley and invited all the workers and their families to a free morning of bowling and fun. That evening we hosted a dinner for the workers that was served by the pastoral and administrative staff members and their spouses. On Sunday morning we printed the names of all the staff and inserted it into the bulletin. During the worship services we invited all of the volunteers listed in the insert to stand and be applauded and prayed for by the senior pastor. This weekend became a tradition during my tenure and created many lasting memories for the team. Appreciation of a job well done goes a long way in helping others deal with the ongoing pressures of ministry.

Too often we take ourselves too seriously. Lightening the load of others means that wholesome humor is a part of our relationships. J. Oswald

Sanders, in his book *Spiritual Leadership*, writes: "Since man is in the image of God, his sense of humor is a gift of God and finds its counterpart in the divine nature. But it is a gift which is to be controlled as well as cultivated. Clean, wholesome humor will relax tension and relieve a difficult situation more than anything else. It can be of untold value in a leader, both for what it does for him and for the use it can be in his work."[6]

This is one area where I feel most deficient as a leader. I err on the serious side in my temperament, so I rely on others around me to offer the lighter, more humorous touch. But I know how important appropriate humor is for the building of relationships and the creation of teams. If we are unable to laugh at ourselves and the situations that are before us, then we are in sad shape as leaders and as teams. When is the last time you had a good laugh?

Be a Leader Who Leads

People don't want to be managed. They want to be led. If you really want to manage someone, then focus on managing yourself. Managing yourself includes the management of your time, talents, and resources. It includes issues of personal stewardship that lead to a well-managed life. Dr. Carl Saylor, a professor of mine in seminary, once said, "Manage your time before it manages you." Do that well and you'll be prepared to stop managing others and start leading them instead.

In a general sense, the church suffers from a leadership crisis. Many who are charged with the responsibility of leadership are not called or equipped for this task. They have been given titles and prestige, but it's shallow because they are misfits for the jobs they carry. This poses a serious dilemma for local church leadership teams and those who service them like our Christian colleges and seminaries. What does it take to truly lead a ministry today? I would summarize the critical tasks of leaders into three major categories.

First, *leaders need to be the keepers of the vision.* They need to be long-term thinkers about what the preferred outcomes and futures are for the ministry. They need to dream big dreams and envision great visions that will inspire others toward lofty ideals and exciting goals. Not only do they need to carry well the vision from a principled perspective, but they need to keep the team focused on the fulfillment of the vision. Every ministry program needs to support and enrich the potential achievement of the vision. The vision needs to be supported by the mission of the church and defined by the activities of each team.

Second, *a leader needs to build a team.* An effective leader knows that the job to be done far exceeds one person's ability to accomplish the task. A leader needs others around who share the vision and mission of the church and are willing to sacrificially participate in the accomplishment of God's will for them. A leader understands that a team goes through a number of stages of development before it reaches peak performance and is willing to walk through each stage with diligent determination. Leaders know when the team is healthy and effective and will go the distance to ensure their quality at all levels of service. Team ministry is a must for all healthy churches.

Third, *a leader empowers others to serve*. Jesus made extraordinary leaders out of ordinary people. He saw the potential within them, and he invested in their lives with the belief that God had something special in mind for them. As we embody the Spirit of Christ, we need to empower others to become all that God intends them to be. We need to give others opportunity to flourish under our guidance and love. We need to share the load with others who are gifted in areas where we are not as strong. We must express tangibly and intangibly that we affirm God's call on them and invest in them so that they utilize their gifts in meaningful ways. We dare not hold others back from the potential that is within them, planted there by God himself.

Howard Hendricks and Bruce Cook suggest eleven characteristics of transformative leaders that also show what it takes to be an effective church leader today.

1. *Persistence*—able to overcome hurdles and obstacles when seeking to accomplish objectives.
2. *Resistance*—capacity both in attitude and actions to handle criticism from others.
3. *Servanthood*—taking the initiative to meet the needs of other people.
4. *Sensitivity*—able to identify with another person's situation and point of view.
5. *Consistent example*—living one's life as a model to others.
6. *Self-mastery*—life characterized by a degree of discipline and self-control.
7. *Virile private life*—involved in a consistent time of self-development and personal growth.
8. *Confidence*—demonstrating a high degree of confidence in one's abilities to make significant accomplishments.
9. *Teachability*—demonstrating openness to new ideas and input from others.
10. *Positive attitude*—showing positive attitudes and a good sense of humor.
11. *Faith*—trusting God for things that only he can do.[7]

From a slightly different but equally worthy perspective, John W. Gardner offers the following nine critical tasks of a leader.

1. *Envision goals*—set goals and create a vision of what the people/organization can achieve.
2. *Affirm values*—shared norms, expectations, and purposes.
3. *Motivate others*—not coming out of thin air; they unlock or channel existing motives.
4. *Managing*—planning, priority setting, agenda setting, decision-making, and exercising political judgment.
5. *Achieve workable unity*—concern for and ability to resolve conflict; and the need to build trust.
6. *Explaining*—sharing information about what is going on and why.
7. *Serve as a symbol*—leaders can rarely afford the luxury of speaking for themselves alone!
8. *Representing the group*—serve as the people's representative with other leaders and groups.
9. *Renewing*—because of inevitable change, always seek renewal of purposes and goals and methods for achieving those goals.[8]

All of these characteristics require that leaders be men and women of prayer and the Word. We cannot perform these functions in our own strength or human ability. Leaders who are healthy and effective have a wholesome dependence on God. The authority of the Scriptures and the lordship of Christ are their primary points of guidance in love, grace, and support. When called to lead, don't forget to lead!

Be a Leader Who Leaves a Legacy

Michael Youseff tells us, "One characteristic of good leaders is that they prepare others to take over. They don't just prepare their followers to 'do well' but prepare them to do everything they are doing themselves."[9]

Could you walk away from your leadership responsibilities and leave your ministry intact today? Are you empowering a new generation of leaders to step in and take over from where you have left off? Are you preparing a foundation from which those who follow you can do greater things than you have done?

Most of us in leadership positions would rather avoid these questions than answer them. We are so engrossed in our responsibilities that we have neglected the preparation of future leadership. Or at least most of us are not proactively and strategically covering this essential ingredient of effective leadership. We don't necessarily mean to do so—many of us are just not sure how to leave a legacy.

I believe that mentoring and discipleship encompass the answer. Investing in the lives of others is the basic principle that we started with at the beginning of this chapter, and it's the place from which we will end. The best leaders are motivated by loving concern for others rather than a desire for personal glory. They are willing to pay the price in mentoring and discipling others.

It was so encouraging to watch how Pastor Stan Allaby of Black Rock Congregational Church, Connecticut, turned over the senior pastor role to one of his associates, Steve Treash. Stan had served for over thirty years in this pastoral position. But when he knew that his retirement was forthcoming, he began the mentoring process with Steve. Today Steve Treash is thriving in his new leadership role, having taken the reins from his mentor and been freed up to serve with the gifts God has bestowed on him.

Closing Question

Henri Nouwen, in his book *In the Name of Jesus*, brings Jesus' question to Peter close to home: "Jesus asks, 'Do you love me?' Jesus sends us out to be shepherds, and Jesus promises a life in which we increasingly have to stretch out our hands and be led to places where we would rather not go. He asks us to move from a concern for relevance to a life of prayer, from worries about popularity to communal and mutual ministry, and from a leadership built on power to a leadership in which we critically discern where God is leading us and our people. Be a leader with outstretched hands, who chooses a life of servanthood. It is contained in the image of the *praying* leader, the *vulnerable* leader, and the *trusting* leader."[10] Jesus' emphasis was not on the authority of a leader who rules but on the humility of a leader who serves. This, then, is the life of a leader worth following.

Lord Jesus, your life and service here on earth captivate my attention as a leader. How I long to lead as you led. I desire this day to acquire the supernatural ability to lead as a servant. I want to please you in how I give of myself to the members of the team that you have entrusted to my care. Give me a heart that is led by your heart. Give me a hunger to grow in my love for you and my desire to love others. Give me a yearning to learn new things about you, your world, your Word, your people, your principles of righteousness and service. Give me ears that are attuned to listening to your still small voice amidst the cacophony of voices all around me. Give me the ability to lighten the load of others by showing me how I can help them in their roles and by creating memories with them. Give me the strength and wisdom to know how to lead as you have led. Give me the insight to mentor and disciple others with a long-term view of passing on the torch of my leadership to a new generation of servants. Only you, Lord, can grant these petitions, so I ask for them boldly as one of your servant-leaders called by your name to lead others in the body in healthy and effective ways. Give ear to these petitions, and bless my life as a leader in ways that only you can. For I pray this day with deep commitment and devotion to you, the Great Shepherd. Amen.

FOR REFLECTION AND RENEWAL

The healthy church identifies and develops individuals whom God has called and given the gift of leadership and challenges them to become servant-leaders.

For church government, the healthy church:

- is led by persons who understand the church's vision, communicate it clearly to the congregation, and organize the body and each of its ministry groups so that the vision becomes reality
- motivates potential leaders by challenging them to serve for the glory of God
- develops a sense of collegiality among leaders—both lay and clergy
- encourages turnover yet stability in lay leadership
- evaluates the church's effectiveness, manages change, and plans for the future
- seeks to unify the congregation behind its leaders

For ministry leadership, the healthy church:

- creates an environment in which men and women with ministry gifts are developed to serve as servant-leaders
- encourages ministries to be led by laypersons as much as possible

- makes sure that ministry leadership is shared widely among congregation members
- works hard to assure that laypersons are partners who are respected, honored, mobilized, and freed to minister both inside and outside the church
- equips and empowers others to serve in ministry

> From him [Christ] the whole body, joined and held together by every supporting ligament, grows and builds itself up in love, as each part does its work.
>
> Ephesians 4:16

1. On a scale of 1 to 10 (1 being not at all important and 10 being most important), rank each of the above statements while answering the question, "How important is this statement for the health of our church; how highly do we value servant-leadership development?"

2. On a scale of 1 to 10 (1 being very ineffective and 10 being very effective), rank each of the above statements while answering the question, "How effective are we as a leadership team at instilling these values in our church?"

3. For each of the above statements, ask your team, "Where do we want to be in the characteristic Servant-Leadership Development in this next year or two?"

4. For each of the above statements, ask your team, "How will we get where we want to be in living out Servant-Leadership Development in this next year?"

5. Overall, on a scale of 1 to 10 (1 being very low and 10 being very high), rank how well you think your church is doing in living out this sixth characteristic of a healthy church, Servant-Leadership Development.

8

An Outward Focus
Characteristic 7

The healthy church places high priority on communicating the truth of Jesus and demonstrating his love to those outside the faith.

"For the Son of Man came to seek and to save what was lost."

Luke 19:10

"It was January 1991, and I went for a walk with you. The streets of Dhaka, Bangladesh, that morning were still quiet. We had walked together many different times in many different countries. But that morning it was a walk that began in me something eternal."

These words were written by Barry Corey to his father, Hugh Corey, in a letter commemorating his dad's seventy-fifth birthday—and reread at his dad's memorial service six months later.

Hugh Corey was a long-time friend and colleague in ministry here in New England. He had a tender, pastoral heart, and he served his Lord with daily love and faithfulness. Hugh was a pastor for many years, a denominational executive, and a member of the Vision New England staff heading up our pastoral mentoring ministry and serving as our minister-at-large. He passed away in January 1998 after suffering with an extended bout of cancer.

As Hugh's days were coming to a close, his son, Barry, revised his letter to his dad. Barry poured out his heart in this letter, and his sentiments became our focus during Hugh's memorial service. One concept in particular that was the hallmark of Hugh's life and ministry is described by Barry through the following story.

"It was that morning, that walk, when you wove into the fabric of my being a part of your life. I did not fully understand then, and am only beginning to grasp today, the full meaning of the early morning walk through the streets of Bangladesh. I had been studying in that country for several months of my yearlong assignment when you and mom paid me a visit. Each morning before breakfast you and I would walk together, catching up on all that was happening in each other's lives.

"This particular morning it was different. As our walk began you started to share with me that in the fifty-three years since you began your pilgrimage with God, so much remained that you did not know about his wisdom and ways. You held no seminary degree. You never completed college. But as we walked, Hugh Corey—the man of God—began to share with me what his life in Christ had taught him.

"'And he that taketh not his cross and followeth after me,' you continued, recounting with me the words of Christ, 'is not worthy of me. He that findeth his life shall lose it; and he that loseth his life for my sake shall find it. He that receiveth you receiveth me, and he that receiveth me receiveth him that sent me.'

"Then you stopped talking for a few minutes and I replayed the words of Christ you had just spoken. 'He who receives you receives me, and he who receives me receives the one who sent me.' Knowing I was the student that moment, I waited for you the teacher to continue. You said, 'Barry, I don't fully understand what Jesus meant when he said, "He who receives you receives me, and he who receives me receives the one who sent me." But this I do know. In everything I do I must make myself receivable to the people God places in my life. If the lives God intersects with mine do not have the opportunity to receive me, how will they ever know the infinite love the Father has for them? I must live my life in a way that strangers, friends, aching, lonely, family . . . they must receive me and receive through me the amazing love God alone has authored.'

"We finished our walk in silence. I knew that although you wanted only to share your heart with me as you have done so many times before and since, this thought was different. Maybe it was different because I had not heard your voice for many months. Maybe it was different because I was trying to make sense of my life in Christ while I lived among some of the world's poorest people. Maybe it was different because I was ready to hear what you had to say.

"As I have gone back to that walk many times over these past seven years, I have come to understand *that* moment as one ordained by God when I would receive my most cherished gift. On the fetid streets of Bangladesh, the bedrock of your faith was being passed on to me, your son. It was as if you had traveled halfway around the world to find me and pass on a truth to your son. And two days after you spoke, I witnessed you demonstrating the profound power of this simple truth in Christ: 'He who receives you receives me, and he who receives me receives the one who sent me.'

"Shamsul was a poor Bangladeshi man of twenty-one who lived in the servant's quarters behind the house where I was staying. He spoke little English and, like many others, had left his family in the villages to seek out work as a day laborer in Dhaka, the nation's largest city. I had noticed you had begun to build a relationship with Shamsul in the few days you and mom were with me. This was nothing new. All my life I have seen you show your love to gas station attendants, cobblers, dentists, tailors, attorneys, and on and on. But it was not until after our walk earlier in the week that I had focused closely on the transforming power of Christ's words, 'He who receives you receives me, and he who receives me receives the one who sent me.'

"You and Shamsul had been struggling to communicate but managed to become friends nonetheless, laughing and talking during those few days you had known each other. I was even a bit envious that you had become closer to him then I had in the months I had been living there. Then one afternoon it happened. The reception moment occurred between Hugh Corey and Shamsul when the words of Christ, as they had so often before, called you to act. 'He who receives you receives me, and he who receives me receives the one who sent me.'

"I was transfixed as you, this sixty-eight-year-old Canadian preacher, reached out your hands in a moment of outpouring compassion and held the face of this poor man Shamsul, looking into his dark eyes. 'Shamsul, my friend,' you said, 'I love you.' Then pulling your face to his, Shamsul leaned forward and kissed you, Hugh Corey, right on the mouth. You both fought back tears. 'He who receives you receives me, and he who receives me receives the one who sent me.' On one day in Bangladesh you told me. A few days later you showed me. And my life has been changed from those words and that deed.

"Hugh Corey, you received this stranger named Shamsul. Jesus said, 'The Son of Man did not come to be served, but to serve, and to give his life as a ransom for many.' I have no doubt that because you have demonstrated the love of Christ and have been well-received in this world, you will soon be well-received by your Father in heaven.

"You were epic in life because you were epic in love. Hugh MacLeod Corey, you are the greatest receiver I have ever known. And I love you. Your son, Barry."[1]

In everything I do I must make myself receivable to the people God places in my life. These words of Hugh Corey define a life poured out for others so that they, too, can know God personally through his Son, our Savior, Jesus Christ. Unless we are able to be received—where it's easy for others to receive us—how will the world he has died to save come to know him? "He who receives you receives me, and he who receives me receives the one who sent me'" (Matt. 10:40).

How receivable are you to the people God places in your life? What spiritual resources are you turning to in your efforts of outreach and service? Is your life marked by the love of Christ that overflows into the hearts and lives of others in need? Hugh Corey was effective in his outreach because he was first and foremost a man of God. He focused his daily energies on growing in the grace and knowledge of God, and it was out of that inner strength that his life of love overflowed to others.

Evangelizing out of Your Overflow

Michael Green, in his book *Evangelism through the Local Church*, offers three helpful definitions for evangelism.

The first comes from the English Archbishop William Temple. Appearing in *Towards the Conversion of England*, it states: "To evangelise is so to present Jesus Christ in the power of the Holy Spirit, that men [and women] shall come to put their trust in God through him, to accept him as their Savior, and serve him as their King in the fellowship of his church."

The second definition is attributed to Charles Spurgeon, the famous nineteenth-century British preacher and evangelist. Evangelism, he said, "is one beggar telling another beggar where to get bread." It draws attention both to the needs of the recipient and to the generosity of the giver: God will not give us a stone when we ask him for bread. It underscores equality. There is no way that an evangelist is any better or on higher ground than the person to whom he or she is talking. The ground is level around the cross of Christ. The only difference between the two hungry beggars is that one has been fed and knows where food is always available. This reminds us that we cannot bring this good news to others unless we personally have come to "taste and see that the Lord is good" (Ps. 34:8).

The third definition, and by far my personal favorite, is found in one word: overflow. It gives the right nuance, of someone who is so full of joy about Jesus Christ that it overflows as surely as a bathtub overflowing with water. It has the quality that so much evangelism today lacks: spontaneity. Incidentally, *overflow* is a passable translation of a Greek word that occurs often in the New Testament to describe the liberated confidence of the Christian, *plarophoria*. The apostle Paul reminds the Thessalonians that "our gospel came to you not simply with words, but also with power, with the Holy Spirit and with [much *plarophoria*]," much confident overflow (1 Thess. 1:5).[2]

The natural, obvious, spontaneous nature of overflow is desperately needed in the church. Imagine if every member of your church found natural ways of sharing the love of Christ with others outside the faith who cross our paths each day. If this ever became a reality, I would suspect that your church would look much different than it does today. How do we get our church leaders and members to pursue a life of contagious, overflowing joy?

Bill Hybels and Mark Mittelberg spell out a creative prescription for effective, everyday evangelism. It reinforces the biblical value of the Willow Creek Community Church, that "all people matter to God." Their biblical formula for influencing our world for Christ is summarized as HP + CP + CC = MI. Which means: our *high potency* as Christ-followers seeking to make a difference in the lives of those we are called to serve plus the *close proximity* we have with those we hope to influence for Christ, plus *clear communication* of the gospel message itself equals the *maximum impact* God desires to emerge in others.[3]

In essence, what Hybels and Mittelberg are promoting is that God loves to use the lives of Christian men and women who are yielded to his will and ways. And so they are excited about the opportunity for maximum impact in the lives of those outside our faith. Having this kind of impact requires that we live yielded lives before God; have open, outstretched hands to receive the Lord's daily love and grace; and then be free to share that with others.

What we experience on the inside of our hearts and souls eventually bubbles up to the surface and overflows to others. So if what you experience with God is pure joy, then what you give away to others is joy. Remember Jeff Poor, who came alive to Christ as a result of commitment to him at Congress '97? For the next year until he died of cancer, his overflowing joy resulted in a powerful witness at his job, in his community, and in a number of churches where he shared his story. His witness was so joyful that his boss shut down the furniture store he worked in so that the staff could attend Jeff's funeral.

On the other hand, if we feed our souls with something less than God's priorities, the overflow either never occurs or what spills out of us is less than pleasing or desirable to him. It's like the old computer slogan, Garbage in, garbage out. Or, We are what we eat. So if what we consume in life is bad for our souls, what is visibly apparent from our words and attitudes is counterproductive for others. Instead of Garbage in, garbage out, it should be Joy in, joy out!

Choose Joy!

What is joy anyway? Where do you discover it? How do you define it? With whom do you have it in common? How do you give it away?

My eight-year-old daughter, Rebekah, and I went sledding on the heels of a surprise springtime snowstorm. It was truly one of the most enjoyable two hours we had spent together in a long time. She had this small, red plastic sled that we took with us. Of course, I needed to carry her in it all the way from our home to the top of the sledding hill. When we finally made it to our hilltop destination, we looked longingly at the snow-covered trail before us.

She was convinced that if we rubbed an ice block on the bottom of this plastic sled, it would go down the hill much faster. So I took her cue, and we worked feverishly to ice up the base as best we could. We both barely fit into the sled but managed it anyway. Rebekah said it was like "Honey I shrunk the sled" with her dad's large backside barely squeezing into the rear of the sled. We wanted to be together each run of the hill, so we were determined to make it work. She hopped on my lap, I barely got my feet around her waist and into the front of the sled, and off we went.

The first run of the hill was the best. We blazed the trail ahead of us for each succeeding ride. We ran into the bushes along the edge of the trail, bumped our way off course several times, and when we reached the bottom, we toppled over into the snow amid our laughter and screaming. We coached each other every step of the way, recounted each run with constructive commentary, and tirelessly walked up and rode down our little hill several times.

When we got back home, we enjoyed a delicious hot chocolate brimming with marshmallows and talked about our experiences together with absolute delight. It certainly was a happy, fun, memorable time together, but what it produced in us was far better. It gave us a new appreciation of joy—joy in our love for God's beautiful creation, and joy in one another as God's children. This father-daughter experience has marked our relationship with special significance. In fact, later that evening, after Ruth and I had tucked Rebekah in, said our prayers, and kissed her goodnight, she called me back into her room to tell me, "Thanks, Dad, I really had fun today sledding with you." That made it all worthwhile!

Now, the Christian life is not always a parallel to this sledding expedition. In fact, most of the time it's much "tougher sledding" than this. No biblical promises tell us it will be smooth sledding all the way. On the contrary, the pain, suffering, sacrifice, and heartaches of life are pictured much more graphically in the pages of Scripture. And the Lord reminds us that we are blessed if we suffer in his name (Acts 5:41; Rom. 5:3; 2 Tim. 1:8; Heb. 2:10; 1 Peter 3:17). What does that mean for us who claim the name of Christ and desire to know his joy and share it with others?

The Scriptures are replete with examples of tough sledding that produces a faith that's joy filled. One passage has become a reference point for me. During my first summer of leadership at Vision New England, the board of directors told me to take some time to study the Scriptures, pray, journal, and seek the mind of Christ for our mission and ministry. I did so with fear and trepidation, not sure what would emerge.

That season of my faith journey had me reflecting on the Psalms each day. In the midst of my study, I landed on Psalm 51 and was transfixed by its significance. David wrote this psalm after his sin with Bathsheba. Second Samuel 11–12 shows us a picture of King David as a man known for his faith in God but greatly distracted from his duties as a king and as a man of God. It all began with his wandering eyes, which landed on the figure of a beautiful woman, Bathsheba.

David's lustful look led to a downward spiral of distraction and destruction. From his initial lust, he called her to himself, had a sexual encounter with her, and she ultimately became pregnant. David sought to cover up his sin. He summoned her faithful husband, Uriah the Hittite, home from the battlefield supposedly to discuss the details of the war. David hoped that once Uriah was home, he would want to sleep with his wife. But faithful Uriah surprised David with his integrity and refused to enjoy his wife when his fellow soldiers did not have such a luxury. Even after being wined and dined by David a second night home, Uriah still refused to go and sleep with his wife.

So David plotted Uriah's death. He sent a note with Uriah to give to his commander, issuing an order for Uriah to be placed on the front line of battle. David set up Uriah's death, and one more commandment was broken by the king. With Uriah dead, David took Bathsheba to be his wife.

Then God intervened with a massive wake-up call for David. He sent the prophet Nathan with a simple story of injustice to awaken David to the reality of his sin and his desperate need for repentance and forgiveness. He confessed to Nathan, "I have sinned against the Lord," (2 Sam. 12:13). Psalm 51 was birthed as a result of this experience.

Such is the experience for every Christian who grapples with his or her own sinfulness, and when confronted by another, confesses and comes clean before God. I have had my share of mishaps in relationships. When I hold back my confession I find my soul begins to rot and wither away. On the other hand, being open with myself and others I have hurt brings healing and restoration. The result is a renewed relationship—with God and with others.

Thank God for Nathan, who loved God enough to respond obediently to his calling and giftedness and loved David enough to be used to expose his sin and rescue him from further distraction and ultimate destruction. All of us need Nathans in our lives to wake us up to our sinfulness, our brokenness, our tough sledding experiences of life that need midcourse corrections.

In the early verses of Psalm 51, David pours out his heart before God and comes clean:

> Have mercy on me, O God,
>   according to your unfailing love;
> according to your great compassion
>   blot out my transgressions.
> Wash away all my iniquity
>   and cleanse me from my sin.
> For I know my transgressions,
>   and my sin is always before me.
> Against you, you only, have I sinned
>   and done what is evil in your sight,
> so that you are proved right when you speak
>   and justified when you judge.
> Surely I was sinful from birth,
>   sinful from the time my mother conceived me.
> Surely you desire truth in the inner parts;
>   you teach me wisdom in the inmost place.
> Cleanse me with hyssop, and I will be clean;
>   wash me, and I will be whiter than snow.
> Let me hear joy and gladness;
>   let the bones you have crushed rejoice.
> Hide your face from my sins
>   and blot out all my iniquity.
>
>   verses 1–9

Now that David was broken before God, he was ready to receive his gift of grace, mercy, love, forgiveness, and joy. The psalm continues,

> Create in me a pure heart, O God,
>   and renew a steadfast spirit within me.
> Do not cast me from your presence
>   or take your Holy Spirit from me.
> Restore to me the joy of your salvation
>   and grant me a willing spirit, to sustain me.
>
>   verses 10–12

Out of David's brokenness came joy—pure, restored, sustained, steadfast joy. A gift that comes from God and God alone.

When we finally give up our own attempts to control our lives and submit to the love and lordship of Christ, we discover true joy for the first time. As children of God, there is no greater joy than to be in relationship with him and with one another as joybearers in this world.

Joy permeates the Scriptures verse after verse. Listed below are some of my favorite passages related to joy.

- Galatians 5:22–23—the apostle Paul outlines for us what the fruit of the Spirit looks like, with joy near the top of the list!
- Philippians—the epistle of joy, most likely written by Paul from a prison cell in Rome.
- Habakkuk 3:17–18—the prophet reminds the people of God that "though the fig tree does not bud and there are no grapes on the vines, though the olive crop fails and the fields produce no food, though there are no sheep in the pen and no cattle in the stalls, yet I will rejoice in the Lord, I will be joyful in God my Savior."
- Nehemiah 8:10—"the joy of the Lord is your strength."

Joy is more than a feel-good emotion. It is rooted in God. Andrew, the disciple of Christ, was so filled with joy when he was found by Jesus that he dragged his brother Peter along to meet him. Zacchaeus was joyfully liberated from the bondage of financial pursuits and was set free to be the friend of the Lord when he met Jesus. When the pearl of great price was discovered by the pearl fancier, he rejoiced. When the bridesmaids went into the wedding feast, they found joy. Finding friendship with God, through Jesus Christ his Son, is the most exhilarating experience in the world. Despite our circumstances, distractions, occupations, or preoccupations, we can choose to receive joy from God. When we face the sins that separate us from God, confess them, and receive his forgiveness and renewal, we will find true joy. From this restoration-based joy then emerges a life of faithfulness. This is the *overflow* of our lives, fulfilling the call of God stamped on our beings. Psalm 51 is like one massive if-then clause. If we are broken and if we find true joy, then we will be found faithful:

- then (v. 13) "I will teach transgressors your ways, and sinners will turn back to you";
- then (vv. 14–15) "my tongue will sing of your righteousness; O Lord, open my lips, and my mouth will declare your praise";

- then (v. 18) "in your good pleasure make Zion prosper; build up the walls of Jerusalem";
- then (v. 19) "there will be righteous sacrifices, whole burnt offerings to delight you."

The faithfulness of God's people is the visible overflow of our joy-filled lives. What Rebekah and I found during our sledding experience was like another cup of joy being poured into our lives by the author and creator of joy, the Lord himself. But when life is not smooth sledding and the tougher times of brokenness come our way, his gift of joy still comes our way. When we find joy in God and in each other as brothers and sisters in Christ, we are filled up to overflowing with the joy of the Lord, and we can't help but give it away to others. If we remain in Christ, he will bear eternal fruit through us as a result of our obedient overflow of his love and joy (see John 15).

One devout woman of God who gives out of the overflow of her joy in Christ is Sarah Small. Thirty-four years ago Sarah was field secretary and youth organizer for the Southern Christian Leadership Conference and a close associate of Martin Luther King Jr. For nearly thirty years she has made the invisible Christ visible to both her African-American brothers and sisters and thousands of others in Boston. She demonstrates what it means to be a born-again Christian activist for justice, racial reconciliation, and mercy.

When Sarah became the director of Packard Manse in Roxbury, Massachusetts, in 1970, the Lord gave her a fifteen-room home as a base of operations for a remarkable career in helping the disadvantaged. She dedicated herself to helping the homeless, drug addicts, single mothers with children—all who needed a meal and a roof over their head. In 1975 she went to work as chaplain at the University of Massachusetts/Boston, counseling hundreds of college students each year. And she funded meals and necessities for others out of her own pocket.

In addition, Sarah has always been actively involved in criminal justice and prison issues. In that role she is known far beyond the borders of Boston. When God created Sarah, he gave her a big heart with unlimited energy to do his bidding. We do know, of course, where that energy comes from. A consistent prayer warrior, she prays every morning from 4:15 to 6:30, having enlisted a dozen others to pray with her at fifteen-minute segments every day. Every Thursday she holds a Bible study at the Packard Manse. That prayer-generated and Bible-informed energy is the source of the overflow of her river of mercy.

Tools of the Trade

Like every person who perfects skills in a select area of expertise, we Christians need to "always be prepared to give an answer to everyone who asks you to give the reason for the hope that you have" (1 Peter 3:15). Yet this frightens off many Christians. We fear potential rejection from our family or friends; we are uncertain of the biblical references that highlight the essentials of the gospel message; we are shy about sharing the ingredients of our own personal testimony; or we are concerned that we may lose the relationship altogether if we start talking too much about spiritual issues. One or more of these hang-ups are the hot buttons for most Christ-followers today as it relates to their understanding and fulfillment of the evangelism mandate.

Jesus' words to go out and make disciples of all the nations (Matt. 28:18–20) are not to be taken lightly. We have God-ordained responsibilities in the areas of evangelism, social concern, and worldwide missions. Imagine what your church would be like if the pastor and leadership team lived out this mandate and empowered others in the congregation to do so as well. For this to occur, we need to equip the saints for the work of outwardly focused ministry.

What are the tools of the trade for an outwardly focused life and church?

The Holy Spirit. The first and most essential tool is the powerful work of the Holy Spirit. Far too often, we Christians who live in North America tend to think we can fix our problems on our own. Unfortunately, we translate this pragmatic optimism to the work of evangelism as well. As Michael Green writes,

> We have the message, the manpower, the methodology, the money: let's go. But it is not like that. God will not give His glory to another. And the pragmatism of so much modern evangelism is an insult to the Almighty. He does not need our publicity drives, our booklets, or our appeals. He may well make use of them, in His grace, from time to time. But it is God Almighty we are talking about! Evangelism is supremely His work. He so loved the world that He became the first evangelist. And there are three areas in particular where the mystery of His working, and His alone, are most evident: the sovereignty of His choice, the authority of His Scriptures, and the power of His Spirit.[4]

The amazing fact of the matter is that he can handle this task all on his own, thank you very much. But, what's even more amazing is that he would choose to use people just like you and me to accomplish his redemptive purposes in this world.

Prayer. The second tool of the Christian in the work of evangelism is prayer. There is no such thing as effective evangelism without fervent prayer. This powerful truth is clearly spelled out for us in passages like 2 Chronicles 7:14: "If my people, who are called by my name, will humble themselves and pray and seek my face and turn from their wicked ways, then will I hear from heaven and will forgive their sin and will heal their land." An outwardly focused community is reinforced by prayers that remind us of our dependency on the God who called us to this task and remains sovereignly responsible for all outcomes. We also need the help of our fellow believers if we are to participate with the Holy Spirit in the work of evangelism. The apostle Paul pleaded for the prayers of the Ephesian church, "That whenever I open my mouth, words may be given me so that I will fearlessly make known the mystery of the gospel" (Eph. 6:19). Prayer is absolutely, positively, without a shadow of a doubt, essential.

Understanding the process. The third tool of the trade is understanding the process of effective evangelism in the life of the seeker. In 1 Thessalonians 2, Paul reminded the new believers in that city about his love for them. "We were gentle among you, like a mother caring for her little children. We loved you so much that we were delighted to share with you not only the gospel of God but our lives as well, because you had become so dear to us. . . . We dealt with each of you as a father deals with his own children, encouraging, comforting and urging you to live lives worthy of God, who calls you into his kingdom and glory" (vv. 7–13). What we see here are personal relationships of authentic love. The apostles took advantage of every opportunity to share the gospel of Christ with the people, but it was done out of genuine concern for their spiritual well-being. They built trust in their relationships by listening to the heart cries of the people, just like mothers and fathers care for their children. By living honorable lives before the Thessalonians, they earned the right to be heard. They took full advantage of the reception they had received and graciously presented the life-changing message of Jesus to all who would give them a hearing. As a result, a new citywide church was born. It takes that kind of bold yet sensitive love to reach this generation as well.

Personal stories. The fourth tool available to Christ-followers is our personal stories. When I was teaching a course on evangelism and discipleship at Gordon College in Wenham, Massachusetts, several years ago, I thought it would be good practice for the students in the class to share their testimony with one another. When we started this sharing routine, one young man offered to lead the way and tell his story first. After twenty long minutes, he finally wrapped up his concluding thought. The cold body language throughout the room emphasized for me the importance of teaching others how to appropriately share their story without boring or frustrating their listeners. We become so engrossed in the details of our own story that we forget how long it is taking for us to disclose every detail. I determined from that night forward that I would focus some of my teaching on helping every student tell the salient points of their story in a short period of time and in a way that is engaging for the listener and focused on what God can do if we yield ourselves to his loving care.

I am convinced that the most effective testimonies are short and to the point, articulated in such a way that the focus is on God and not the believer telling the story. Testimonies should lead the way into further dialogue with the listener—not for the purpose of further embellishment of "our" details but as an encouragement to all who hear. "I will tell of the kindnesses of the Lord, the deeds for which he is to be praised, according to all the Lord has done for us—yes, the many good things he has done for the house of Israel, according to his compassion and many kindnesses" (Isa. 63:7).

Preferred style. The fifth tool for life-changing witness is your preferred style of sharing the gospel. The prophet Jeremiah describes in vivid detail what it feels like to hold back the desire to speak out truth, "But if I say, 'I will not mention him or speak any more in his name,' his word is in my heart like a fire, a fire shut up in my bones. I am weary of holding it in; indeed, I cannot" (20:9). So it is for the on-fire evangelist with the gift for sharing the gospel in a strident fashion. We are not all gifted as the evangelist is, yet we all are still called to the work of evangelism.

The key here is to be comfortable in our own style and gift mix, letting the overflow come out of us in natural ways. We cannot all share his love in the same style, nor is the world monolithic enough to be reached via a single style of sharing. For those of us who are strident confronters, we need to confront. For those of us who are relational in our approach, we need to maximize our giftedness and lead others into the kingdom out of trusted and true friendship building. For the servers in our midst, they are to be freed up to serve and give and love so that out of those angel of mercy acts of kindness others will see Jesus and will choose to follow him. For the intellectual persuaders in our congregations, we need to free them up to dialogue and debate with the learned in our midst. Whatever the gift mix, passion, and preferred style might be, let's give each other permission to be all that God intended us to be, without any unhealthy comparison, envy, or discord.

The gospel. The sixth tool to be utilized is the profound message of the gospel itself. The holy work of evangelism and discipleship is empty without God's story of redemption. In our evangelism endeavors we eventually need to get verbal! The early church is a stunning example of a verbal witness of the gospel message (see Acts 5:20–21; 22:14–15). We know that faith comes from hearing the message (Rom. 10:17). It is incumbent upon us to share the Good News with others. "How, then, can they call on the one they have not believed in? And how can they believe in the one of whom they have not heard? *And how can they hear without someone preaching to them?* And how can they preach unless they are sent? As it is written, 'How beautiful are the feet of those who bring good news!'" (Rom. 10:14–15, emphasis added). There are a plethora of resources available today for learning how to give a crisp and concise gospel presentation. I would recommend getting a copy of *Becoming a Contagious Christian* and perusing the appendixes that include a number of methods from which to choose.

The body of Christ. The seventh tool to be taken advantage of is the potent nature of the body of Christ. God did not call us to this work on our own—let's team up and tackle the job together! Our identity in Christ is not of natural descent, but of God. Therefore, as his children, we need one another in order to survive in this world and to be a part of adding others to the family. In Acts 2 we are told about how the early believers devoted themselves to teaching, fellowship, breaking bread, prayer, worship, community life, praising God, and witnessing the daily expansion of their fellowship via "those who were being saved" (v. 47). By working side by side in unity, the growing work of the gospel was fruitful and multiplied in their midst. When we choose to work within our common unity then the result of our efforts will be a healthy, vibrant community of believers, knit together by the love of God the Father. He longs to see his children united: "May they be brought to complete unity to let the world know that you sent me and have loved them even as you have loved me" (John 17:23).

What we cannot do alone, we can do together. The church family of Groton Bible Chapel in Groton, Connecticut, has lived out this principle and experienced tremendous growth over the past thirty years, in large part due to the creative evangelistic efforts they have pursued as a congregation. They publish a Saturday night column on the religion page in the local newspaper, produce their Sunday morning service on their local cable channel, enter floats in the communitywide Fourth of July parade each year, set up a booth at the local county fairs, host outreach banquets in their local high school cafeteria or restaurant, initiate community-based youth outreach initiatives, have a choir sing at Christmas in the local mall, and lead evangelistic Bible studies in the homes of their members. How exciting to see how God has blessed these efforts over the years in building them up as a healthy congregation in our region.

Going Beyond Our Points of Contact

The next concentric circle of concern includes those who are much less fortunate than most of us in the evangelical church today, who live in communities where monetary and relational poverty reside together. This is known as social concern or bridge building to the urban poor, or ethnic minority populations within our service area who are spiritually, emotionally, and physically neglected. This kind of ministry includes not only soup kitchens, rescue missions, street ministries, and the like. It also includes prison ministries, ministries with persons with disabilities, troubled-youth ministry, ministries to the chemically dependent, the hearing impaired community, and even to the fifty-plus who are in shelters, nursing homes, and rehabilitation centers.[5]

My heart goes out to those who live so close and yet exist on limited resources. The healthy church reaches out to the "least of these" with empathy, compassion, love, gifts, and service.

One such person was Mark, a man who entered the rehabilitation facility of the Lynn, Massachusetts, Salvation Army several years ago. After attending one of the Lynn Corps Sunday morning services, he liked it so much he returned the following Sunday. When Captain Stoops greeted Mark by his first name, he was so impressed that on the spot he decided this was where he wanted to be.

In the following weeks he came to faith in Christ during one of the chapel meetings at the rehabilitation facility and entered actively into the life of the church. Today Mark is the greeter for visitors at the Lynn Corps Sunday service—and serving in the Corps full-time as a key link to the community, serving the needs of others in Jesus' name. In Mark's own words, he stayed at the church for one simple reason: because someone remembered his name. His name is now permanently etched in the Book of Life.

When questioned by the "expert in the law" as to "What must I do to inherit eternal life?" Jesus not only urges him to love the Lord his God with all his heart and all his soul and all his mind but to love his neighbor as himself (Luke 10:25–28). He continued to probe Jesus with the question, "And who is my neighbor?" Jesus answers with the parable of the Good Samaritan. This is Christ's clarion call for mercy-based ministry—a call we are to follow in our personal lives and in our local churches.

Claire Sullivan of the Emmanuel Gospel Center's Starlight Ministries has been a Good Samaritan to many individuals and families over the years in Boston. In one of her recent newsletters, Claire shares the story of a fifty-six-year-old woman who grew up in Boston's South End. She was once a

CPA until she started drinking at the age of forty. She has grown sons, and she used to take them to church on Sundays when they were little, but she became a victim of domestic violence and now lives on the streets of Boston.

One day Claire found this woman on the floor near an automated teller machine with a cut going down her back at least a foot long, bleeding profusely. Nobody had touched her or even asked if she needed help. Nobody was willing to get involved—not even just to call 911 on her behalf. When Claire arrived, she called for help and stayed by her side until medical personnel attended to her wounds.

Claire calls the ATM a symbol of our times. We get instant cash from such a machine because we are too busy to enter a bank during business hours. She says, "Maybe instead of 'automated teller machine' it should stand for 'at the moment.' At the moment, I'm too busy to drop a quarter into the pay phone to dial 911 because . . ." Claire is concerned that our society avoids the poor, discards the unborn, abandons the elderly, and neglects our children, all because "at the moment" we are too busy.

Is your congregation too busy to be a Good Samaritan neighbor to those in need outside your regular circle of contact but within your reachable circle of concern? The Root Cellar in Portland, Maine, is one such Good Samaritan ministry, in one of the poorest white slums in America. Each day of the year they mobilize Christians from area churches to serve children and families in the name of Jesus. Their resources are limited, but those who are involved not only believe in the mission of the Root Cellar but invest their time and talents in a myriad of after school programs for the neighborhood children and practical services to their families.

Getting involved in this type of outreach sensitizes us to God's heart for the downtrodden and neglected ones of our society. His heart is torn by the sheer numbers of people in this pocket of need. He wants us to be his arms and legs and ears and eyes and heart and hands to reach out tangibly to others, offering them a cup of cold water in Jesus' name. Where are you and your church family involved in this type of Good Samaritan ministry, beyond merely sending a donation of food, clothing, or cash? We need people in our congregations who are willing to be champions for the impoverished within our reach. What about you? Are you willing to get involved and tangibly love your neighbor as yourself?

Till the Whole World Knows!

When Sol Vedrine first came to New England at the end of 1972 with a law degree from the Haiti State University, there were two Haitian churches in New England. Now there are well over seventy-five Haitian churches from Manchester, New Hampshire, to Hartford, Connecticut. Sol's role as liaison with these churches through the Haitian ministry association in our region has been a significant factor in the success of these bold initiatives. On top of the aggressive church planting efforts over the past twenty-five years, Sol and his church have been involved in effective ministry in his homeland of Haiti and with the Haitian community in the Bahamas, where he and other Haitian leaders in New England conduct annual crusades. His team also does youth ministry, participates in medical outreach, and helps stimulate microeconomic enterprises abroad.

Sol Vedrine pastors the Boston Missionary Baptist Church, which has served as the mother church to four other Missionary Baptist churches in Hartford and Norwich, Connecticut; Providence, Rhode Island; and Brockton, Massachusetts. He reports that, "There are significant Haitian communities in fifteen different countries. We cannot only focus on getting them established economically, we must challenge our churches in those countries to become strongly missionary minded." Pastor Vedrine is excited about the evangelistic momentum that is gaining strength in the youth and young adult groups within their churches and are seeing many Haitians become trained in Christian college and seminary settings. The need for leadership is tremendous, and the opportunities for local and worldwide missions is growing each year.

We can learn a lot about local and international missions from people like Sol Vedrine. I was fortunate many years ago to go to Haiti with a group from Sol's church where we ministered to the children and families of that poverty-stricken land. The international community of needs is great today and growing exponentially each year. The Christian community has the greatest resource for transformation in these countries through the message of hope contained in the Good News of Christ. We are called in the Great Commission to go into all the world and preach the gospel. We are to be his witnesses in Jerusalem, and in all Judea and Samaria, and to the ends of the earth (Acts 1:8).

What does it mean for us to go to the ends of the earth with the gospel of Christ? My dear friend Paul Borthwick, an expert on the subject of international missions, calls the body of Christ to become world-class Christians, "whose lifestyle and obedience are compatible, in cooperation, and in accord with what God is doing and wants to do in our world." David Bryant, the president of Concerts of Prayer International, reminds us that "God's primary goal is *not* to get each of us into the Great Commission. His goal is to get the Great Commission *into us!*" The Lausanne Covenant challenges the whole church to carry the whole gospel to the whole world. ACMC (Advancing Churches in Missions Commitment) encourages Christians to be bifocal . . . nearsighted (evangelism and discipleship) and farsighted (international missions). All of these groups and individuals offer a sense of urgency to the task at hand, one which requires us to be fully informed about the needs of this world, prayerful in our missionary endeavors, involved in our giving and our going, and sacrificing our creature comforts to accomplish this daunting task.

One church that has done all of this is Grace Community Church in Rochester, New Hampshire. When the people of this small congregation heard of the plight of fellow Christians in Romania from their pastor, the Reverend Steve Poole, they vowed to do something about it in addition to praying. After sending a four-person delegation from the church to assess the needs and report back on what the Bucharest congregation wanted, the church voted to lend a helping hand.

Speaking for his people, John Ceuta (Chey-woot-sa), pastor of Biserica Harul Bucuresti, asked Grace to build an American-style church building on a fifteen-hundred-square-meter lot the Romanian church already owned. Grace Community in New Hampshire had already dug deep and raised $10,000 for the project. When merchants, community members, and other churches in the area learned what was going on, they pitched in with additional cash and building materials totaling more than $42,000. The total cost of materials for the new building was over $70,000, plus shipping expenses and the airfares of those construction crew members who supervised the erection of the new structure in a building blitz over a three-week period. Considering that Grace's annual budget is about $150,000, the Romanian project became an "over and above the budget" venture.

Biserica Harul Bucuresti, which roughly translates "Grace Community Church" in honor of their American benefactors, today includes a food pantry, clothing exchange, and various other social service programs in addition to providing a meeting place for the Bucharest congregation. "I wanted people to see and believe that we could do things much bigger than ourselves if we would step out in faith," says Pastor Poole. The Bucharest church building project has brought together churches in the Rochester, New Hampshire, area for an Eastern European task force. Six men agreed to join the team that each summer will tackle a construction project in Romania.

Now that's a church with a healthy missions program. They are not out to conquer the world, but the corner of the planet they have targeted will be well served because of their faithfulness.

A Dollar a Day Can Save a Life

Alfred Magandi's photo overlooks the desk in my home office. Each day, I look at the bright face of a handsome young boy in Africa whom I have never met. I see in his eyes a world of opportunity and need. My heart extends in his direction as I pray for him and commit his needs to the Lord. I know Alfred only through our friends at Compassion International who introduced us to him when our family began sponsoring him several years ago.

Alfred is a bright young man who has a heart for God. His letters recount for us his daily routines, progress in school, and concerns for his family and friends. He writes very simple letters, yet they are keepers for the family scrapbook. We have fallen in love with this young man through the gifts, prayers, letters, and love we send his way each month. It's amazing to see what a dollar a day can do to save a life.

Alfred would be considered "one of the least of these" that Jesus teaches us about. He lives in a land of poverty and desperate spiritual need. The needs of the poorest of the poor in our world are overwhelming. Every time I see a video produced by Compassion, World Relief, or World Vision, I am overwrought with emotion. The tears flow easily as I see the pictures of how so many hundreds of thousands of people—especially the very young—live each day. The faces of hungry children are compelling to me. How can we ignore their plight?

The healthy church sees the needs of children like Alfred and does everything possible to end the struggles children like this face each day. As a family, we knew we couldn't tackle the problems of the poor around the world all by ourselves. But we could take on at least one life and try to offer hope in the name of Jesus. That's what we are trying to do for Alfred. What about you? Who among us can't afford one dollar a day to save the life of another in the name of Jesus?

Anyone who had the resources to purchase this book can afford this gift for another in need. Doing one thing a day (minimum) for someone else is the best way to start your own outreach efforts. One prayer for someone in need, one dollar for a poverty-stricken child, one kind deed for your unlovable neighbor, one note of encouragement for a friend who's sad, one anonymous gift to bolster the spirits of another, one word of affirmation to a colleague, one phone call to a family member, one e-mail message to a missionary. This is how the world is changed—one life at a time.

Lord, Make Me an Instrument

Individual lives and local churches with a healthy outward focus will reflect God's heart—a heart of sacrifice, obedience, and stewardship. They will overflow onto others with the joy of the Lord. They will creatively reach out to everyone with the life-changing message of hope in Jesus Christ. They will love their neighbor as themselves. They will consider the needs of others as more important than their own. They will die to themselves out of love for God and concern for the eternal life of their friends. In everything they do, they make themselves receivable to the people God places in their lives. Is this a description of your life and the ministry of your church?

Lord, make me an instrument of your peace.
Make me receivable to the people you place in my life.
Where there is hatred, let me sow love.
Where there is hopelessness, let me offer a word of comforting peace.
Where my neighbors feel unloved, neglected, or abused, may my arms of love
    wrapped around them be your arms too.
Where there are broken relationships, let me be your vessel of forgiveness and rec-
    onciliation.
Where there are weary and hurting wanderers on the road of life, help me never
    to walk past them but reach out and offer a helping hand.
Where there is complacency in me or in my church to the desperate needs of oth-
    ers, may I be a mouthpiece for your clarion call to action.
Where there are cities, counties, countries, and continents that are being missed
    along the way, may I be a champion for their cause and prayerfully consider
    ways that the family of God can reach out and touch them for Christ.
The needs of this world are great and getting greater.
Build within your people the best we have to offer so that we may be missions-
    minded in all of our ways.
For I delight to serve you this day and look forward to the ways in which you will
    overflow from within me with your will and your ways for this world and the
    next.
All for the love of God and each life along the way, I desire to be your instrument
    of peace.
For Jesus' sake. Amen.

▬▬▬ FOR REFLECTION AND RENEWAL ▬▬▬

The healthy church places high priority on communicating the truth of Jesus and demonstrating his love to those outside the faith.

Specifically, the church with an outward focus has a growing sense of the importance of outreach ministries of evangelism, social concern, and international missions and:

- intentionally communicates the message of Christ in culturally relevant ways to those outside the family of God
- commits to passing on our faith to the next generation
- demonstrates to the world through acts of love, justice, and mercy that "God became flesh"
- welcomes a steady stream of new people at all stages of their spiritual journey:

    nonbelieving seekers
    recent converts
    enthusiastic young Christians
    believers with questions, doubts, and struggles
    active kingdom builders
    wiser, older Christians

- experiments continually to find more effective ways to communicate the gospel to nonbelievers in the family, marketplace, community, and neighborhood
- develops a strategy for global awareness and international missions involvement

> For the Son of Man came to seek and to save what was lost.
>
> Luke 19:10

1. On a scale of 1 to 10 (1 being not at all important and 10 being most important), rank each of the above statements while answering the question, "How important is this statement for the health of our church; how highly do we value an outward focus?"

2. On a scale of 1 to 10 (1 being very ineffective and 10 being very effective), rank each of the above statements while answering the question, "How effective are we as a leadership team at instilling these values in our church?"

3. For each of the above statements, ask your team, "Where do we want to be in the characteristic aspect of An Outward Focus in this next year or two?"

4. For each of the above statements, ask your team, "How will we get where we want to be in living out An Outward Focus in this next year?"

5. Overall, on a scale of 1 to 10 (1 being very low and 10 being very high), rank how well you think your church is doing in living out this seventh characteristic of a healthy church, An Outward Focus.

9

Wise Administration and Accountability
Characteristic 8

The healthy church utilizes appropriate facilities, equipment, and systems to provide maximum support for the growth and development of its ministries.

"So if you have not been trustworthy in handling worldly wealth, who will trust you with true riches?"

Luke 16:11

n many churches the wise administrator might not be the senior pastor but someone God has gifted and trained for that role. The pastor's role is to find that person (or persons), rather than struggle along, hoping to learn on the job.

"We frankly should not expect pastors to be good administrators," according to Robert Ludwig, VNE's new executive vice president and former executive pastor at Grace Chapel in Lexington, Massachusetts. "Seminary did not train them in administration, and few have the experience in it or the God-given gift of administration. That's why so many churches suffer from unwise administration."

Handing over administrative duties to someone else, however, even in a small church, can be a tough decision for a senior pastor.

"The biggest fear of a senior pastor is that he will get an administrator that he cannot control—and control is what many pastors feel is all-important. Somewhere along the line they turned over an administrative duty to someone, and that person blew it. And the pastor feels, 'I just can't trust anyone else to do it right,'" says Ludwig.

The solution? Careful, Holy Spirit–led selection of an administrator who has the same vision and commitment to the Lord and the church as the pastor. And good chemistry between the pastor and the administrative person is vital.

"Both the senior pastor and the administrator need to realize that God has given them different skills—and that they respect each other for those gifts and skills," says Ludwig. "They also need to like each other, not just tolerate each other."

Just as in business, the first person engaged as administrator might not work out. That is not fatal, for the learning process might have been important, and what was learned might be applied for the second person engaged as administrator.

"Not that this person won't make mistakes as well, for all of us make mistakes. But when the vision meshes with that of the pastor and the commitment and training is there, mistakes become stepping stones to greater teamwork and success," says Ludwig.

If there are complementary skills and good chemistry, the administrator can relieve the senior pastor of a great number of headaches. It will also let the administrator work in his or her area of giftedness. So what kind of persons ought to be considered for administrative responsibilities?

"You don't need a senior vice president of a major corporation as administrator in a small church. A housewife who has developed administrative skills running a household with three or four children may well be able to do the work on a part-time basis. The small- or medium-sized church may also have an engineer who managed a team of people or a retired small businessman," suggests Ludwig. "There is more talent available than most people assume."

The situation is quite different at a large church, where the administrative pastor might be called an executive pastor, with all staff reporting to him instead of to the senior pastor. Again the chemistry on the team is vital.

"In my conversations with many pastors across the country, I found that many preferred to report to an executive pastor because he was a more effective manager of people and programs, while the senior pastor was the most effective in the pulpit and/or as a counselor," reveals Ludwig. "Now if the senior pastor is a good manager as well, then an executive pastor is just considered another level of bureaucracy."

What congregations sometimes consider poor administration might only be poor communication. "Frequently the person in the pew believes that decisions are made in church government very arbitrarily. They sometimes believe that there is a great deal of favoritism. To change those feelings means that the administrator needs to demonstrate that he has taken everyone's point of view into consideration. And that means establishing listening opportunities," says Ludwig. "He needs to be able to say, 'I cannot guarantee what you are saying will be acted on, but I will pass it on to the right board or committee.' People need to believe that management is trying to be fair."

Wise administration ought not to be the prerogative of merely the business community. The early church recognized that—and so should churches today. But as in the early church, someone had to identify the need for a separation of responsibilities, so pastors today need to recognize when they are not gifted in administration. God will have someone in the congregation who can do it.

The Administrative Agenda

The tasks of wise administration and accountability in the local church are varied and require ongoing attention by those assigned to oversee this area of the local church ministry. The administrators are critical to the success of the ministry of the church and are to be treated as vital participants in all of the church's ministries. They are not to be treated as second-class citizens, gofers, or to be assigned tasks that are considered 'grunt work" by other members of the congregation. I have learned over the years that most servants who give themselves to the administrative responsibilities are often treated poorly by others in leadership and by the average parishioner. This is unacceptable in a healthy church. They are to be affirmed and appreciated for the gifts they offer to the ministry and included in the major planning elements related to administration.

What is on the administrative agenda for the healthy church? First of all, there is the *strategic planning* required in understanding the defined call of God upon your local church. Second, *goal setting* by departments and individuals assigned to lead areas of the ministry. Third, *accountability* structures designed to keep everyone on target in the fulfillment of God's will in your ministry setting. Fourth, *ongoing assessment and evaluation* that grows out of the value of accountability in relationships and service. Fifth and finally, *change management* that keeps the ministry moving forward so that long-term, lasting effectiveness can be achieved for the service within the church, throughout the community, and around the world amidst the inevitable changes that will occur. Let's tackle these one at a time.

1. Strategic Planning

To effectively enter the strategic planning process, the leaders in the church need to put on the hat of the diagnostician. Diagnosing the current realties of your ministry might require a hard hat so that the debris that falls along the way won't knock you out! A diagnosis is the careful examination and analysis of the facts that is needed in order to understand or explain the current condition. Some in the business world have defined the work of the diagnostic team in the term SWOT analysis (Strengths, Weaknesses, Opportunities, Threats).

If you were to perform a SWOT analysis on your church, what do you think you would discover? I challenge you to do it at your next leadership team meeting or retreat—the results will be fascinating to review. What are your current strengths and weaknesses? What are the ministry opportunities ahead, and what is threatening your success today and potentially into the future? We have done this exercise several times at Vision New England, both with the board of directors and with the staff team. I am always amazed at the analysis these questions generate. The first responsibility of every great leader, according to Max De Pree is "to define reality. The last is to say thank you. In between the two, the leader must become a servant and a debtor. That sums up the progress of an artful leader."[1] I couldn't agree more. We must be able to wrap our arms around our current realities if we are to think beyond them and plan for an exciting future.

A good diagnostician analyzes the condition of the hearts and lives of those in leadership and within the congregation. What are their devotional and prayer lives like? How are they manifesting a deep love for God in their attitudes and actions? An effective diagnosis includes an analysis of our current roles and responsibilities as leaders: How deep is the dedication index reading on each leader in the church? What are their desires in fulfilling faithfully their call to service within the body? It includes assessing the condition of our relationships with one another: Are we actively caring for each other at all of our points of need? Are we communicating effectively with one another and resolving every conflict that comes our way? What about the condition of our relationships within the congregation as a whole? Diagnosing our current realities also includes in-depth looks into the condition of our overall ministry and each individual department of service. Taken one at a time, how are things going at every layer of ministry? When these questions are posed to leaders throughout the congregation, it's amazing what can be discovered.

Serving in the role of diagnostician means that you observe the nature of your current condition by identifying and specifying the facts that define your reality. A good diagnostician examines the potential root issues or symptoms that explain the results of your self-examination. By understanding empathetically the realities you face, a leadership team can concentrate efforts appropriately and establish goals and plans that build on this defined situation. It's important, too, that all diagnosticians in the process effectively communicate with one another and pursue wise counsel from inside and outside the church so that a realistic picture is gained. Acting prayerfully, the leadership team can remedy problems that must be addressed while at the same time begin planning for the future. Diagnosing your condition—it's the best place to begin in the strategic planning process because it unpackages for the leadership team the areas that need your greatest attention and reveals the best opportunities for service in the short- and long-term future.

Many churches are unwilling to take this first essential step in the strategic planning process. But unless you do so, you are planning for the future in a vacuum, void of an accurate understanding of who you are today and what potential you have for growth and health in the future. This step is especially critical for the church as we enter into the twenty-first century.

There are not only new realities within the congregation, but the world we live in is filled with issues that impact our ability to lead the church into the new millennium. There are the changing global climates, changing demographics, new technologies, shifts in government, and the explosion of traditional values, just to name a few. There are external realities like the secular agenda of pluralism, new economic realities of the rich becoming richer and the poor becoming poorer, family breakdown, busyness of society, and growing hostility among ethnic groups and within neighborhoods.

When Walnut Hill Community Church in Bethel, Connecticut, completed its internal assessment as part of a strategic planning initiative, they set out to determine their environment. They brought together twenty-five members of the church who represented all ages, from high school to senior citizens, and a variety of occupations for two Saturdays of listening and discussion.

For the first all-day session they had invited five representatives of the greater Danbury community. Each was given twenty minutes for a presentation and ten minutes for interaction on what they saw happening that might affect the church and its ministry. Making presentations were the school board superintendent, a bank manager, a vice president of the United Way, a state representative, and the vice president of communications for Vision New England, who represented the larger religious picture in New England. After lunch the group assembled to discuss what they had heard and interact further with representatives who stayed. Then they broke into groups to discuss specifics.

Two weeks later the group gathered for a much more detailed analysis of the church's environment, charting the information gleaned on a flip chart and posting it. Then they broke into groups for more detailed strategic planning for the church in light of the information received. This was then presented to the board of elders for their action. All in all, this was a productive experience for the church and had positive effects on their planning process.

There are other overarching realities that the Christian community must face within the walls of our churches. We have a high rate of biblical illiteracy in our pews. We are addicted to our Christian consumerism, buying books we never read and attending events only to bring home as many Christian trinkets as possible. We are dealing on the local level with the intrusion of distant ministries calling for our attention and resources. What about the mobility of our congregation and the anti-institutionalism that affects the attitudes of our members? Then there's the growing polarization of the religious communities, where the Christian right and the moderates are fighting with one another about a "Christian" response to the issues of the day.

Add to all of this the shifts we are experiencing in local church ministry. We are gradually moving away from an outward ministry focus and turning inward. We have shifted from the priority of developing our people to informing them. We are discovering that instead of being building- and property-centered as churches we are becoming technology driven. Instead of maintaining a monolithic cultural identity we are needing to consider multicultural approaches to serve the broader needs of the church. We are seeing a shift away from the top-down approach to leadership, embracing instead a new paradigm of clergy and lay team partnerships. Independent churches know they cannot get the job done on their own, and since we are not all self-contained megachurches, we are forced to consider a new way of becoming interdependent.

As if all of this weren't enough change to swallow, there are the new realities facing pastors today. Fifty years ago, the demand on pastors was much simpler. They were called to the basic tasks of preaching and teaching the Bible, calling on the sick and bereaved, being on call for emergency aid, having basic financial management skills, and shepherding the people through all of the seasons of life. Today the expectations are outstripping the best of us, with the ever-expanding needs of congregations for multitalented servants of Christ who are: excellent communicators; trained psychotherapists; theologians and philosophers who can address all the pertinent issues of the day intellectually; have the ability to serve as a small group leader; be a social worker for the detailed real-life cases presented each week; financial wizard and fundraiser; have the ability to speak into the unchurched, secular mind of the day and persuade them with the gospel; serve as a futurist and strategic thinker; manage the overall organization and the many programs offered in the church; and at the same time have a healthy marriage and two (or more) wonderfully talented children.

The new realities of our society and the complex condition of the church are staggering. But once you have gone through this exercise and defined your realities as a congregation, it's time to begin dreaming about the future. Resist the temptation to skip over the first step of diagnosing your realities to jump ahead to this stage, even if it hurts.

The Strategic Planning Process

In the midst of a trying time in my personal life and in my ministry at Vision New England, God comforted me with the words of some simple yet profound truths. They are found in Jeremiah 29:11–13, "'For I know the plans I have for you,' declares the Lord, 'plans to prosper you and not to harm you, plans to give you hope and a future. Then you will call upon me and come and pray to me, and I will listen to you. You will seek me and find me when you seek me with all your heart.'" It was heartwarming to remember that God remains sovereignly in control and delights to reveal his will to his people when we take the time to hop off the treadmill of activity that consumes us and hear from him about his good and perfect will for us.

Another wonderful passage to ruminate on as you begin the process of vision casting and priority setting with your congregation is Proverbs 3:5–8:

> Trust in the Lord with all your heart
>   and lean not on your own understanding;
> in all your ways acknowledge him,
>   and he will make your paths straight.
> Do not be wise in your own eyes;
>   fear the Lord and shun evil.
> This will bring health to your body
>   and nourishment to your bones.

Trust him for making the pathway clear. Don't lean on your own understanding. Pray that his ways will be revealed. Look forward to the health of the body and the nourishment for the ministry that will result.

Strategic thinking and planning help us integrate the will of the Holy Spirit, our own church's uniqueness, and our ongoing responsibilities as leaders to develop a Christ-centered church. It lays down the tracks in a systematic fashion so that the train we are traveling on together doesn't go off course and land in the woods. It identifies what you will do together as a church; how you will live out your strategy; when you will accomplish stated goals; where you will focus your energies; why you will do what you do; and with whom you will partner to accomplish the tasks ahead. It integrates a clear understanding of your past ministry activities and accomplishments and bridges you through your present realities into an exciting future.

In addition, the strategic planning process helps each church and leader identify the right things to be done and the right way to execute them. The process builds a sense of unity among all participants at every level of the discussion. It reinforces the need to be proactive rather than reactive in your ministry pursuits. It maximizes your effectiveness in the utilization of time, resources, coordination, and communication within the leadership team and throughout the church. Finally, it helps you measure your effectiveness by providing a baseline from which to grow and a target you hope to hit. (See the bibliography for resources to assist you in designing the best approach for your congregation.)

This process is exhilarating for all involved. By saying yes to a strategy-development exercise, you are learning together through Bible study, prayer, strategic thinking, research, and discussion about what God wants you as a local church to become as you pursue your health and vitality as a ministry. It is in this process that you accentuate what you do well, analyze your strengths and weaknesses, while at the same time determine improvement criteria for the future. You abandon those things that no longer work or which never were effective in helping you achieve the results you had hoped for in the past. It requires that the pastor and leadership team have the stamina for the task, which is not to be taken lightly. In fact, it needs to be repeated at least every two to four years in order to be relevant in this fast-changing world we are called to serve.

The big picture strategy should be shared by all who will bring it to fruition. Therefore, it is incumbent upon the pastor and leadership team to communicate with the congregation every step of the way, involving them in the discussions as much as possible. But when all is said and done, the lion's share of the strategy design will be done by a small group who track together throughout the process. It is important that each member of the church remain prayerfully involved on the sidelines and actively participate when opportunities arise for data gathering and input into the documents being formulated. Final sign off by the church leaders is key before presenting the concluding report to the congregation. The steps along the way will vary according to the governance of each local church. Be sensitive to the process, to the Holy Spirit, and to one another, and the product will honor him and propel his people to greater effectiveness, health, and vitality.

The bite-sized pieces of implementing the strategy are left to those who are charged with the responsibility to lead various components of the ministry. The fleshing out of the ministry plan is therefore owned within each department where more and more members will have an opportunity to put their own thumbprint on the plan. This is where the strategy hits the grassroots and spreads fortuitously throughout the life of the church. Everyone who has an interest in the life and future of the church gets to touch the strategy somewhere along the way, even if it's in the final implementation of hands-on service.

The Ministry Platform

On our most recent round of strategy development at Vision New England, a friend of the ministry and a former board member, Jim Van Yperen, assisted us in the process of defining our ministry platform. He described it to us in the following way: "Every Christian organization must have a 'ministry platform' if it is to be effective and truly account-able to God. The ministry platform will inform how decisions are made, goals are determined, and success is measured. A platform consists of at least seven critical elements, each defined in priority order, each build-ing upon the one previous and further defining the unique ministry of the organization. These critical elements are: Affirmation of Faith (doc-trinal statement); Audition (hearing from God); Vision; Core Values and Beliefs (or motivational values); Missional Purpose; Culture (or philos-ophy); and Goals/Strategy. The final aspect of the ministry platform are the ministries, all of which are derived from the previous seven elements that define who you are as a people called for a specific purpose." We followed Van Yperen's outline for Vision New England's ministry plat-form (see the appendix).

The *affirmation of faith* is the doctrinal position founded upon God's Word. For us, we have selected the National Association of Evangeli-cals (NAE) statement of faith and have adopted it as our guide for healthy doctrinal underpinnings. For others, there may be a statement of faith from your denomination or fellowship that can be reviewed and affirmed.

The *auditioning process* is the Bible study and prayer times that you do individually and collectively in an effort to hear the still small voice of God and what he is saying to you about your current and future min-istry. It is a dynamic process led by the Spirit of God when you wait on him, listen for his voice, interpret what you sense is his direction, and discover what shape the plan takes for maximizing your effectiveness. The auditioning process is based on the Scriptures, experienced in com-munity, in light of the needs that surround you and the environment you are placed in as a people of God. Martin Luther once said, "In order to see God we must learn to stick our eyes in our ears." This mysterious process of listening to God needs to be affirmed by the group involved in the strategy design and not dominated by one strong person who claims sole listening ability! What do you sense together that the Spirit is saying to you regarding the ministry he has called you to lead?

The *vision* statement can be described as "what your eyes see your ears hear." It is a specific view of a preferred future, based on what you believe the Holy Spirit is calling your unique community of believers to be and do. It is based on where you would like to be several years from now, so that by stating the vision you encourage the congregation to pursue a big dream together.

Vision is not an option for the church today. We have one whether we care to admit it or not. Some have lofty ones, others have ones that are less than mighty. Some prefer to keep it to themselves or don't dabble in the subject because that's for "God alone to know and to reveal if he wills." Vision indeed is God directed, God inspired, and for the glory and purposes of him alone. However, he longs for every church to understand what it is that he desires them to fulfill, and he reveals it to those who take the time to hear him and respond to his initiatives on their behalf.

The *core beliefs and values* are the beliefs, intuition, and values that motivate your church. These are the spiritual and philosophical underpinnings that inspire you to action. We need to ask ourselves, What is it that we value the most in our relationships and ministries? What intrinsically motivates us to serve the Lord and others in the way we do? Brainstorm together and see what emerges from your discussion. I think you'll be surprised to hear the wisdom around the circle.

The *missional purpose* is the historic, philosophical statement of your general, global purpose. What do you believe God wills for you to do and for whom? This is the mission statement exercise that for many churches is excruciating, but once the words are written out and memorized by the body, it's amazing to see the excitement build. Take the time necessary to work on a mission statement that's crisp, concise, and inspirational. Look at other church mission statements, and glean from them the concepts that work in your setting too. However, it is important that your mission statement be exactly that—yours. There are many ways to unpack God's mission for the church today.

The *culture* is the description of how your values, commitments, and attitudes shape how your church will execute your vision. Also described as your philosophy of ministry, this is your statement of passion that depicts the kind of people you intend to be and how you proactively choose to serve together in fulfilling your ministry agenda. What are you committed to as the people of God? What will you aspire to in your relationships and service? How will you be united in accomplishing the task before you? If someone were to observe and describe your church, what would they see in you, what words or phrases would they use to define what they perceive? This is your culture.

The *goals* are the qualitative and quantitative objectives that you believe God would have you strive to accomplish. They are tangible ways to measure ministry and guide planning. In broad strokes, this is where your strategy for service is defined. The goals that are presented here are not the specified objectives of a particular department or aspect of the ministry. This is what you hope to do, Lord willing, in a combined fashion as a local church. Your overarching strategy is general enough that all other ministries of the church can reinforce it, yet specific enough that it connotes the boundaries whereby you will or will not invest energies and resources. In other words, it is in this arena that you state clearly what your strategy is as a church as opposed to any other nonprofit Christian ministry. Why do you exist and for what purpose? State it here clearly.

The *ministries* are what you do together in worship, fellowship, caring, service, and outreach. On this page are written the various ways God is using your faith community to introduce and strengthen the faith of others. The ministry listing describes in simple words or phrases the specific programs and services God is growing in your community, based on the Holy Spirit's equipping of spiritual gifts among your members.

Taking one step at a time, starting with the affirmation of faith and working your way down to specific ministries, will create a complementary framework from which all additional information about your church will apply. The idea here is that each piece of the ministry platform grows out of and supports the preceding layer. When you are finished with this exercise, you are ready to move forward in fleshing out the details of the ministry strategy you have outlined together. Be as creative as possible, including as many as possible along the way (for input and reflection), and the product will be owned by the body and acted on by each subdivision of the ministry. But remember, the process must be carried by the pastor and key leadership team from beginning to end. Don't pass off the responsibility to any group not central to the long-term leadership of the church. What is created in the crucible of community will last throughout the seasons of your shared ministry. Visit this document often so that it is a living resource, reviewed and revised along the way.

2. Goal Setting

If any strategic initiative taxes and challenges a pastor's administrative skills, it is a church building program. Senior Pastor George Cope of Bethany Assembly of God in Agawam, Massachusetts, knows all about this, since this church recently completed an aggressive goal—a three-million-dollar building program. Pastor Cope came to Bethany Assembly of God seven years ago, following a twenty-five-year tenured pastor who had been promoted to district superintendent just prior to Cope's arrival. At the time attendance was about 800—now it is over 1500, and the church has sent off 250 members to found one church and 80 to start another. They are now planning a third church plant! They have seven full-time pastors and thirteen board members.

Almost all of the church growth at Bethany Assembly of God has been through conversions. People come to know Christ at every service, including Wednesday nights.

"When I came to Bethany I wanted to be a loving, transparent, and consistent pastor. When I said I would do something, people should know that it would happen," says Pastor Cope. According to Cope, it took him a solid five and a half years to prove himself and win over the people. Part of the process was to honor the previous pastor, inviting him into the pulpit once a year and recognizing the great contribution he had made.

Pastor Cope brought with him a clearly developed administrative style, one which was comfortable with establishing and achieving large goals. But he knew that in order to accomplish these goals he would need a strong team.

"I believe firmly in team ministry. I hire people to work around me whom I can trust. So I share my load with those on our staff or on our board in areas of personal weakness," says Pastor Cope. "I am not afraid to say, 'I need your help because I am not skilled in this area.'" Each staff person has a full job description, ongoing communication with the pastor, vision-casting days with the team to discuss what they want to see happening in their area of responsibility, and the opportunity to set goals for their area of the ministry.

When the church recognized the need to build a larger facility, Pastor Cope said to the board and building committee, "My role is not that of a builder. That's why we have a building committee." That, however, did not mean Pastor Cope sat back to see what would develop. "We met frequently as a staff to discuss what was necessary for us to work effectively," he says. "Each staff member was asked to provide input, what was needed for him to function. We compiled our needs, worked up a document that stated our goals for the project, and presented it to the building committee."

The pastoral team and the committee met every week for about two years to work out all of the details. Today they have a beautiful, fully functional facility that is meeting their needs and serving their community beyond their greatest hopes and dreams. It truly is a goal worthy of celebration not only by the family at Bethany Assembly of God but by the broader Christian community.

Goal setting is strenuous work for the average pastor and leadership team. And yet the value of meaningful goals far exceeds the labor required to write them effectively. What are those values? First, goals concentrate attention, energy, and resources to accomplish effective results. Second, goals make it possible to design strategy to move toward significant accomplishments. Third, goals tend to inspire even greater effort than they articulate. Fourth, goals provide a basis for periodically evaluating our performance and effectiveness. Fifth, goals can bring discipline into our life together, by excluding the less desirable objectives in favor of a well-thought-out direction. Sixth, goals encourage consistency and stability among the church leaders who are charged with reinforcing them with effective ministries.

The goal-oriented leader helps others in writing good goals that are worthy of accomplishing. When I first introduced the concept of goal setting both in the church setting and at Vision New England, I was not met with enthusiastic applause. In both settings there was great resistance at every level in seeing the need for such an exercise. And yet those who have embraced the challenge and have written good goals are delighted to see them become a reality in their ministry and rejoice, like Pastor Cope and his team, when they are fulfilled beyond expectation.

Each spring, after the ministry platform has been reviewed by the board and staff leaders, and the big picture strategic initiatives for the coming year have been determined, it's time for our board and staff teams to write their SMART goals. The board has a list of goals that they hold each other accountable to accomplish, each department has their goals, and each individual writes specific goals they hope to achieve over the next year.

SMART is an acronym that refers to Specific, Measurable, Achievable, Results-oriented, and Time-dated. In other words, each goal that is written must abide by these five principles and is evaluated accordingly. I have designed a worksheet (see VNE's website) for each staff member and the board of directors to use in thinking through each goal. The goal is evaluated according to SMART language (is it specific, measurable, achievable, results oriented, and time dated?), which basically describes what, where, and why. Action steps are then listed beneath each stated goal, which spell out the manner in which this goal will be achieved. Stretching across the sheet are four additional columns: Who will be involved? What are your starting and stopping dates? How are you going to resource the fulfillment of this goal? and, Is the goal complete?

I have found this exercise extremely beneficial to both groups and individuals and those who will supervise the ministry referred to in each goal. Goal setting is a discipline and therefore requires diligent effort on the part of all team members. But the rewards are phenomenal, and the gains for the kingdom are eternal.

3. Accountability

Once the ministry platform and the SMART goals have been agreed on, we need to be held accountable to accomplishing what we have set out to do. Like the previous two agenda items, accountability is also a discipline. It's hard work to hold one another accountable, and yet the value in doing so outstrips the effort. When we allow ourselves to be accountable to another group or individual, we say in essence that we need help in becoming all God intends us to be. We let others see both our accomplishments and our shortcomings. We express interest in hearing objective feedback that will sharpen our focus and realign our efforts. We say that in order for me to stay on course in fulfillment of my goals, I will need the support, advice, counsel, and prayers of others. And we admit that if we are left on our own, we may compromise our goals or forget that they exist. The need for accountability is great, and yet too few churches and individuals have accountability structures in place that are capable of producing fruit that lasts.

One of the neediest areas of local church accountability is in the area of finances. What are your internal structures of accountability as it relates to your budget? Brian Kluth, president of the Christian Stewardship Association, says financial accountability is linked to the vision, mission, and ministries of the local church. Where our treasures are, there will our heart be as well.

"I could be giving $100,000 a year to my church, but their biggest vision is to paint the bathrooms," one church member told Kluth. "That church did not get his giving to the Lord. His position demonstrates again that accountability is tied to a well-developed and articulated vision for the church that goes beyond the upkeep of the property."

Brian Kluth has found that there are four key vision points at the local church level.

- Staffing issues
- Facilities and equipment needs
- Outreach initiatives
- International missions

When a church has visions and goals surrounding these major initiatives, the resources usually follow in line with the stated direction of the leadership. But the goals need to be written down and articulated in ways that average church attendees can understand, affirm, and ultimately support with their gifts. When church members know that the leadership is open to maintaining accountability for the fulfillment of these goals, their confidence rises to new heights.

"If you look into the Bible, you will find that before God resourced any ministry, the plans for it were written down," says Kluth. "For example, consider the case of Moses building the tabernacle in the desert. Before anything happened, Moses had to write down detailed plans that God gave him (Exod. 30–33). Then the funds came in as the people gave gladly (Exod. 34–36). David wrote a plan for the temple, and we read in 1 Chronicles 29 that there was a huge offering from the people toward fulfilling those plans.

"Even the apostle Paul wrote a letter to churches on what they were going to give to. He made it clear what he was going to do with the money—and then he collected the funds for relief purposes in Jerusalem."

Today, most people want the answers to three questions when they give to a church, reveals Kluth.

- How much money came in?
- Where did the money go?
- Are all the bills of the church paid?

So how do you provide the accountability answers to these three questions? One way is to prepare a detailed budget and present it to the church at the annual meeting.

"Normally that is a disaster," says Kluth. "Ninety percent of the people in the congregation do not understand the budget. And you always have some who start picky arguments that upset everybody. A pie chart of the budget allocations works best, I have found, with pieces in the pie indicating funding for missions, building and grounds, staff, Christian education, etc."

At the annual meeting, present the pie chart and announce that anyone who wants a detailed handout can pick one up at the end of the meeting. The chairman or member of the budget committee can then meet with this person and go over the budget to make sure it is clearly understood.

"We've taken this approach at our church for five years and it has had wonderful results. Only one person ever wanted to see the thirty-page budget report," says Kluth.

It is also important to communicate with the congregation more than once a year, says Kluth. Four times a year is much better. But that communication needs to be accompanied by a statement of that person's giving or not giving—and a newsletter that ties in people's giving to how the money is used for ministry and missions.

"Putting financial information in the Sunday bulletin or making financial announcements from up front is ineffective. On top of that, 25 percent of the congregation is generally absent each Sunday. And those who have brought their friends don't want them to hear or read about money," says Kluth. "The mail route provides higher mutual accountability, it helps people see how their money is tied to ministry, and the communication is going to the people who want to know the information."

Finally, financial accountability means more than a couple or three members of the church looking over the books, according to Kluth. In today's world, a CPA examining the church's financial structure is important, for this person can alert the church to problem areas. You simply don't want the pastor being the sole arbiter on what is ethical and what is not, and what is legal and what is not. Accountability, especially in relationship to financial resources, is absolutely essential for a healthy church in the twenty-first century. Take the time to establish accountability systems in your church that maintain the vitality of the personnel, finances, facilities, ministries, missions, and day-to-day programs under your care.

4. Ongoing Assessment and Evaluation

One of the most helpful aspects of the ministry of the board of directors to whom I am accountable is the ongoing assessment and evaluation they offer. I thrive on their input, both the affirmation on a job well done and the constructive criticism when things don't materialize as we had all hoped. I recognize that without this assessment and evaluation in place I would stagnate as a leader. There is always something new I can learn in the various responsibilities I carry in my leadership role.

Each week I face new challenges, and each new opportunity means I have new skills to develop and new experiences to explore. Sometimes I make wise choices in handling each issue, and other times I blow it. If I did not have a structure of trusted relationships in place to assess my progress and evaluate my effectiveness, I would be less of a leader. I need the board and other members of the team to become actively involved in this process—not only for my sake but for our shared ministry efforts in our region. The same is true for the average pastor and ministry leader in the local church.

You may think it rather peculiar, but I have files in my office with over twenty years of weekly reports from my days in ministry here in New England. I learned long ago that unless I establish for myself a system for weekly personal assessment and evaluation, I am less than fully accountable to God for the work he has called me to. So from the time I was a junior-high director, I have kept a record of my time and ministry contacts. One of my mentors, Gordon MacDonald, once said to us as younger members of his staff team, "You have the privileges of most executives in the business world who manage their own schedules, so don't abuse the privilege."

I took his counsel seriously and have sought ever since to steward my time, talent, and resources in ways that honor God and best serve those I am charged to lead. I have established a weekly habit of meeting with God on Sunday evenings to plan out my week. I take a look at the past week, examine the schedule of appointments for the coming week, and establish reasonable goals to accomplish in each of my roles as a child of God, a family mentor, a teacher-student of the Word, a staff team leader, a partner with our board of directors, a fund-raiser, and a pastor-ministry leader encourager. This enables me to have a way to assess my progress each Sunday night, looking back and looking ahead, always with an eye toward the fulfillment of what I sense is God's mission for me.

The assessment and evaluation process begins with your own personal disciplines, similar to what I have shared above. But it does not end there. We need others in our sphere of influence to offer their honest input into our lives. One of the systems I have established for our team are weekly and monthly reports. The weekly reports can be written in a format suitable to each staff member. I urge them all to look back on the progress they have made in the prior week, recording as many contacts and projects completed as possible, and then look ahead to the coming week. Weekly staff reports should be done by noon on Monday so that full days are not lost in the process of planning and evaluation. I try not to be rigid about this requirement, stressing always the importance of doing so not only for their sake but for the sake of the overall ministry.

The monthly reports are usually generated by the staff who minister on the field in various assignments, like prison ministry, women's ministry, and recovery ministry. Their reports cover the following areas:

- Significant contacts of this past month
- Major accomplishments of this past month
- Issues, concerns, needs that arose this past month which your supervisor needs to be aware of

- Plans and goals for the upcoming month
- Issues of personal growth and balance:

  Relationship with Jesus
  Good books that have stimulated my thinking
  Update on diet, exercise, rest, and days off
  Friendship and social life beyond ministry

It always fascinates me to read these reports each month, because it gives me a glimpse into their ministry priorities, their relationships, and their personal concerns. I want the team to know that I deeply care about them and want them to succeed. I don't abuse the information they share with me and don't hold it against them if they are struggling with serious issues. Many times the red flags that emerge become opportunities for me to invest in their lives in ways that will serve as relationship builders and enhance our service together.

On top of the ongoing assessment and evaluation that occurs on a weekly or monthly basis is the annual performance evaluation. I see this as a chance to sit down with each leader and reflect together on the past year of ministry, talk honestly about the pros and cons of the year, discuss major accomplishments and highlights, and look ahead to next year with growing enthusiasm and defined strategies. Most of the staff enjoy this concentrated time where we are able to focus on the big picture over against the weekly minutia. Annual evaluations should be free from administrative clutter and are best handled in a more comfortable setting for each participant in the process.

We have three different forms for evaluation of our team, one for the administrative staff, the ministry coordinators, and the staff directors (see VNE's website). We have tried to develop forms that are most applicable to the specific responsibilities and have made them as interactive as possible. They are to be treated as discussion starters more than anything else. As a result of the dialogue, appropriate changes can be pursued in the months ahead. Nine times out of ten in each annual review, specific actions can be taken by both the supervisor and the staff member to enhance the environment and responsibilities of the team in an effort to build on the prior year of ministry. The children of assessment and evaluation are change, renewal, and hopefulness . . . a generation worthy of encouragement.

Specifically in the church setting, the assessment and evaluation of the senior pastor and any staff members employed by the church is a must. If you do not have a structure in place to do so, I urge you to act swiftly to correct this situation. Everyone benefits from meaningful assessment and evaluation. Then in addition to the paid staff, each volunteer leader and team member should receive similar assessment and evaluation at least on an annual basis. If you hope to enhance what you currently have available to you in your local church setting, this process is simply irreplaceable.

All of the team building and accountability for goal setting looks like a business environment where a CEO is in charge. In reality, it represents a lot of mutuality, where the focus is on the giftedness of team members at the staff and lay level. And it is the key to multiplication of the laity and its giftedness. But it is the drafting of job descriptions for every leadership position and the continual reporting at all levels, with an annual performance review, that keeps the church on target with its vision.

5. Change Management

One thing is absolutely certain in every ministry setting—the inevitability of change. The changes we are facing in our world and in our churches are staggering. Globalization, technological access to the world, demographic shifts, and economic changes are altering the way we look at our world in incomprehensible proportions. In the church we are facing the increase in lack of commitment, the growth of dysfunctional families, the overwhelming needs of each generation within the church, the lack of visionary leaders, the jeopardizing of pastoral credibility, the desire for the latest fad, or jumping on the bandwagon of the hottest megachurch.

On the positive side, we have access to the world like we've never had before. The technological advances of our day are increasing the ways in which we can communicate with our missionaries and with one another. The demographic shifts have broadened our horizons and deepened our connections with people who are different from us. The teachable moments to discuss the subject of healthy relationships and renewed commitments to Christ and one another are ripe for the picking. And the megachurch movement offers substantial resources to leaders in churches of all sizes who are not threatened by someone else's "success" and are willing to apply the transferable concepts to their ministry environment.

The question to wrestle with related to change remains, Is the glass half empty or half full? Will you face your changes with optimism about what God has in store for you, or will you moan and groan about the changes and let discouragement get the best of you? Hannah Whitall Smith, in her classic *The Christian's Secret of a Happy Life*, reminds us of the difficulty of seeing God in everything—yes, I said everything, even the massively overwhelming changes that surround us. She writes,

What is needed, then, is to see God in everything, and to receive everything directly from His hands, with no intervention of second causes; and it is to just this that we must be brought before we can know an abiding experience of entire abandonment and perfect trust. Our abandonment must be to God, not to man; and our trust must be in Him, not in any arm of flesh, or we shall fail at the first trial. To the children of God, everything comes directly from their Father's hand, no matter who or what may have been the apparent agents . . . by the time it reaches us it has become God's will for us, and must be accepted as directly from His hands."[2]

If all the changes in the world, within the culture, and ultimately the church are allowed to occur from the hand of almighty God, then we need to learn how to appropriately handle them. When a high level of discomfort occurs in our society or within the walls of the church, a change can be born that will provide the energy to cope with or resolve the discomfort. If healthy relationships, plans, and strategies are in place within the church to deal with changes that come your way, then the changes won't collide with the community but will coalesce with what God has in store for you. We need to be a people who celebrate our histories and heritages, implement changes in incremental steps, and recognize that in every change there is a letting go of something (or someone) to embrace what is destined to come next from the hand of God.

The best posture for dealing with change is the posture of the open, outstretched hand. When a staff member told me he was leaving for a new ministry assignment recently, the Lord (through my spiritual director) took me to Jeremiah 18—the story of the potter and the clay. "So I went down to the potter's house, and I saw him working at the wheel. But the pot he was shaping from the clay was marred in his hands; so the potter formed it into another pot, shaping it as seemed best to him. . . . Like clay in the hand of the potter, so are you in my hand" (vv. 3–4, 6).

I knew after reading this passage that I needed to take my hand off the clay that was on the potter's wheel. Was I the one who was marring the clay because of my desire to cling to this staff member a bit longer and not embrace the change destined by the Potter himself? By releasing my hands from the clay and allowing the Potter to shape it "as seemed best to him," I was able to release this man of God to go and serve elsewhere, knowing that I too was being shaped by the Potter.

The difficulty in the inevitability of change is the disruption that changes can cause in the building of ministry for the long haul. Longevity is a value in ministry that I ascribe to with great fervency. I am committed to the fact that the best and deepest contribution I can make to a person, a ministry, or a project is if I am willing to hang in there for a lengthy stream of seasons of life. It's attractive at times to pack it up and leave behind what you have invested in, even if it was for a short while. We tend to lean in this direction when we are weary and discouraged. But when we trust in the Lord to give us the energy to sustain us for the long haul, we will see blessing upon blessing as God works steadily and methodically to grow his people over time and seasons.

Do you have a long view of ministry, and are you willing to hang in there through the changes that come your way? The changes are yours to learn from, and sometimes the changes are yours to lead. Whatever the case may be, make sure you manage them in ways that honor the Lord who allowed them in the first place. Take your hand off the wheel and let the Potter do his shaping work. He is trustworthy to handle it because he loves what he has created.

Almighty God, you are wise in all your ways and patient in all your dealings with your children. You are the potter, we are the clay; mold us and make us to reflect your radiant splendor throughout our days of service here on earth. We want to be wise in all of our dealings with one another, in all of our planning for the future, in all of our responsible acts of leadership and oversight of the ministries you have called us to serve. Teach us what it means to trust you as we manage the changes that come our way. Love us as we assess and evaluate ourselves and one another—may this be affirming and building for all. Give us a renewed sense of our accountability first and foremost to you, and secondarily to each other as brothers and sisters in Christ. Help us to dream big dreams for you and your kingdom, and set realistic goals for accomplishing what you have destined for us to do. In all ways and in every day, keep us in the center of your will, held securely in the palms of your loving hands. Our love for you continues to grow with each succeeding day. Refresh us in our love and service. For your name's sake. Amen.

■ FOR REFLECTION AND RENEWAL ■

The healthy church utilizes appropriate facilities, equipment, and systems to provide maximum support for the growth and development of its ministries.

The healthy church fosters wise administration and accountability as it:

- strives for excellence, effectiveness, and efficiency through management practices that emphasize responsibility and accountability
- creates support systems to meet the functional needs of the ministry
- conducts an ongoing evaluation of church progress against its mission and vision
- develops a broad base of support among its members
- provides appropriately for its staff
- plans for the longevity of the ministry and for leadership transitions
- conducts an honest assessment of the strengths and weaknesses, opportunities and threats to its ministry
- thinks and acts strategically

> So if you have not been trustworthy in handling worldly wealth, who will trust you with true riches?
>
> Luke 16:11

1. On a scale of 1 to 10 (1 being not at all important and 10 being most important), rank each of the above statements while answering the question, "How important is this statement for the health of our church; how highly do we value wise administration and accountability?"
2. On a scale of 1 to 10 (1 being very ineffective and 10 being very effective), rank each of the above statements while answering the question, "How effective are we as a leadership team at instilling these values in our church?"
3. For each of the above statements, ask your team, "Where do we want to be in the characteristic Wise Administration and Accountability in this next year or two?"
4. For each of the above statements, ask your team, "How will we get where we want to be in living out Wise Administration and Accountability in this next year?"
5. Overall, on a scale of 1 to 10 (1 being very low and 10 being very high), rank how well you think your church is doing in living out this eighth characteristic of a healthy church, Wise Administration and Accountability.

10

Networking with the Body of Christ
Characteristic 9

The healthy church reaches out to others in the body of Christ for collaboration, resource sharing, learning opportunities, and united celebrations of worship.

"May they [the church] be brought to complete unity to let the world know that you sent me and have loved them even as you have loved me."

John 17:23

When five to six thousand witches from all over the United States, England, and France descend on Salem, Massachusetts, at the end of October each year, they attract up to 150,000 tourists. But they also bring out loving believers in Christ from eighteen churches in the region. This proactive networking is bathed in prayer prior to the big events surrounding the witches' holiday of Halloween.

"Pastors from these eighteen churches gather every Wednesday morning to pray. Every third Tuesday evening we have another time of prayer. Then on October 31 we sponsor a concert of prayer in Salem," reports Pastor Ken Steigler of Wesley United Methodist Church, the center for much of the activity aimed at bringing hope to the Wiccan community. "We have about five hundred come out for that concert of prayer, which is organized by the New England Concerts of Prayer and led by Rev. Jeff Marks."

Pastor Steigler is now in his seventh year at Wesley United Methodist Church and has been at the forefront of the region's evangelistic efforts aimed at the Wiccan community and those who come every October. But he realizes that there is no way the ministry to the witches could occur if he were left on his own. The networking of the body of Christ in his region is the key to effective outreach each October.

"God has brought eighty-two former witches to faith in Christ over the years. I work with three ex-witches to help disciple new believers and am in contact with them three to four times a week," reports Pastor Steigler. Despite their constant efforts to reach witches, it is still a shock when members of the congregation discover they are standing next to a witch in typical Wiccan attire. They are, however, effectively reaching out to them in love. "I tell my congregation that they are to love them, sharing their love for Christ with them," he says.

From October 10 to 31, Wesley United Methodist Church and many other Christians from area churches jointly sponsor singers, speakers, fairs, dinners—anything to try to impact those who have come for the Wiccan festival. "Last year a group of fifteen musicians came from all over the country. They came from as far away as Texas and Kansas, all at their own expense, and served for four days. We had eighteen people sleeping in our parsonage during that time," says Pastor Steigler. "A dynamic evangelist, Dr. Harvey Brown, came from Asbury College in Kentucky last year and will be coming again this fall. With a speaker like Dr. Brown, an extraordinary musical group, and the loving environment of many believers joined together in love and service, we invite witches to 'Come see the alternative,'" says Pastor Steigler.

Powerfully facing opposition to the gospel becomes a reality when those in the body of Christ unite to pool their resources and energy. Years of relationship building have formed the foundation for effective collaboration and service, which has resulted in life-changing ministry. By choosing to work side by side, these eighteen churches have forged a strategic alliance that has impacted their corner of the region for Christ in a wonderful way.

In what ways are you and your congregation developing meaningful supradenominational relationships with others of like mind and heart in your region? Are you coming together for the purposes of friendship building, prayer, worship, resource sharing, collaboration, strategic alliances, or ministry partnerships? The healthy church reaches out to brothers and sisters in Christ, recognizing that the work of ministry cannot effectively be accomplished without such connections.

Worldwide, National, and Regional Networking

Christians all over the world are seeing the need for effective networking in order for the church to accomplish the mission set before us. The World Evangelical Fellowship (WEF) has been encouraging such alliances for several decades since its inception in 1951. Based in Singapore, this worldwide movement has seen fabulous success in nations where few advances for the gospel were achieved before Christian communities banded together to form national fellowships and collaborative ministries. It's phenomenal to hear the WEF story of whole nations being impacted through such networking.

"When pastors and church leaders get outside of their own church building or church denomination, they realize the commonality of opportunities and problems that they face. It is a natural tendency to become isolationist and think you are the only one that has a certain problem. I am continually amazed in my work at WEF how common are the opportunities and problems faced not only within a state or region but across national borders," says Dwight Gibson, North American Director for WEF.

Gibson continues, "It seems that for people to seek to move beyond their own bounds, they need to have a vision beyond themselves. In this sense the opportunity or the problem has to be bigger than their one church or their single ministry. I think there has to be a realization of the true strength and breadth of God impacting all areas of our lives. If our concept of God is small, our concept of working together in the body of Christ will probably also be equally small. On the other hand, if we realize the breadth and strength in the body of Christ, we will have a more open mind for interaction."

On a national scene, there is no more exciting story than the Evangelical Alliance (EA) in Great Britain. Founded in 1846, the EA has grown to become the largest Christian organization in Great Britain, representing well over 1.5 million Christians from over thirty denominations and nearly one thousand other Christian organizations. "The original emphasis of the EA, still strong today, was religious liberty. In subsequent years, through tough times and good times, the alliance has emphasized prayer, the renewal of the church, and the advancement of the gospel."[1]

Under the unifying leadership of Clive Calver, the EA has grown significantly since 1983 (Calver resigned in 1997 to become president of World Relief Corporation, leaving the EA as a strong and vital movement). Tim Stafford, in a *Christianity Today* article, elaborates.

When Calver took over in 1983, he and his team established a two-track strategy: (1) To develop greater credibility with the larger evangelical community in the U.K. and (2) To achieve visibility and credibility with the media and political leaders in Britain. It succeeded in building trust with evangelicals by providing leadership in key areas of concern. And, over time, both the media and political leaders in Parliament were educated by the alliance about evangelical Christianity, its constituency, and views on religious, social, and political issues.

The objectives of the Evangelical Alliance today are straight-forward:

- to promote unity in the church;
- to stimulate prayer;
- to encourage evangelism; and
- to enable Christians to act as salt and light in society.

One way EA seeks to achieve these goals is to sponsor an annual event called Spring Harvest. This yearly conference attracts evangelicals from house churches, and Baptist, Methodist, and Anglican congregations, along with Pentecostals, charismatics, and many ethnic congregations. Worship and prayer are the vital core of Spring Harvest. But there is an educational component as well: leading evangelical scholars from the U.K. and beyond are tapped to educate evangelicals on the history, theology, and social implications of their faith.[2]

On the American scene, networking with the body of Christ is taking on a new dimension of cooperation. "For many years, the term *partnership* has been somewhat of a misnomer in the Christian church in the United States," says Dr. Paul Cedar, chairman of Mission America. "For the most part, a given ministry has developed a strategic plan and then has invited other ministries, denominations and/or churches to partner with them. That scenario is changing in a remarkable way. Denominations, churches, and other ministries across America are now asking the question, What is God calling us to do together rather than alone?"

Mission America is seeing authentic partnerships being formed in many parts of the United States as well as on the national level, where each member of the partnership is an equal. For example, more than thirty national ministry networks focus today on prayer and evangelism in America. Scores of churches, denominations, and ministries are all equal partners in these ministry networks. This is obviously the work of the Holy Spirit.

The primary national movement is the National Association of Evangelicals (NAE), which has developed into a strong voice, forum, and resource for the church through their member denominations partnering for a strong evangelical witness in America. The member denominations are united around a common affirmation of faith; racial reconciliation initiatives; an active office for Governmental Affairs in Washington, D.C.; affiliate ministries like the Christian Stewardship Association, the Evangelical Fellowship of Mission Agencies (EFMA), the Evangelical Child and Family Agency, and National Religious Broadcasters; and a burgeoning subsidiary ministry to the world's poor, World Relief Corporation.

The NAE comprises approximately 42,500 congregations nationwide. The membership also includes more than 250 parachurch ministries and educational institutions. Through the cooperative ministry of these members, NAE benefits over 27 million people. Its reputation for impeccable integrity and effective service has been a tribute to the strength of the evangelical Christian community across America.

On a regional basis, there are very few ministries like Vision New England. Founded in 1887 by a group of committed Christian business leaders in Boston, Vision New England (formerly the Evangelistic Association of New England) has grown dramatically over the years. Today we serve nearly four thousand congregations from six New England states (Maine, New Hampshire, Vermont, Massachusetts, Connecticut, and Rhode Island), representing eighty denominations. Our staff of thirty-five ministry specialists serves the body of Christ by advancing the healthy church philosophy in local church settings, specifically focusing on worship, servant-leadership development, outreach ministries, and networking opportunities.

Vision New England exists for the purpose of uniting Christians in effective evangelism. We believe firmly that for this task to be accomplished, we need to share a common philosophy of ministry, which is wrapped around the ten characteristics of a healthy church. In order for the local church to be effective in her daily witness and service to the communities she has been called to reach, we must embrace the supradenominational agenda of Christ. By uniting the body of Christ across cultural, religious, denominational, ethnic, and urban, suburban, and rural boundaries, we are seeing the body truly become all that God intends for us to be.

We have developed a strong relationship with the Hawaiian Islands Ministry (HIM) located in Honolulu. They are doing a great work uniting the Christian community of the islands, with their conferences for pastors and church leaders having proven to be a vital resource for the health and vitality of their region. Other ministries have grown as a result, and the body is truly united in a place where opposition to the gospel exists. Will you embrace a similar challenge and rally your region around a common agenda for unity and effective witness?

United We Stand

Clive Calver and Rob Warner wrote a wonderful book on this subject in 1996, titled *Together We Stand*. In defining our unity as Christians, they write:

Evangelical Christians have always maintained a particular obsession with individuality. Some of this owes its origin to the understanding of personal conversion. Yet while this is individual at the beginning, it is the entry into a community. While the word 'saint' is used only once in Scripture, 'saints' occurs no less than 61 times. . . .

As individuals God gives us his Spirit, but collectively he gives us each other. It is vital that we recognize that, apart from the Holy Spirit, the greatest gift we receive from God is one another. For we were never meant to have to struggle along solo, instead we were designed to be indispensable to each other. This point is strongly maintained by the Apostle Paul when he insists that we are the people of God, and individually members of Christ's body (1 Corinthians 12:12, 27). The analogy he draws is a vivid one, because no single person is the body of Christ, that identity is a collective privilege. The picture is not of an arm, some toes, an ear and legs desperately seeking to unite together. Instead under Christ as our head, we naturally fit together to form a unit suitable for him to operate in and through us as his body. . . .

Just as eyes need ears and vice versa, so we remain incomplete when apart from each other (1 Corinthians 12:15–20). This offers us a clear illustration of unity in diversity. We are not designed to be the same as each other, nor to perform identical functions, but we are inextricably linked to each other. The only possible division would be created by amputation, if we were forcibly cut off from the rest of the body. . . .

We are therefore 'one' body just as God is 'one' (1 Timothy 2:5). . . .

Similarly there is one God in the one Lord Jesus Christ (John 10:30; 17:11, 21). There is also one God in the one Spirit of Christ (Ephesians 2:18; 1 Corinthians 12:9–11). Each believer's unity with Christ is not a physical one, it is a spiritual unity (1 Corinthians 6:17). Therefore, we are brothers and sisters, united in the body of Christ through the Holy Spirit (1 Corinthians 12:12; Galatians 3:28; Ephesians 4:4; Colossians 3:15; Hebrews 2:11).[3]

While we may be dissimilar in our styles of worship, our form of church polity, or our denominational affiliation, a basic conviction of our unity in Christ lies at the heart of our coming together. The vast majority of evangelical opinion is united in five clear-cut responses to the prevailing climate of contemporary opinion:

1. We agree that cultural pluralism is bad news for the church.
2. We agree that Christianity is not to be reduced to the level of a privatized faith.
3. We agree that all religions are not the same.
4. We agree that tolerance and endorsement are not the same.
5. We agree that conversion lies at the heart of the Christian faith.

This, then, is our unity—it is not just contained in our fellowship or our common beliefs and practices but in a mutual commitment to maintain the exclusive claims of Christ against the rising tide of pluralism.[4] Those exclusive claims can be summarized in the supreme authority of the Word of God, the unique redemption available through Jesus Christ, the need for personal conversion of individual lives, and the urgent need for effective evangelism. Every man or woman, young or old, who claims the name of Jesus Christ as their Lord and Savior is united with one another around these biblical truths. They will inevitably be resisted by others who resent our distinctiveness and label us as exclusivist. But our response as the people of God is not to compromise but to present them lovingly as Christ-honoring truths for a heartsick world.

The overwhelming strength that emerges from a united church will overpower the forces of evil in our world today. If we really believe in heaven and hell, we have no other option than to unite around heavenly priorities and do everything possible to keep others from going to hell.

Citywide Initiatives

For my friend Ted Haggard, founder and pastor of New Life Church in Colorado Springs, Colorado, his lifelong mission is to do everything possible to keep people from going to hell. In his book *Primary Purpose*, Ted reminds us that we have the resources, the spiritual power, and the will of God in our favor to accomplish this task. The message of Christ is in our trust as his people. He calls the church to combine efforts in our cities so that the people within our reach can hear the claims of Christ in clear, relevant ways. Ted says,

We are the church . . .

- We are the only ones with the message that guarantees eternal life;
- We are the only ones with unlimited access to God the Father;
- We are the only ones with the power of the Holy Spirit and the authority to negate the influence of demonic strategies;
- We are the only ones who are able to overcome "the gates of hell";
- We are the only ones in our cities who can do His job;
- We are the only ones who are exclusively responsible because we are His Body, His co-workers, His ambassadors, His friends.

He gave us His name, His will, His plan, His Spirit, His grace, His love, and His anointing. Therefore, our role as liberators is a life-giving responsibility.[5]

Ted spends the bulk of his book telling the story of how the body of Christ in Colorado Springs has been united around a common agenda for their city, centering on five primary principles: Focus on the absolutes of Scripture; promote the ministry of Christ and his Word above our own mission or method; pray to raise the "water level" of the Holy Spirit's activity in our city; appreciate one another's respected interpretations of Scripture; and practice supportive speech and actions toward others. Colorado Springs has been significantly impacted by the churches in that community who have practiced these principles and combined their efforts for effective service for the cause of Christ.

What will it take for the like-minded and like-hearted churches in your city or town to develop a renewed "parish mentality" for reaching your community for Christ? Are there principles to replicate in your region so that the unity that's experienced will have an eternal effect on those you have been called to serve? There certainly are—five, in fact.

1. Pastors as Friends in Prayer

Forty pastors from all over Vermont met at Smugglers' Notch to pray for revival in the state. "Our objective was to pray on the highest peak in the state. Smugglers' Notch is symbolic of the rebellious attitudes in Vermont, so it was important that we gather there for what is being called 'representational repentance,'" says Pastor Craig Benson of Cambridge United Church in Cambridge, Vermont. "Other gatherings of pastors have set up stone altars of prayer at entry points into Vermont. We believe God has been preparing us for revival, and we are getting ready for it by repenting of our sin."

The oldest network of pastors in northwestern Vermont is the Greater Burlington Evangelical Association. Out of forty-five churches in the region, twenty to twenty-five gather for breakfast once a month for fellowship and networking opportunities. Spun out of that group were creative evangelism initiatives, jointly sponsored seminars, the annual March for Jesus, and quarterly concerts of prayer. It all began with quality relationships among the pastors.

In Hopkinton, Massachusetts, Pastor Dick Germaine has been a leader in their John 17:23 Fellowship for area pastors. Over the years, God has brought these pastors together for heartfelt support and encouragement, as well as networking among the churches represented. Their stated mission is to "offer every believing pastor in central Massachusetts the opportunity to be a part of a John 17:23-type fellowship where he can receive support and encouragement, healing and help, and pray and work together for revival and unity in the church and the winning of many to Christ."

Currently, the John 17:23 Fellowship has thirteen pastors actively involved. They come from charismatic, mainline, evangelical, independent, and Pentecostal churches. They meet every other Thursday for three hours. They also go on retreats together, and through the depth of relationships that have been formed, they are opening up their hearts to one another in meaningful ways. "We are finding pastors with some deep hurts, some with problems in their marriages, and as we pray fervently for one another we are seeing God bring healing to those who are hurting," says Pastor Germaine.

A similar meeting of pastors has been going on for fifteen years in the Haverhill, Massachusetts, area. "When you have been meeting as many years as we have, you really get to know the other pastors. And we are very close to each other in our care groups," says the Reverend Charles Barton, rector of St. James Episcopal Church in Groveland, Massachusetts.

Meeting at the Trinity Episcopal Church in Haverhill, the ministers' fellowship was started when a Nazarene pastor called pastors together to pray for revival. This group has been meeting regularly ever since. Attendance has been as high as fifteen pastors, who meet monthly for personal sharing and prayer for revival in the community. "We attract a rather diverse group of ministers, including two women pastors from a United Methodist Church," reports Rev. Barton.

When the Cape Cod Evangelical Ministers Fellowship was organized more than thirty years ago, it was primarily seen as a once-a-month fellowship that provided the pastors with the emotional and spiritual support they all needed. "We are now looking to form smaller groups that will meet more than once a month and provide more intensive fellowship opportunities," says Pastor Mike Rowe of Osterville Baptist Church and current president of the Fellowship.

"I challenged the ministers in our association to change how we think of ourselves," says Rowe. "We are thirty-five churches spread from Plymouth to Wellfleet, and it is easy for us to think of ourselves as a collection of small churches. So we look at big churches like Willow Creek Community Church and feel we could never do what they have done on Cape Cod. What we really need to do is to think of ourselves as a large church spread over a larger region. When we do this we begin to picture ourselves as the church on Cape Cod—and we as pastors are the staff of this large church. Suddenly we are seeing ourselves as a church of three or four thousand, instead of seventy-five or one hundred struggling to stay alive. And just think of the facilities we have available to us!"

These ministers' fellowship groups represent scores of others like them that have sprung up around our region and across the nation. When the pastors grow to love and trust one another within immediate geographic boundaries, then the local churches they represent begin to unite for celebrations of worship and prayer, ministry opportunities, and healthy relationship building. The health of the community emerges out of the strength of relationships, which begin with the leaders of each church.

2. Resource Sharing

What do you do when you are too small to afford a full-time youth pastor? In Stamford, Connecticut, three churches facing that dilemma decided to pool their resources, combine their young people, and engage the services of one youth pastor. "We are delighted with how well our youth ministry is going," says Pastor Bob Childs of the Long Ridge Congregational Church. "The Evangelical Community Church, the Alliance Church of Stamford, and we agreed that it was better to work together and genuinely minister to our young people than to try to protect our own turf. The ministry has gone so well we are now considering hiring a youth pastor of the middle-school-aged kids."

The senior high youth ministry is being carried on at the Evangelical Community Church, while the ministry to middle schoolers will likely be at the Long Ridge Congregational Church.

Having developed a closer relationship through this cooperative youth ministry, the three churches cosponsor a series of five Picnics in July. Each Wednesday evening the churches share a meal and sing together, followed by a joint vacation Bible school program. Since the meetings are in a public park, information is handed out to anyone there, inviting them to join the group.

Such cooperation has grown out of various levels of networking in Fairfield County and Stamford in particular. "Around fifteen pastors meet once a month for breakfast. Half a dozen are meeting every two weeks for prayer. And I am in a support group with two other pastors," says Pastor Childs.

In Boston there is another cooperative youth ministry venture between Emmanuel Gospel Center and the Ten Point Coalition. The Youth Ministry Development Project is designed to spearhead the placement of twenty new full-time youth workers in urban churches by the year 2006. Since most of the ethnic churches in Boston are typically too small to be able to support a full-time youth pastor, this project is bringing together resources in a focused effort to place youth pastors in churches already reaching out to urban youth.

The need for such ministry is staggering. An extensive survey of existing youth ministry efforts in Boston, conducted by the Emmanuel Gospel Center, revealed that only 15 percent of 561 churches surveyed have programs for youth who do not already come to church. Yet teens in Boston face a growing gauntlet of problems, including violence, pregnancy, lack of opportunity, abuse, crime, poverty. On top of that, the number of teens in urban areas will grow 17 percent by the year 2005. It is predicted that this demographic tidal wave of children growing up in moral poverty will create a major crime wave within the next few years of "super-predators, more terrorist than criminal."

The goal is to gain greater church participation in outreach efforts to nonchurched youth, involve thousands of young people in church-based programs and in church life, and develop a strong ministry support system for existing youth workers—in addition to the placement of twenty new full-time youth workers. These aggressive goals are visionary in their scope but necessary if the next generation of young people are to be reached with the gospel. And the only way these aggressive goals will be achieved is if churches partner to accomplish what God desires for the city.

What resources are you willing to share with others in your community or region? Are there ministries that can be launched or reinforced if you combine your efforts with others of common faith and witness? The healthy church finds ways to multiply its resources and ultimately the impact of its ministry. Join hands and share resources with your brothers and sisters in Christ and watch how the Lord blesses your efforts.

3. Citywide Covenant

On March 24, 1996, representatives of the churches of Brockton, Massachusetts, gathered to make a public commitment to one another and to the city. Serving under the banner of CURE (Christians United for Renewal and Evangelism), fourteen pastors and their respective churches sealed their relationship with each other in a worship service that concluded with a formal signing of a covenant of cooperation. "The foundation of church networking is the pastors' relationship with each other," says Pastor David Holland of the Brockton Foursquare Gospel Church.

This covenant was made possible by the pastors meeting for prayer for two years. In addition, they had begun sponsoring quarterly concerts of prayer attended by more than five hundred people on the National Day of Prayer and between two hundred to three hundred people the rest of the year. For five years the churches had also jointly sponsored discipleship conferences.

The covenant reads as follows:

> *Whereas, Christians United for Renewal and Evangelism* join in common belief in the Trinity of the Godhead, the lordship of Christ, the authority of the Bible, and the lostness of humanity apart from faith in Jesus Christ;
>
> *Whereas*, we do acknowledge it is God's will that "none should perish but that all should come to repentance" according to 2 Peter 3:9;
>
> *Therefore Be It Resolved* that we commit to the following directives:
>
> *To work together for renewal and evangelism.* We propose to meet monthly; spending additional time with each other as the Lord gives opportunity.
>
> *To respect, honor, and love one another.* To listen and learn from each other, especially during times of disagreement, seeking first to understand and then be understood; to speak well of each other, without criticism; to edify in all situations.
>
> *In accordance* with Ephesians 4:3 we recognize God's will for believers of the Lord Jesus Christ to "endeavor to keep the unity of the Spirit in the bond of peace."
>
> *In One Accord*, we the undersigned ministers do hereby covenant together on this twenty-fourth day of March, in the year of our Lord nineteen hundred ninety-six.

The covenant-signing ceremony has truly sealed the relationship among the Brockton pastors and their pledge of serving side by side for the sake of Christ has impacted the city. Their promises to one another are a living example of Psalm 133:1, "How good and pleasant it is when brothers live together in unity!"

Several significant initiatives have been tackled by the churches aligned with CURE. "For four Saturdays about three hundred volunteers went block by block throughout our community, praying in front of every home," reports Pastor Holland. As a result, more than ninety thousand people were prayed for, a truly astonishing achievement. This prayer effort resulted in a huge community park party cooperatively sponsored by the churches. "At the height of the party we had more than two thousand people from the community in the park," says Pastor Holland. "We wanted to serve the community in a way that would enable us to demonstrate the love of God to the people in it. So we served fourteen hundred free meals and gave away hundreds of prizes. We had clowns, balloons, three-on-three basketball games, puppet shows." All day people were given raffle tickets toward one of the ten bicycles that would be awarded at intervals during the day. "A team of men repaired over one hundred children's bicycles, having brought parts with them," says Holland.

The climax of the party was a gospel presentation by a team from the Brockton Teen Challenge ministry. The pastors were responsible for preparing counselors. The Holy Spirit had prepared hearts, and more than three hundred came forward to make a decision to follow Jesus. "Everyone who came forward received a New Testament. The counselors had response cards that were in duplicate form. The person who led someone to the Lord kept one to do the follow-up," reveals Pastor Holland. "Our real goal was to raise the spiritual water table of Brockton, and we believe we achieved that."

Whether done formally or informally, the healthy church joins hearts and hands with other Christians and churches in their community in pledging their support of one another. Networking with the body of Christ is not an option for the healthy church, and committing yourself to this endeavor by covenanting with brothers and sisters in Christ seals these relationships for the long term.

When I addressed this group of pastors and churches on that glorious covenant-signing day, I reminded them that the signatures they add to the document are not signed in pencil, to be easily erased if the going gets tough. Instead, the commitment to one another is in ink—permanently sealing their promises to one another. Taken seriously, the impact of such a commitment has eternal value for entire cities and towns. This pledge shows the world that we are united in faith, witness, and service—all for the glory of God.

4. United Outreach Efforts

Although the churches in the greater Burlington, Vermont, region had been cooperating for a variety of activities over the years, the concept of a "city church" presented the theological basis for networking and helped galvanize a new level of cooperation.

"Pastors who move into this area are amazed at the networking and cooperation under the banner of Vermont Arise," says Rick Callahan, senior pastor at Maranatha Christian Church, one of the largest churches in the area. "Today we have a dozen churches working together on community projects."

One of the reasons for organizing Vermont Arise was the March for Jesus. The churches have since participated in jointly sponsored training events, monthlong series of evangelistic outreaches, and summer rallies in City Hall Park, at which food and clothing are given away. They are even banding together in promoting the biblical value of heterosexual marriages versus same-sex marriages in the state.

Another form of collaboration is in supporting Burlington Street Ministries, which sponsors a feeding program each Friday in the park or at the Restoration Baptist Church. On the cobblestones of Church Street, in the downtown business district, tables are set up every day most of the summer for the distribution of Bibles and tracts to visitors to Burlington. In the summer of 1997 more than five thousand Bibles were given away. "As churches we provide financial resources and volunteers for this ministry in the heart of Burlington," says Pastor Callahan.

Mission America has been promoting Celebrate Jesus 2000 across the country. The stated goal of this initiative is to pray for and witness to every person in America by the end of the year 2000. Many churches and communities like Burlington are fully engaged in seeking to reach this goal. Vision New England is spearheading this initiative regionally, as are hundreds of other ministries across the country. With the arrival of a new millenium, the time is ripe for churches to come together under this banner or to create a citywide network on their own.

Vision New England and our urban ministry partners, the Emmanuel Gospel Center, have forged a united front around Project ONE. Project ONE has been designed to help pastors and churches build relationships with other Christians, while also working as one toward a common, grassroots approach to community evangelism. This project is developing new models of cooperative service and facilitating pastor and leadership team dialogue among churches. Out of this interaction, local evangelistic approaches keyed specifically to the community's social and cultural environment will emerge as directed by the Holy Spirit. Because these approaches are locally initiated, they will contain the seeds for strategies that will be ongoing for many years.

Not only are churches cooperating in citywide initiatives, but they are also combining efforts related to international missions. When a national mission board associated with International Fellowship of Mission Agencies or Evangelical Fellowship of Mission Agencies appoints a missionary from one of nine churches in Connecticut, a unique network takes over to get the missionary onto the field in a hurry. As a member of one of these churches, the missionary can apply for full financial support, and if approved by the executive committee of the Connecticut Missions Consortium, he or she can count on leaving for the mission field much sooner—fully funded.

"The church in which the missionary candidate is a member provides 30 percent of the candidate's support, with the other churches each providing 10 percent on a voluntary basis," says Larry Fullerton, the missions pastor at Black Rock Congregational Church, who serves as coordinator for the consortium. "Over the past ten years, seven couples and two single missionaries have received such support. This past year two couples and two singles are also leaving for the mission field with full support from the consortium. That will put our total budget at over $500,000 for the support of consortium missionaries."

Originally organized by churches in southern Connecticut, the consortium now includes churches throughout the state. "When these missionaries return on furlough, we expect them to settle in our region and establish firm relationships with the participating churches, rather than having to travel all over the country to raise support," says Pastor Fullerton.

The impact of shared outreach initiatives explodes when churches unite in their city or region. What we cannot do alone, we certainly can accomplish together.

5. Regional Interdependence

Networking with the body of Christ also occurs when Christians join to worship God and affirm their unity in Christ in areawide celebrations. One of the nation's premier Christian gatherings each year happens here in New England, under the auspices of Vision New England. Known affectionately as Congress, this annual event attracts upwards of ten thousand believers. It has been scheduled each midwinter since the early 1960s, when it was originally established as a pastor's conference focusing on evangelism.

Each Congress features nearly a dozen nationally recognized speakers, powerful God-exalting worship, more than fifty practical workshops, an exhibit hall teeming with nearly three hundred ministry booths, and lots of new friends in the body of Christ. For John and Carol Baer of Candia, New Hampshire, Congress '98 was their best Congress experience yet.

"We have made Congress our annual 'mini winter-vacation,' with the Sunday after Congress as our time to visit a different church," writes Carol Baer. "This year we had an unbelievable experience. After hearing the workshop on warfare prayer, I mentioned to the woman sitting beside me that I would really like to visit the workshop leader's church, New Covenant Christian Church. Coincidentally, this woman was a member there.

"Since our family did not bring our car to Boston, I asked her for directions using public transportation. She chuckled and told me that the church was just outside the city and therefore not easily accessible using public transportation. She then offered to pick us up early Sunday morning, take us to her home, then to her church, and drive us back to the hotel. I could hardly believe or accept her gracious offer. We were strangers to each other. She had never even seen my husband, since he wasn't at this workshop.

"But as the Spirit was instructing us during Congress, we were indeed one family in Christ," continues Carol. "Sunday morning was unforgettable. We thought the blessings ended with the last Congress session. Instead, when Pat picked us up, we were treated to a tour of Boston. Then she brought us to her home, where we met her family. Funny how discussions of trying to raise godly children or loving loved ones cross all barriers of race, culture, denomination, or age. We regularly worship at a church in New Hampshire that sits on a hill in the middle of a small country town. Our church is historic, dynamic, blessed by God, and we love it. But this morning we worshiped in a big, predominantly African-American, inner city, 'done over shopping center' church, where we had to wait in line for the parking attendant to let us into the lot. It was also dynamic, blessed by God, and we loved it. We felt at home because we were surrounded by sisters and brothers in the faith. Color, size, or style was no boundary to the richness of our worship experience."

Carol ends her letter, "Sunday afternoon we exchanged addresses and phone numbers with Pat. As we parted, we knew it was just the beginning of a friendship graced by God."

Regional interdependence can be fostered in a number of different ways. For the Baers, it came through the richness of fellowship at an annual gathering of the body of Christ in our region. For you and your church, it can come when churches in your community share in Holy Week services; united efforts of outreach and service; joining couples, singles, or youth groups in shared activities; or in concerts of prayer. The opportunities for developing regional interdependence are endless. One step in the right direction is merely to reach out to one another, extend words of love and support, share a meal with another leader or pastor in the community, and open yourself up to deepening your friendships with your brothers and sisters in Christ. Then watch how God blesses your relationships and your united efforts of love and service!

From the pages of the New Testament we discover how the early church sought to encourage and learn from one another. They learned more and more about how there was a relational unity founded upon Jesus Christ that bonded them together. Imagine for a moment if Jesus' prayer in John 17 was fulfilled in our lifetime. We'd see Christians in churches across America working interdependently—united in their collective efforts to reach their region for Christ.

Technology and the diminishing distances between us in modern society have allowed us unprecedented opportunities to bring about an ever-growing closeness among the body of Christ. As we prepare to enter a new century and a new millenium, there is a movement among his church that is filled with joyful anticipation. It is a movement characterized by interdenominational advances for the gospel. It is a movement emerging through prayer, shared learning and resources, loving relationships, and ministry partnerships.

Don't miss out on the movement . . . choose interdependence as a churchwide posture of love, service, and witness. Instead of merely focusing on the growth and development of your local church, link up with the family of God as we influence our communities, our nation, and our world for Christ—together! For the healthy church, there is no other alternative.

Please join me in praying for the church, the body of Christ.

For this reason we kneel before the Father, from whom his whole family in heaven and on earth derives its name. We pray that out of his glorious riches he may strengthen his church with power through his Spirit in the inner being of the body, so that Christ may dwell in their hearts through faith. And we pray that the church triumphant will be rooted and established in love, may have power, together with all the saints, to grasp how wide and long and high and deep is the love of Christ, and to know this love that surpasses knowledge—that they may be filled to the measure of all the fullness of God. Now to him who is able to do immeasurably more than all we ask or imagine, according to his power that is at work within us, to him be glory in the church and in Christ Jesus throughout all generations, forever and ever! Amen.

(prayer adapted from Ephesians 3:14–21)

FOR REFLECTION AND RENEWAL

The healthy church reaches out to others in the body of Christ for collaboration, resource sharing, learning opportunities, and united celebrations of worship.

Networking with the regional church includes such things as:

- pastors within the same town meeting regularly to pray for and encourage each other

- churches developing ministry specialties that meet the needs of their community without overlapping or competing with each other
- ministry leaders receiving training for their specific ministry with other leaders throughout the entire region
- areawide celebrations where Christians join to worship God and affirm their unity in Christ
- the gathering of the church in a variety of training and networking settings
- sharing resources between churches
- fostering interdependence across denominational boundaries
- communicating with one another through the use of new and effective technologies, such as the internet

> May they [the church] be brought to complete unity to let the world know that you sent me and have loved them even as you have loved me.
>
> John 17:23

1. On a scale of 1 to 10 (1 being not at all important and 10 being most important), rank each of the above statements while answering the question, "How important is this statement for the health of our church; how highly do we value networking with the body of Christ?"

2. On a scale of 1 to 10 (1 being very ineffective and 10 being very effective), rank each of the above statements while answering the question, "How effective are we as a leadership team at instilling these values in our church?"

3. For each of the above statements, ask your team, "Where do we want to be in the characteristic Networking with the Body of Christ in this next year or two?"

4. For each of the above statements, ask your team, "How will we get where we want to be in living out Networking with the Body of Christ in this next year?"

5. Overall, on a scale of 1 to 10 (1 being very low and 10 being very high), rank how well you think your church is doing in living out this ninth characteristic of a healthy church, Networking with the Body of Christ.

11

Stewardship and Generosity
Characteristic 10

The healthy church teaches its members that they are stewards of their God-given resources and challenges them to sacrificial generosity in sharing with others.

Remember this: Whoever sows sparingly will also reap sparingly, and whoever sows generously will also reap generously.

2 Corinthians 9:6

On March 26, 1997, John G. Bennett Jr. pleaded no contest to an eighty-two-count indictment charging him with mail fraud, wire fraud, false statements, filing false tax returns, impeding the IRS, and money laundering. Because Bennett had been found guilty of all of the charges against him, there was no trial for this case.

Dubbed as one of the biggest stories in the Christian community in the 1990s, the Ponzi scheme of the Foundation for New Era Philanthropy affected many well-intentioned donors and scores of Christian ministries. This "too good to be true" concept of doubling your donation dollars because of the supposed generosity of behind-the-scenes philanthropists was exactly that, too good to be true.

The major donors that believed in Bennett's integrity invested millions of dollars in New Era, hoping to see many of their favorite charities benefit from doubled donations. It actually worked for a few years, and word spread throughout the world of highly esteemed philanthropists. No one suspected they were being taken advantage of. Everyone who knew the man found him to be a man of his word—until it all caught up with Bennett, and the scheme that he masterminded exploded. The ripple effects are still being felt in many ministries today.

The Evangelical Council for Financial Accountability (ECFA) quickly jumped into the fray and offered their services as reconcilers of this terrible situation. The ECFA became the rallying agency for all of the evangelical ministries that were affected by the fallout from New Era. They became the single most redemptive initiator of a fair and peaceful resolution to this potential catastrophe. Trusted implicitly for their rock-solid integrity, the ECFA helped the well-meaning philanthropists, the affected ministries, the attorneys, and the government officials come to an equitable solution over several difficult months. The ECFA team upheld the standards of Christ-honoring stewardship and generosity, and the broader Christian community is indebted to them for their outstanding service on behalf of us all.[1]

Stewardship and generosity are where the rubber meets the road in our lifestyle as Christians. The healthy church is filled with generous, well-intentioned and cheerful givers of time, talent, and finances. By contrast, we live in a world that is absorbed with the almighty dollar. We are encouraged to pursue financial gain at all costs, even at risk of our own reputations. But we better not get so caught up in these pursuits that we find ourselves involved in schemes that will hurt the expansion of the gospel or our collective witness as the body of Christ. Steps can be taken to avoid anything close to another New Era scandal by assisting local church leaders in addressing the subject of healthy stewardship in many aspects of church life.

The Christian Stewardship Association (CSA), an impeccable ministry supporting the work of local churches and parachurch ministries, has done extensive research on the trends affecting finances and the Christian life. "We as believers have experienced a great outpouring of generosity from the hand of God," insists Brian Kluth, president of CSA. "Anything good that happens in your church is from the hand of God. That being the case, giving is a matter of consecration."

Stewardship has become the silent subject in evangelical churches during the past forty years. A recent survey conducted by CSA reveals that few churches are teaching biblical stewardship. Why the lack of teaching on generosity?

"Our survey showed that 85 percent of the pastors never had a course on stewardship in seminary, so how can they teach it in the churches they pastor? Eighty-one percent of the pastors say that their congregation does not have a high view of giving—and 83 percent define stewardship as 'meeting the budget,' instead of stewardship of life," reported Kluth. "When I called 15 denominations, I discovered none had materials for a holistic, year-round teaching on stewardship. No wonder that

Christian giving has declined for twenty-six years—and is still declining—even though 97 percent of the pastors surveyed said their people are making more money than ever. The average evangelical believer is giving only 3 ½ percent of his income back to God.

"God builds momentum when the leading people in a congregation give joyously, in keeping with his generosity to them," says Kluth. "They then experience the vital nature of giving in the experience of the Christian—even in the midst of difficult situations." According to Kluth, giving breaks the power of the dragon of materialism because joyous stewardship puts God first in our life. "Every checkbook is a theological document. It tells you where your treasure is—and thus where your heart is."

The issue of stewardship in the healthy local church and in the lives of individual Christians needs to be unpacked in light of well over 2,300 scriptural references about finances and material possessions. There are justifiable reasons why Jesus spoke so extensively on this subject, "For where your treasure is, there your heart will be also" (Matt. 6:21). There is so much truth contained in this short verse!

A Matter of the Heart

In the healthy church the subject of stewardship is more than financial, with healthy giving flowing out of a lifestyle of stewardship. Life management and stewardship are opposite sides of the same coin—the terms are interchangeable. The central issue is our love for God with all of our heart, soul, mind, and strength and our love for our neighbors as ourselves. It grows into an ever-deepening understanding of our own temperament, passion, gift mix, and personal mission. It lives itself out in our focus on serving the needs of people within our sphere of influence. And it all begins with a heart fully devoted to loving the Lord and the people of his world in a manner most befitting his heart.

When New England Patriots rookie running back and committed Christian Curtis Martin found himself buried at the bottom of a pile of three-hundred-pound linemen—folks who resemble refrigerators with feet—they would curse him and punch him when they had him where the referee couldn't see him. "No one hundred-yard game today, you [expletive] rookie!" they'd say when they finally rolled off him. "Martin would spring to his feet, flip the football to the official, and respond to the behemoths who had just tried to hurt and intimidate him. 'God bless you,' he'd say, every time. Then he would take the next handoff from

Patriots quarterback Drew Bledsoe and juke his way upfield for another ten yards."[2]

Curtis Martin's God-honoring response has been an inspiration to me. I see him as a man who tried consistently to be a good steward of the gifts he was given as a child of God, even when he was literally being crushed by others. For us, the crush will not come from three-hundred-pound linemen but from the pressures to succeed, the stresses of our jobs, the demands on our ministries, the needs of our families, the struggles in relationships, the hunger to be released from the unending rat race of life. What is a God-honoring response to this?

Let me suggest that a hearty "God bless you" is an excellent place to start. Why? Because it's a reflection of our hearts, a picture of our "being" that diminishes the crushing blows we will inevitably experience and allows the Lord to use these situations to grow us into the people he intends us to become. Stewardship is a matter of the heart, and unless we deal with the condition of our hearts, we will merely deal on the surface, cataloging ways we can structure programs of stewardship rather than grooming a generation of stewards who live out God's priorities in a more natural, healthy manner.

After a season of reading devotionally through the Gospel of Matthew, the words of Jesus only, I realized that everywhere Jesus spoke he was penetrating the hearts of his listeners. He was speaking to issues of the soul, our personhood, our relationship with God. There was a distinct focus of his teaching on our *becoming* more like him over against our *doing* active service for him. The balance of doing and being that we covered earlier in this book was unearthed here as well, but the weight was definitely more on being than on doing. He truly cares more about who we are and who we are becoming as his children than what we are doing or accomplishing in life. He's much more interested in our souls than our schedules. Our schedules, then, need to reflect the condition of our souls (just like our checkbooks reflect the condition of our life of stewardship). The inner circle of concern—namely, our hearts—dominates the outer circle of influence—namely, our lifestyle and our relationships. This is a difficult principle for us to swallow, given the fact that so much of the value of our lives is attached to our activity level over against our soul.

This principle gets tested when we sing wonderful hymns like "I'd Rather Have Jesus," the words of which are illuminating. The lyrics go through a litany of things from our world that capture our attention much more than Jesus does, like silver, gold, riches, houses, land, people's applause, and fame. And then it ends with a powerful phrase: "I'd rather have Jesus than anything this world affords today."[3] I love this hymn by George Beverly Shea, but I am troubled when forced to answer the question, "Would I really rather have Jesus more than anything?" In my heart of hearts the answer is a resounding "Yes!" but in my daily life I'm quite sure this does not always translate in my relationships, decisions, and lifestyle choices. However, by saying yes, I am convinced that the merciful and loving Lord begins a new work in us, guiding us in being and becoming all he intends us to be.

Maintaining this focus will result in our hearing those long-awaited words from the Father, "Well done, good and faithful servant! You have been faithful with a few things; I will put you in charge of many things. Come and share your master's happiness!" (Matt. 25:21). Who among us doesn't desire receiving such words from the Lord when we are ushered into glory, as well as whispered in our ears along the way of life on this earth?

Pastor Paul Bertolino of Calvary Bible Church in Meredith, New Hampshire, believes in the importance of verbalizing "well done, good and faithful servant" to members of his congregation. One-on-one and public appreciation for quality ministry is an ongoing part of his leadership. "During the Sunday morning service we will often recognize exceptional service," says Pastor Bertolino. "For example, recently one of our young women who serves in puppetry with our young people was recognized with a community award for her volunteer services—and on Sunday morning we also recognized her with a Certificate of Appreciation. When a church member retired after thirty years of missionary service in the Philippines, we organized a banquet in her honor."

With that consistent attitude of gratitude stimulating volunteerism in the church, is it any wonder that the church three years ago received the Governor's Award for Volunteerism? Recognition and reward, key elements in Pastor Bertolino's total quality ministry approach, combined with an emphasis on giving as an expression of faith have become the key ingredients for building an attitude of stewardship at Calvary Bible Church.

Multiplied Talents

The parable of the talents in Matthew 25 is an excellent place to stop and reflect on the subject of life stewardship. It is set amid two full chapters of teaching from Jesus on the subject of the Kingdom of God. It speaks of judgment, anticipation of Jesus' ultimate return, and our response as his children. It is a simple story with powerful and profound implications for all of us as followers of Christ.

Scattered throughout this Gospel is the main theme of Jesus as King. The subject of the kingly rule of Jesus is something we need to pay careful attention to—he is the reigning King of the universe. He holds our past, present, and future securely in his hands, and he wants us to trust in his kingly rule over our lives.

When Jesus spoke of the kingdom of God, he was not referring to land mass. It was not the physical domain of the earth he was referring to, although it is true that he is King over all the earth. What he was speaking of here was the dominion of God—the territory of our hearts and souls and minds and wills. William Barclay explains it this way.

> Any man (or woman) in any age and generation who has done God's will was in the Kingdom; those who do God's will are in the Kingdom; but the final consummation when the whole world will do God's will is something which is still to come. So when Jesus spoke of the Kingdom of God He thought of doing God's will as perfectly on earth as it was done in heaven. He Himself always did that, not just sometimes as others had done, but always. That is why the Kingdom perfectly begins with Him. He thought of how happy men would be if only they did that; of what a wonderful world this would be if it was ruled by God's will; of how God's heart would be glad when men did perfectly accept His will. Truly when that happened there would be heaven on earth. That is why for Jesus the Kingdom was the most important thing of all. And that is why for so long men did not understand Him. When they spoke of the Kingdom they were still thinking of the old nationalistic dreams of world power and they would have liked to make Him a king like that. *But He was thinking of doing the will of God and it was in their hearts and not on their earthly thrones He wished to reign.*[4]

It is therefore essential that we as Christians, followers of the King of Kings, Jesus himself, understand the serious nature of these passages of Scripture—spoken directly by Jesus—and respond affirmatively to the call for action outlined here. In all of our labor and in all of our leisure we are to honor our King so that the fruit of our labors will bring him glory. Jesus, all throughout the Gospels, seeks to capture the hearts of his listeners, for it is in our hearts and not on our earthly thrones that He wishes to reign.

I would encourage you as church leaders to be familiar with kingdom teachings so that you can instill kingdom values into your congregations, thus stewarding the resources of God's kingdom here on earth in ways that reflect his teachings on the subject. Some passages to study include:

Matthew 21:33–46—the parable of the tenants
Luke 19:11–27—the parable of the ten minas

Mark 13:32–37—the unknown day and hour of Jesus' return

Matthew 24 and 25—provide additional kingdom teachings and parables

Luke 13:28—past prophets who spoke of the kingdom

Luke 17:21—the kingdom in the midst of you or within you

Luke 12:32—God's good pleasure to give his disciples the kingdom, clearly at some point in the future

The parable of the talents (Matthew 25:14–30) is a simple story of a man who entrusts five talents to one of his servants, two talents to another, and one talent to a third. We know that the man in the story is one of obvious wealth, because the word Jesus uses for talent represents a large sum of money—not a mere coin but the weight of the coinage, comparable to a hefty sum today.

Jesus is telling about a master who intended to be away from his servants for some considerable block of time. Not wishing to leave his estate unattended during his absence, he divides up his wealth among his servants in proportion to their ability to handle it. After a long time he came home again and summoned the servants to a reckoning. The first two servants had actually doubled the money entrusted to them. But the third, making the excuse that he had been afraid to risk his talent by trading with it, had simply hidden the money in the ground. And now he handed it back with no increase, thinking he knew the master's heart.

The third servant, the lazy, not-so-bright one, reminds me of the young boy in Shel Silverstein's book *Where the Sidewalk Ends* in the poem "SMART":

My dad gave me one dollar bill 'cause I'm his smartest son,
And I swapped it for two shiny quarters 'cause two is more than one!
And then I took the quarters and traded them to Lou
For three dimes—I guess he don't know that three is more than two!
Just then, along came old blind Bates and just 'cause he can't see
He gave me four nickels for my three dimes, and four is more than three!
And I took the nickels to Hiram Coombs down at the seed-feed store,
And the fool gave me five pennies for them, and five is more than four!
And then I went and showed my dad, and he got red in the cheeks
And closed his eyes and shook his head—too proud of me to speak![5]

The boy thought he was smart with all his wheeling and dealing, but his entrusted amount of one dollar shrunk down to five measly pennies. So, too, is the brilliance of the lazy servant in this parable. At least the little boy in the poem tried to do something with his "talent"; the lazy servant did nothing but hide it. Notice that Jesus describes such a servant as wicked or mean. He's not only lazy in multiplying what was entrusted to him, but he has a mean streak as well—almost vindictive toward the Master.

So the first two servants were praised and given promise of greater things to come. But the third servant was condemned and shut out in the outer darkness forever. Like the scribes and Pharisees of Jesus' day, so those who refuse to multiply the talents entrusted into their care for the purpose of introducing others to the life-changing message of Jesus will be judged.

Divine Ownership

In this parable and its parallel passages, there is a consistent character in every account. He is referred to as either a master or a man of noble birth or a king—the point is that in every incident a divine Owner generously entrusts his possessions to his people. He is ultimately in control of his land, servants, possessions—everything—whether he is physically present or absent from the scene. He takes a risk every time, trusting that instead of the possessions being squandered, they will be multiplied by his servants. That is his obvious expectation.

No one in any of the stories was able to predict his return. Jesus is explicit in his warning to "keep watch" over the talents entrusted into our care and to anticipate his return. The issue here is one of control. If the master entrusted the resources to the servants, does the servant control the talents? Obviously not for the long haul, but there is an element of control in stewarding the talent that comes into play here. The first two servants took control in a positive way and sought to multiply their talents. The wicked, lazy servant took control in a negative way and hid the talent in the ground. So who's ultimately in control, the master or the servant? The master, because on his return he took back what was rightly his, multiplied for his good pleasure or hidden for his dismay.

Each leader and member of a healthy church should consider the following questions:

Who's in control of your resources—God or you?

Who's in control of your soul? The best way to evaluate that is to spend time in prayer and in the study of his Word, asking him to help you make wise choices related to all of your possessions, given to you by the gracious hand of God.

Who's in control of your resources? A surefire way to evaluate this area is to review your checkbook—are you willing to open it up for a stewardship audit?

Who's in control of your relationships? Are you trying to cling to them and manipulate them, or is God guiding you to be loving, giving, and forgiving to all?

Who's in control of your vocational pursuits? Are you living out his mission in the workplace, community, and church as God has called you to serve, or are you in the driver's seat?

To test your level of control, try the open hand test. Are you willing to live out a posture in your life of open, outstretched hands, ready to receive from God and give yourself freely back to him? Are you willing to serve others and receive their kindness and love? Control is a critical issue in most churches today. The question is, What posture best describes your life and the life of your community of faith—open, outstretched hands of love and service or clenched fists of control, anger, and manipulation? I guarantee the posture of your lives will impact your stewardship. Jesus is in control; he has given everything to you for a purpose. He is there to guide and empower you to use all he has given for his glory. You may need to relinquish control today and allow him to be in the driver's seat once again.

All of life is a gift from God, the divine Owner of the Universe. Everything comes from his almighty hand. What is your response?

Interdependent Partnerships

The concept of interdependence has become a significant one for us at Vision New England. In our pursuit of unity in the body of Christ, we are encouraging the formation of interdependent partnerships among healthy churches all over the region. We recognize that no single church or denomination can get the job of regional ministry done on its own. The word *interdependent* means interconnected, complementary, synergistic—when two or more parties understand the value they have to offer and see the exponential results of working with others who also have something of value to offer.

This principle is like a continuum of relationships. On one end of the spectrum are the independents—the ones who don't need anyone else, thank you very much. On the other end are the dependents—the ones who are desperate for the help of others and will drain people dry as a result. In the center of the continuum are the interdependents—the ones who know the contributions they can offer, see the need to work together, and energize others in the process. The healthiest families, churches, communities, ministries, and businesses are those that pursue interdependence.

In the parable of the talents, and in all of the related passages referenced earlier, there is that sense that we need to work together, side by side for the sake of Christ and his priorities for us. Unfortunately, in each of the passages there is one party who chooses to go it alone, doing his own thing, and the result is devastating. It is so unfortunate when servants of Christ do not team up with one another. In the case of this parable, it could have saved the lazy, wicked servant's life. And so, more out of absence than prominence in this parable, I suggest the importance of interdependent partnerships for healthy stewardship. The return on our collective investments of time, energy, and resources will be far greater when done in unity.

None of us can accomplish his complete will without turning to one another for partnership and support. That's what the body of Christ, the church, is all about. We need to be fellow servants of one another, encouraging, affirming, supporting, serving, and praying so that the massive work set before us can be accomplished in our day and time. We need each other—do you agree?

It reminds me of the time when my wife and I purchased a new portable basketball hoop for our son, Nathan. It was the one birthday present he was longing for. We got the kind that requires some set-up, with the large poles to support the fiberglass rim that elevates up to nine feet tall, supported by a base that you fill with water or sand. We picked it up at the department store and brought it home with confidence that we could handle this task. After all, we had constructed other toys for the children in the past, what would be so tough about this?

Well, when we opened the box, we discovered hundreds of pieces to put together. Ruth and I looked at each other and decided quickly not to risk the task (or the potential of marital conflict!) and chose instead to seek out the help of our neighbor, Chris. Just because we could read the instructions didn't guarantee that we could follow them and accomplish the goal. I called Chris and asked him if he would be willing to give me a hand in putting the basketball set together. He readily agreed to help, and within two hours my son and his friends were enjoying basketball court action on our driveway. Had Ruth and I gone much further, we would have made a mess. But by teaming up with someone who had the necessary talent, it was actually fun to do it. In the same way, the body of Christ will serve effectively and in a healthy manner when we lean on each other's strengths to get the job done.

Leading people to accept the lordship of Jesus Christ is paramount to establishing a biblical basis for stewardship of life among God's people, according to Senior Pastor J. Jey Deifell Jr. of First Church of Christ in Wethersfield, Connecticut. "I believe you have to lift up the lordship of Jesus Christ. If a congregation can accept that, celebrate it, and be obedient to him together, then matters of stewardship fall into place. An understanding of who we are and how we use what has been given us in response to the grace of God sets the stage for healthy stewardship. Then it doesn't become a tedious, negative, or laborious process, but a positive, joyous experience. The strongest focus for me is that stewardship is not a season. It is to be carried out in all areas of our personal life and church life as we lift up the vision where the Lord wants us to go. As people catch the vision, stewardship of life and resources happen more naturally and spontaneously."

I don't know about you, but the last thing I want for the church of Jesus Christ is to be in someone else's way, tripping up their giftedness, and pulling them off course in using their talent for God. I want to maximize my own giftedness and effectiveness, and I want to see others flourish too. There is no greater joy for me as a servant-leader than to see the people around me abound in love and good works. There is no greater alternative as stewards of the talents entrusted in our care than to encourage good stewardship in the lives of our brothers and sisters in Christ. Let's strive together to hear the words "well done, good and faithful servant" directly from the lips of Jesus.

Personal Stewardship

God has entrusted us with all the property, time, talent, and resources we have. Those in the parable who acted as responsible stewards were rewarded with honor, while the lazy, disobedient, noncompliant servant was earmarked for doom. Each individual who is a part of the kingdom has his or her own talents, responsibilities, relationships, and "assigned tasks." The question remains as to whether we will multiply them for the sake of the King who has generously entrusted them into our care.

The bottom line here is this: personal stewardship of life. Regardless of our status, occupation, ethnicity, economic means, or whether we are a full-time grandparent, a retiree, a professional in our field, a student, a stay-at-home mother, the key for us is to multiply our "talents" for God's glory. We may not be equal in what has been entrusted into our care, but we can be equal in our efforts to use what's been given.

It's not what we give but what we keep that reflects our stewardship commitment, according to Pastor Ralph Wetherington of West Congregational Church in Peabody, Massachusetts. "It is my personal conviction that God is not as concerned with the portion of money I give away in his name as he is with what we do with the portion that I keep for myself. The heart of the disciple is revealed in the portion we keep. As I understand the teaching of God's Word, Christian stewardship of life is a simple and straightforward expectation for all believers. Everything we are and have belongs to God, according to Romans 11:36, therefore our preaching and teaching on stewardship is a much larger topic than money. What we do with our money is important! Jesus said that where our treasure is, there will our heart be also. This applies to poor people as well as to the wealthy. Each of us needs to lay aside from our firstfruits to God as an act of worship and obedience."

Healthy local churches, filled with people who take their stewardship seriously, will live out a rule of life that is universally true. It tells us that to the one who has, more will be given; and the one who has not will lose even what he or she has. If a child of God has a talent and exercises it, that person is progressively able to do more of it. But if that same person has a talent and fails to exercise it, he or she will inevitably lose it. If we are proficient in a sport or an art, or if we are a gifted musician, the more we exercise that expertise and that gift, the harder the work and the bigger the task we will be able to tackle. But if we fail to use it, we lose it.

What matters most to Jesus, and should matter to us as well—is that we be good stewards of the gift of life handed to us by the divine King of the universe who loves us with an endless love and desires that we work together as members of his family for his greater glory. Taking our stewardship seriously, and encouraging it in others, is a refreshing alternative to digging a hole and hiding away the gifts he has given so generously.

The first two servants in the parable were excellent stewards. They did everything they could to multiply their talents. What about you and your church? How can you increase the congregation's understanding of stewardship and hold one another accountable to a new standard of excellence in this area as leaders in the church? Your deepening commitment to biblical stewardship will have a positive ripple effect throughout the community of faith under your care.

Give out of Substance, Not Surplus

How do you finally break through the emotional barrier against teaching on stewardship—especially when your church is experiencing a financial crisis? "I'm part of a group of pastors who hold each other accountable, and they began telling my copastor and me we needed to teach on stewardship," says Pastor Eric Hanson of Hosanna New Testament Church in Oxford, Maine. "As a result we began a series of four messages on the stewardship of life."

Hosanna New Testament Church ministers in a community with a population of ten thousand that has lost its manufacturing base. Unemployment is almost twice as high as the national average in the state of Maine. Many in the congregation are working on subsistence wages. In addition, two years ago a group of families left, taking about 60 percent of the children in the church's Christian day school with them, because of parents who persuaded the families that only parents should teach their children. The resulting financial belt-tightening, though, has not prevented the church from increasing its commitment to world missions.

"A few years ago we made a leap of faith and committed ourselves as a church to tithing our church income," says Pastor Hanson. "We started at 10 percent and now are giving 13 percent of our budget to missions. Our goal is to give 20 percent to missions over the next few years. What this has done is really made us globally minded as a congregation, since we support ministries in New York City, Haiti, and many other countries."

The sermon series was designed to put financial giving in the church within the framework of stewardship of life. This emphasis is especially important to the many newer believers in the congregation for whom stewardship of life is a new concept.

Right now Hosanna's local priority is paving its parking lot, "a sea of mud right now." This will cost eighteen to twenty thousand dollars. The church building needs upgrading as well, but that will have to wait. At the moment there is no thought of reducing the pastoral staff because of the high ministry load in the community. "We have elected to cut back in other areas rather than on pastoral staff," says Pastor Hanson.

The church has also elected to keep its Christian day school going, even though the drastic decline in student enrollment meant cutting teaching staff. In fact, members who are active tithers can receive up to a 50 percent reduction in tuition costs at the school if needed. And when a family cannot afford even that, anonymous donors are encouraged to help.

For the members of Hosanna New Testament Church, there is no such thing as surplus. They give out of substance, and as a result their giving is truly sacrificial. So many of us give out of our surplus and cannot identify with the experiences of others who sacrifice to maintain integrity in tithing. Teaching and emulating this principle is a challenge to most churches, and especially to wealthier congregations. Does it hurt to give to the Lord's service, or is your giving considered more like paying your electric bill?

Giving out of substance heightens the awareness of generosity within the community of believers. Several years ago the Vision New England board of directors made a substantial decision about our annual Congress offering. Congress has been in existence for almost forty years in New England. Every year for the first thirty or so years an offering was taken that was designated for our ministry. In 1992 we decided to split the offering 50-50 between our ministry and other needy ministries in the region. In 1992 the amount of the offering was double what it was in 1991! The Lord honored our decision, and the amount that came to our ministry was no less than the year before.

Ever since 1992 we have split the offering with other notable ministries that exemplify the priorities of our regional ministry and the theme of each congress. Consequently, more than $150,000 has been given away to fifty-nine ministries in our region and around the world. In 1998 the decision was to split the offering three ways, with only 33 percent of the offering coming to our ministry. You guessed it—the amount we received was higher than the year before, with a record-breaking offering received once again.

The concept of giving out of our substance rather than our surplus is magnified when the giving is sacrificial and from the heart.

God Loves a Cheerful Giver

And now, brothers, we want you to know about the grace that God has given the Macedonian churches. Out of the most severe trial, their *overflowing joy* and their extreme poverty welled up in *rich generosity*. For I testify that they *gave as much as they were able*, and *even beyond their ability*. Entirely *on their own*, they urgently pleaded with us for the *privilege of sharing in this service to the saints*. And they did not do as we expected, but they *gave themselves first to the Lord and then to us in keeping with God's will*. So we urged Titus, since he had earlier made a beginning, to bring also to completion this act of grace on your part. *But just as you excel in everything—in faith, in speech, in knowledge, in complete earnestness and in your love for us—see that you also excel in this grace of giving.*

I am not commanding you, but I want to test the *sincerity* of your love by comparing it with the *earnestness* of others. For you know the *grace* of our Lord Jesus Christ, that though he was rich, yet *for your sakes he became poor*, so that you through his poverty might become rich.

And here is my advice about what is best for you in this matter: Last year you were the first not only to give but also to have the desire to do so. Now finish the work, so that your *eager willingness* to do it may be matched by your completion of it, according to your means. For if the willingness is there, the *gift is acceptable* according to what one has, not according to what he does not have.

Our desire is not that others might be relieved while you are hard pressed, but that there might be *equality*. At the present time your plenty will supply what they need, so that in turn their plenty will supply what you need. Then there will be *equality*, as it is written: "He who gathered much did not have too much, and he who gathered little did not have too little."

2 Corinthians 8:1–15, emphasis added

To excel in the grace of giving is Paul's urging in this powerful passage of Scripture. I have italicized key words and phrases that pop off the page when considering the need for cheerful, generous giving from the heart. A good steward excels in generous giving, and our goal as church leaders is to model this principle and see it lived out in the lives of our congregation.

To get to that place in our churches, we need a strategy that begins with an articulated vision and mission for the church. The people need to believe in and support this mission in order to participate in the church's ministry. The congregation needs to trust the pastor and leadership team, recognizing the importance of effective leadership in the fulfillment of the church's stated mission. The clarion call for bold stewardship needs to be sounded, not only for a season but on a regular, consistent basis. Then the congregation, at all ages and levels, will target their time, energy, prayers, and resources to teaching life-stewardship principles for all.

Healthy stewardship-training initiatives will not grow on their own. Leaders must take charge in this area and offer extensive education. It can begin with preaching and teaching in large and small groups on parables like the ones we have looked at in this chapter, or it can take place through in-depth dialogue on the implications of 2 Corinthians 8. It could include special gatherings to explore this topic in more relaxed settings. It may require that you offer a seminar on life stewardship and a follow-up session on financial management. You might want to invite a financial planner to come and meet with members of your congregation for free. Or you might want to offer a planned giving workshop, a budgeting seminar for teens, a finance course for single moms, or an extensive session for the deacons or trustees on the subject of effective church budgeting. The opportunities are endless, so begin by assessing your needs and filling the gaps with effective learning strategies designed for your congregation.

The Christian Stewardship Association offers the following keys to church financial fitness:

1. Teach about stewardship.
2. Handle donations and church funds properly.
3. Strategize planning and budgeting.
4. Exercise caution with debt.
5. Compensate your staff fairly.
6. Review finances with others often.
7. Model giving as an act of worship.

In addition to the above steps, CSA suggests each church develop an integrated stewardship strategy that includes:

- Christian education courses on finances, giving, budgeting, career guidance, new member giving orientations;
- communications and gift processing efforts such as mailing quarterly statements to members, financial newsletters, designated giving options;
- stewardship counseling and advising on matters such as volunteering and using your spiritual gifts, career assessments, budget and debt counseling;
- Sunday morning church services emphasizing this topic sensitively through stewardship testimonies, annual giving series, messages on tithing;
- special funding emphases and campaigns designed to raise funds for missions, renovations, building expansions, annual giving increases;
- care ministries offered to members who are in debt and need budget counsel, for unwed mothers, the unemployed, missionaries, single parents;
- leadership providing the role modeling necessary in order for the congregation to follow their example in all aspects of stewardship of life;
- fiscal management and integrity in all aspects of record keeping, written policies about budgeting and expenditures, staff reviews and salary increases.[6]

The goal for the healthy church is to raise the standards for the congregation in effectively loving God through Christ-honoring generosity. What's the next step you will take in providing leadership for this to happen in your local church?

Lord, the need for a healthy understanding of stewardship and generosity begins in my heart today. I give you full permission to conduct an audit of my life. My books are open for review today by the King of heaven. I want to be a faithful steward of the time, talents, and treasures entrusted to my care. I long to be a generous person who gives out of a heart that is willing to sacrifice for the needs of others, rather than continue to give out of my surplus, as if my giving were merely a part of paying my bills instead of an act of worship. Renew my understanding of the biblical principles of steward-

ship, tithing, generosity, servanthood, leadership, and mission, and wrap them all together in a combined understanding of what you desire of me and members of my local church. Help me not to look over my shoulder to see how others are giving for kingdom purposes; but instead, may I shut my eyes and focus on what you would have of me in this life-shaping matter. I offer myself to you with open, outstretched hands that are willing and ready to receive from you and in turn offer all of who I am back to you. You are King of all ages and Lord of my life . . . consecrate each gift I give to you, for the glory of your name and the purposes of your kingdom. Amen.

FOR REFLECTION AND RENEWAL

The healthy church teaches its members that they are stewards of their God-given resources and challenges them to sacrificial generosity in sharing with others.

The attitude of the leaders and members of the local church express tangibly the attitude of Jesus, who taught that to whom much is given, much is required (Luke 12:48), and where our treasure is, our hearts will be also (Matt. 6:21). It also includes:

- teaching on generosity and financial planning
- sharing facilities and programs with others
- giving a generous portion of the annual budget to local and international missions
- providing abundantly for those in need within the fellowship of believers, including the unemployed, the widowed, single parents, etc.
- operates within its income and can account for all contributions
- operates in accordance with the principles of the Evangelical Council for Financial Accountability

Remember this: Whoever sows sparingly will also reap sparingly, and whoever sows generously will also reap generously.

2 Corinthians 9:6

1. On a scale of 1 to 10 (1 being not at all important and 10 being most important), rank each of the above statements while answering the question, "How important is this statement for the health of our church; how highly do we value stewardship and generosity?"
2. On a scale of 1 to 10 (1 being very ineffective and 10 being very effective), rank each of the above statements while answering the question, "How effective are we as a leadership team at instilling these values in our church?"
3. For each of the above statements, ask your team, "Where do we want to be in the characteristic Stewardship and Generosity in this next year or two?"
4. For each of the above statements, ask your team, "How will we get where we want to be in living out Stewardship and Generosity in this next year?"
5. Overall, on a scale of 1 to 10 (1 being very low and 10 being very high), rank how well you think your church is doing in living out this tenth characteristic of a healthy church, Stewardship and Generosity.

12

The Process of Becoming a Healthy Church

On the heels of completing the bulk of this manuscript for Baker Book House, our family was hit hard with news of a forthcoming surgery for our son, Nathan. Nate was born with a rare congenital defect in his right tibia. He has had three corrective surgeries to implant bone next to his tibia to provide the strength necessary to sustain his body weight and activity level. He wears a brace on his right leg as a measure of protection from the dangers of potential fracturing. He is unable to participate in contact sports and is restricted from any activity that might endanger his leg.

He handles his disability with great courage and is my hero when it comes to the management of his daily pain and disappointment. He is a typical teenager now and would like to be involved in all the activities his friends are doing, but he is learning each day how to cope with the realities of his limitations. He rarely complains about his situation and has confronted every season of life with an attitude befitting the graces of God. Amid all the surgeries, setbacks, fractures, casts, and braces on his leg, he has made great progress. Even though he doesn't have the healthiest of right legs in this world, he does have a heart that reflects the joy of the Lord. His life is a testimony to me of how a person can walk with imperfections in as healthy a manner as possible. It can be done!

Nate's life is a picture of the body of Christ. All of us in the body walk with a limp of some sort. Our goal in life is not perfection—we are not perfect beings, nor is the church a perfect entity. We are all works in progress, and we are all dependent on God to give us the courage to face each new day of our life and ministry. We will encounter our own shortcomings for the rest of our lives until the Lord returns to usher us into a perfected glory in heaven. In the meantime, we need to assist one another in the process of becoming a healthy church—the pursuit of health and vitality, regardless of the limiting conditions of our lives.

The key for us is to pursue healthy balances and perspectives that reflect the heart and mind of Christ. As we study the Scriptures and bathe our lives in prayer, we are better prepared to confront the issues we face together in the church. We need to work on one issue at a time and not allow each other to get overwhelmed. The purpose of this book has been to raise your consciousness about principles that are of vital importance for the church of Jesus Christ today in hopes that you will take a look at these ten characteristics from the vantage point of your own ministry. I have sought to heighten your awareness of these issues without telling you "how to fix" your congregation. I trust that you and members of your church leadership team will discuss these principles extensively and determine together the ways you will live out each of the ten characteristics of a healthy church. Take it one step at a time, and hold fast to realistic expectations about the anticipated results of your work together as you become a healthier congregation.

The apostle Paul writes about the effective work of the church when he uses the analogy of the body. In 1 Corinthians 12 we are reminded that "the body is a unit, though it is made up of many parts; and though all its parts are many, they form one body" (v. 12). The parts of the body are arranged by God—just as he wanted them to be. Therefore,

> The eye cannot say to the hand, "I don't need you!" And the head cannot say to the feet, "I don't need you!" On the contrary, those parts of the body that seem to be weaker are indispensable, and the parts that we think are less honorable we treat with special honor. And the parts that are unpresentable are treated with special modesty, while our presentable parts need no special treatment. But God has combined the members of the body and has given greater honor to the parts that lacked it, so that there should be no division in the body, but that its parts should have equal concern for each other. If one part suffers, every part suffers with it; if one part is honored, every part rejoices with it."

> verses 21–26

We are members of the body of Christ. We are interwoven into one another's lives. We cannot function effectively without each part of the body serving in its God-given capacity. God has placed us where he wills, and our job is to cooperate with his design for our lives while encouraging the members of the body to do the same. Once this is discovered we are free to serve within the calling and gifting of the Spirit. This applies to our families, our local church, the churches in our communities, and the universal church. Are we fit for effective, vibrant, enduring service for the King and his kingdom?

Maintain the Proper Balance

"And Jesus grew in wisdom and stature, and in favor with God and men" (Luke 2:52). In the midst of a busy ministry life, Jesus was known as a man of balance. As he was going about his work for the Father, he did so in a wholesome, balanced approach. In attitude, intellect, body, and spirit, Jesus was the perfect example of a proper, healthy balance.

How do we develop and maintain a similar equilibrium for ourselves, especially in an atmosphere of stress and exhaustion?

The first year we were at Vision New England, our family was stressed almost to our maximum capacity. In March 1989 we left a ministry assignment that we had loved for eleven wonderful years. Saying good-bye was traumatic for us. At our farewell reception we noticed our son favoring his right leg, and within a few days we were back in the hospital preparing for his second surgery. When he came home from the hospital he was in a full leg cast for eight weeks. During this time my wife Ruth was seven and eight months pregnant while she was carting around our four-year-old son through the hot months of summer. By September Nathan was out of his cast and into a new brace just in time for the birth of our daughter, Rebekah. In the meantime we also were searching for a new church home and adjusting to a new job filled with challenges. You might imagine that the stress level was relatively high.

The only way we could deal with this stress was to put our trust in God, believing that he had our best interests in mind throughout these ordeals. He proved himself faithful over and over again and sustained us through some of our darkest and most difficult days. Adding to our spiritual lives was the support of friends, extended family members, and ministry colleagues. In addition, we were able to get a short respite in the summer that helped considerably. And we kept moving forward in spite of ourselves. Only by God's good graces were we able to cope.

Gone are the days of leisurely lifestyles. Gone are the seasons of quietness that offset the ones filled with frenetic activity. Gone are the simple pleasures of casually strolling through life. We are caught up in the busyness of our lives—and yes, even our churches—so much so that we don't dare stop to smell the roses or conduct any kind of self-analysis. Yet this is what we need the most. That's why at the end of every chapter I urge you to reflect on the content you have read. What difference will all of this make in your church? If you don't take the time to ask the hard questions, then you will merely continue to spin your wheels and return to business as usual. Please don't succumb to this pressure! We need to become churches that are not afraid to hop off our treadmills and do some serious self-evaluation—even when we feel stretched to the max. It's all the more important that we do so if we are feeling the pinch. This is the only way we will discover the balance God desires for us and our ministries.

Embrace a Season of Growth and Change

How do you spell change: h-o-p-e? Or, d-i-s-a-s-t-e-r? When my father took early retirement from his mechanical engineering career of more than thirty years, he did so because he wanted to pursue further education and become a teacher. So back to school he went to finish his teaching degree, complete his student teaching, receive his certificate, and proceed to teach for over twelve years in a local technical high school. I was amazed that he took such steps and was so open to continuing his growth and development. He took a huge risk and chose the avenue of change and growth. He did not want to stagnate, and he willingly accepted the adjustments that would be required along the way.

How about you? As you and your leadership team consider the ten principles presented in this book and apply them to your church, are you willing to take some risks and pursue a lifestyle of long-term growth? Even if it requires some changes along the way? If you take the principles presented in this book seriously, then I promise you will need to consider some changes.

What is your attitude about lifelong growth? How does an oak tree grow to full maturity? From the seedling to a fully mature tree there are seasons of growth, nurture, and patience. And yet the oak is one of the strongest trees God ever created. He even likens it to his people in Isaiah 61:3: "They will be called oaks of righteousness, a planting of the Lord for the display of his splendor." With deep, healthy roots, the oak grows tall and strong, produces broad leaves, strong wood, and is able to reproduce itself with the drop of an acorn.

God's people, the living church, are to become like the oak—strong and healthy, full of life, and able to reproduce themselves. Pursuing the ten principles of becoming a healthy church will assist you in the process of becoming an oak tree for the display of the Lord's splendor in your heart and in this world. But in order for us to become oaks of righteousness, we need to be open and willing to be changed by God so that we can grow more like him. The essence of who he has created us to be does not radically change, but the process of growth over the seasons of life and ministry together will shape us in becoming all that he intends us to be—and that certainly is a change.

In order for us to embrace a season of growth and change, there are four "tions" that we dare not shun:

1. *Reflection*—taking the time to hop off the treadmills of our hectic ministry lives and ask ourselves some basic questions about who we are, what we are accomplishing together, where we would like to go in the future, and how we hope to get there.
2. *Affirmation*—acknowledging the truth about ourselves and our church and affirming the gifts that have been planted in our midst as a result of his work of grace in our lives and in our common kingdom-building service. What are our greatest strengths, our most obvious needs, our ability to maximize our strengths, and our openness to change?
3. *Evaluation*—observing together our relationships, knowledge, skill levels, and the best ways to enhance our ministry initiatives in the days to come. By loving each other enough to be honest with each other, we will be able to give each other permission to fail, restore conflicts as they inevitably occur, and strive for true change in the hearts, minds, and wills of the people in our care.
4. *Application*—bringing to fruition the changes and growth we anticipate prayerfully as a result of the self-analysis we have completed. Learning how to master the basics and seek improvements over time will lead to a maturing of the body and build far more effective service in unity. In this stage the leadership team is called on to identify the places where we would like to grow and specific direction for how we will get there.

Pursue Requisites for Renewal

When all is said and done, my hope is that churches all across the country will prayerfully strive for the renewal of the their faith communities so that our neighbors, friends, work associates, and families will be reached with the gospel of Christ. In summarizing the ten principles of a healthy church presented in this book, let me close with a few challenges to consider as requisites for this renewal.

First, we need to pray more than we have ever prayed in our lives. In our prayer closets daily, in our prayer cells on a regular basis, within our praying congregations each week, and in regional prayer gatherings within our communities, cities, or counties. The only way we will ever witness a marked change in the landscape of Christendom throughout our country is if we become a praying nation.

Second, we need to repent and come clean of past and present sin so that who we are and what we are becoming is a fragrant offering to the Lord. When my beloved mother passed away in March 1997, her death birthed new life in people all around her. By her literal dying to herself, her sacrificial love and servanthood brought about life and vitality in many individuals. We need to die to ourselves so that others may live. We need to offer up to the Lord our own agendas, our stubbornness, our self-centeredness, and embrace instead the biblical mandate to consider the needs of others as more important than our own. Death precedes resurrection life. Dying to ourselves precedes new life in others. What will be your choice?

Third, we need to fully engage the hearts, minds, and souls of God's people in rich and meaningful worship experiences. The heart cry of God's people today is for worship that is fully alive in the Spirit. Too many believers are worshiping more in their cars with the aid of excellent worship tapes because their worship leaders at church are ill-equipped.

Fourth, we need to renew old structures that hinder our effectiveness. Some old structures within our church governments need to be thrown away forever, while others may need to be surgically altered. Whatever the case may be, we need to honor healthy traditions that are still effective and radically change those that need to be altered or discarded. How people are given responsibilities, the way programs are developed and designed, the use of technology, the allocation of space and resources, and the need for strategic ministry plans are but a few of the areas to be considered here.

Fifth, the servant-leaders of the congregation need to build and empower strong ministry teams in every aspect of church life and service. The greatest value of church leadership today is in the team concept. When individual believers are equipped to understand their spiritual gifts and are called on to serve cooperatively on a team, then the common mission of the church is more fully realized. Don't attempt the leadership of the church among a handful of faithful servants. Develop teams at every level of the ministry, and watch the explosion of maturity and development occur all around you.

Six, we need to unite with like hearts and minds in interdependent partnerships of true "parish" ministry. When we acknowledge together that we are called to build up the body of Christ within our community more than being called to build up one single congregation, we will be freed up to serve the common mission of the church. We desperately need one another to fulfill the Great Commission through living out the Great Commandment. Don't even attempt to reach every person on your own—it can't be done. Link arms and hands and hearts and voices with others outside your church but within your Christian faith to impact your region together.

Seven, endure the seasons of ministry and hang in there for the long haul. You earn the right to lead others when you prove to them that you truly care about their best interests and are willing to stick it out through thick and thin. It usually takes about three years for a pastor and team to be accepted, recognized, and blessed as the leadership core of the church. Once the blessing of the congregation has been received, then the fruitfulness of the ministry is multiplied. An apple doesn't grow overnight; it ripens over time.

Eight, we need to be patient and loving with each other as brothers and sisters in Chirst. Some of us in the body have greater disabilities to work through and are hurting more than others. Others are dealing with personal pain beyond comprehension. Still others are coping with disappointment, discouragement, and disillusionment. Whatever issues we may be facing in life, the worst we can do is live in isolation. The need for healthy, loving community-building is growing right before our eyes. Let's respond in ways that honor the Lord and uphold the family of faith.

Finally, lots and lots of creative efforts of evangelism are needed to meet the spiritual hunger in the people of our day. The Christian church has the best answer for those who hunger and thirst—Jesus. We present Jesus through the loving overflow of our lives. If the life-changing message of Jesus is to be shared with others, it must come out of a genuine-hearted believer. The pages of our history are being written right before our eyes. Will we be faithful to the task and creative in our approach, or will we settle with how it has been done in the past and possibly lose out on the greatest opportunity for the gospel in the history of humankind? It's up to us to pursue health and vitality and then, out of the overflow of our experience with God, give his love away to all. May it be so in our generation.

Lord, we walk today with our own shortcomings. We are dependent on you for daily strength and mercy. We long for healthy attitudes about you, your world, your people, and all you have died to save. We look to you for guidance in assisting one another as members of your body, the church, throughout the process of becoming a healthy church. Renew within us today a hopefulness for our generation that includes both the maturing of your church and effective outreach to the unbelievers in our midst. You are writing the pages of our history and have charted the pathway for our journey. Reveal your will to us now and in the days to come, and we will thank and praise you for the joy of loving and serving you for such a time as this. With a heart of love and gratitude and for Jesus' sake, we pray. Amen.

■■■■ IMPLEMENTING THE TEN CHARACTERISTICS ■■■■

After each chapter, I have suggested questions for discussion for your church leadership team and your congregation. These questions are a great place to begin implementing the ten characteristics in your church.

If you would like to deepen this dialogue and determine together how to execute this philosophy of ministry, you will want Vision New England's *Ten Characteristics of a Healthy Church Leadership Team Discussion Tool.* This tool is designed for team processing of the information in this book and will give you insight into four basic questions about each characteristic:

1. How highly do we value this characteristic?
2. How well are we implementing this characteristic?
3. Regarding this characteristic, where do we want to be in the future?
4. What is our plan for fulfilling our goals for this characteristic?

We have discovered that churches using this tool on a regular basis, during retreats and special meetings, have begun to understand God's unique design for their ministry and have developed strategies that reflect their calling and giftedness for service. For more information about the Leadership Team Discussion Tool or other healthy church resources, contact us:

Vision New England
468 Great Road
Acton, MA 01720
Phone: 978-929-9800
Fax: 978-929-9898
E-mail: info@vision4ne.org
Website: www.vision4ne.org

Afterword

I came to New England as a young pastor more than twenty-five years ago. Frankly, had I known all the scuttlebutt about the apparent impossibility of successful ministry in most parts of the Northeast, I fear I would have been intimidated and stayed away.

"New England is the graveyard of pastors," one once heard over and over again. "New England is a burned-out area; churches can't grow here." "It might happen in Florida, but it will never happen here." A quarter for every time I heard those comments would have made me a rich man by now.

Well, here I am more than twenty-five years later. I admit I have accumulated scars, stories, and a list of aborted ministry scenarios that prove ministry is tough here, perhaps tougher than any other part of the United States. Indeed, I've seen leaders who felt they failed here go on to other parts of the country and enjoy remarkable success. I've seen leaders who were remarkable successes in other parts of the country come here and, after a few years, leave feeling a total failure. Go figure!

Virtually every well-known ministry in the country has come here and put on conferences and seminars anticipating that they would change us. And, true, almost all of them have been helpful in one way or another. But almost none of them, speakers and programmers, ever understood the uniqueness of the culture of the Northeast, which more resembles Europe, I believe, than other parts of America.

Here weather is harsh and unpredictable, property is scarce and wildly expensive. A secularity pervades community life and often results in the use of every kind of regulatory initiative to impede a church's life and growth. New England people are very "town conscious" and come from a culture that is town-meeting oriented. Remember the hidden character in the town meetings of the Bob Newhart show? Periodically, the gravelly voice would sound out, "I disagree!" We all think we know that person. Third row, left-hand side of the sanctuary.

New Englanders like to hold leaders under suspicion, tend to distrust anything that gets too big and out of their personal scrutiny. They are suspicious of things that happen west of the Hudson River—especially in California and Texas. Outsiders call this snobbery; we like to think of it as the wisdom of the ages.

We are a region that once knew revival and awakening; then outrageous heresy. We are known for an almost idolatrous worship of intellectualism and independence. Sectarianism is deeply entrenched in ethnic identities; family networks are tight, and therefore change is difficult.

But we are a region that is also the idea center of the world. More world leaders in business and government are trained in our region than any other place. Our influence in Washington is enormous. What happens in this six-state area can leverage the world. And has!

What does all of this mean for the church? Unfortunately, sometimes regional culture seeps into the church and affects its spiritual culture. That's why we evangelicals have struggled with a history of ecclesiastical independence and isolationism. It's why church divisions have seemed almost a way of life, why change in our small world comes slowly and painfully, why many good young pastors have left the region in tears.

And yet, having said all this, I love New England, and I love New Englanders. These are my people, and this is my soil. Some of my ancestors walked the main street (a path then) of my town of Lexington, Massachusetts, in 1640. The place is in my blood. And I believe God has some powerful purposes for New England just ahead.

I have painted this gloomy picture because I want you to know that all this is changing. That has been the joy of my twenty-five years or so here in the Northeast. I have been treated to the vista of God's renewing Spirit changing the church. Leaders have come together to pray, to talk, to share ideas. Churches are learning from one another. Congregations are beginning to look beyond their politics and ask how they can reach, serve, and connect with their communities.

If there is a catalyst to this spiritual renaissance in New England it is the annual Vision New England Congress, at which almost ten thousand people gather at the end of January for three days of worship, teaching, and learning. I remember when Congress was fortunate to gather a few hundred. We "old guys" are astounded at the thousands who now register months in advance, lay everything aside for those days, and gobble up everything they can from the resource people who staff that conference. I don't know of anything like it in the country.

How has this happened? The answer lies largely in what Steve Macchia has told you in this book. He's dealt with ministry principles which are as old as church history. They are not necessarily the new techniques of organizational development we are reading about in books streaming out of publishing houses today. They are not the observations of psychologists, managers, and consultants. Rather, they are the accumulated experiences of scores of pastors of different denominations and traditions who have "stuck to their knitting" and found that perseverance and faithfulness are rewarded by God. I have met most of the men and women Macchia quotes in this book. What they have said is not trivial or idealistic speculation. They've been working at it, and the results are now in. The church in New England is coming alive all over the place because these principles are being carried out.

The Holy Spirit is anointing the work of faithful people; new churches are being planted every week; godly people are gaining a burden for reconciliation across racial, gender, and generational lines. Young adults are gathering for praise, for missions projects, for intercessory prayer.

This is not my father's New England—a place where pastors gave up in despair. This is my son's New England—a place where the sky's the limit as the church proclaims the gospel to a region increasingly open to a biblical perspective on reality. If you've read this book carefully, you'll know why it's happening and what the church is doing about it. Quite probably, what we've learned here can be done anywhere—even in Texas and California.

—Gordon MacDonald

Appendix

Ministry Platform of Vision New England

Restore to me the joy of your salvation
and grant me a willing spirit, to sustain me.
Then I will teach transgressors your ways,
and sinners will turn back to you.

Psalm 51:12–13

Ministry Platform

Affirmation of Faith

Vision

Core Beliefs

Core Values

Mission

Philosophy

Strategy

Ministries

Ministry Profile

Affirmation of Faith

We affirm . . .

1. The Bible to be the inspired, the only infallible, authoritative Word of God.
2. There is one God, eternally existent in three persons: Father, Son, and Holy Spirit.
3. The deity of our Lord Jesus Christ, his virgin birth, his sinless life, his miracles, his vicarious and atoning death through his shed

blood, his bodily resurrection, his ascension to the right hand of the Father, and his personal return in power and glory.

4. That for the salvation of lost and sinful man, regeneration by the Holy Spirit is absolutely essential.
5. The present ministry of the Holy Spirit, by whose indwelling the Christian is enabled to live a godly life.
6. The resurrection of both the saved and the lost; they that are saved unto the resurrection of life, and they that are lost unto the resurrection of damnation.
7. The spiritual unity of believers in our Lord Jesus Christ.

Vision

Our vision is to see God restore in New England the joy of his salvation, by creating a future in which . . .

- every church is healthy and vital.
- every Christian is involved in everyday evangelism.
- every people group is reached with the gospel.

Core Beliefs

We believe . . .

1. All people need a personal relationship with Jesus Christ as Savior and Lord.
2. Every person is valued and loved by God and so must be valued and loved by us.
3. The Word of God is the primary tool for evangelism.
4. Local churches working with one another are God's agents for effective evangelism.
5. There is no one way to evangelize. Through multiple contacts and a variety of methods Christians can sensitively reach all people.
6. It is the role of every Christian to proclaim the Good News of salvation and the role of the Holy Spirit to convict and convert sinners.
7. Prayer is requisite to effectiveness and will undergird all we do.

Further, we believe God has equipped his people with all that is needed to reach New England for Christ. Vision New England functions to bring people and resources together to lift up Christ, to unite and encourage the church, and to help every Christian joyfully share the gospel.

Core Values

We value . . .

Vision New England is an interdependent network of individual Christians and local churches who are committed to evangelizing New England. We value the process of developing healthy churches throughout our region.

We assert that a healthy church is prayerful in all of the following aspects of church life and ministry, is reliant upon God's power and the authority of his Word, and values:

1. God's Empowering Presence
2. God-Exalting Worship
3. Spiritual Disciplines
4. Learning and Growing in Community
5. A Commitment to Loving, Caring Relationships
6. Servant-Leadership Development
7. An Outward Focus: evangelism, social concern, and international missions
8. Wise Administration and Accountability
9. Networking with the Body of Christ
10. Stewardship and Generosity

Mission

Our mission is to grow strong and vital churches in every community in order to transform New England for Christ. To that end we will serve and enhance the local church through . . .

- An outward focus: equipping Christians in everyday evangelism.
- Servant-leadership development: equipping church leaders to respond more effectively to the challenges facing today's church.
- Networking with the body of Christ: providing relational networks, training events, and ministry resources for local church life and outreach.

Philosophy

Our passion is to see New England transformed for Jesus Christ. To that end we will strive to be an excellent resource for equipping Christians in everyday evangelism, developing effective leaders, and growing a network of healthy churches.

We will . . .

- maintain an unqualified commitment to the local church.
- work with the local church to empower leaders and teams of leaders.
- lovingly work with and challenge one another.
- tirelessly pursue excellence.
- encourage creativity and freedom.
- operate as a body, a team.
- be proactive and affirming.
- provide urgent forward movement to renew joy in everyday evangelism.
- unite believers from diverse backgrounds.

Strategy

Our strategy is to invest our personnel and ministries in aggressively assisting individuals and local churches who embrace the goal of becoming a healthy church. The health and vitality of these churches will be assessed according to the ten characteristics of a healthy church stated in our core values.

While we assist many churches in developing the ten characteristics of a healthy church, our current focus is on three values best suited to our strengths and opportunities for service:

- An outward focus
- Servant-leadership development
- Networking with the body of Christ

All of our training, networking, and outreach ministries will be available to local churches and individuals in our association. However, our priority will be those churches most receptive to becoming healthy vessels of effective ministry in our region.

Ministries

Our current ministry is to be a resource for equipping Christians in everyday evangelism, developing effective leaders, and growing a network of healthy churches through . . .

Outward Focus
- Becoming a Contagious Christian seminars
- Celebrate Jesus 2000
- Project One
- Deaf ministries
- Ministries with the disabled
- Prison ministries
- Prison family ministries
- Recovery ministries
- Care ministries
- Urban Youth Ministry Initiative

Servant-Leadership Development
- Church leadership services
- Church leadership seminars
- Pastoral mentoring
- Pastors' wives network
- Christian education ministries
- Network of youth workers
- Church planters network
- Men's ministries
- Women's ministries
- Family builders ministries
- Worship renewal ministries

Networking Ministries
- Annual Congress
- Equip: church ministries and Christian education convention
- Interdependent Church Network
- Leadership conferences
- Pastors' prayer summits

Ministry Profile

Vision New England (formerly known as the Evangelistic Association of New England):

- Founded in 1887
- Serving five thousand congregations from eighty denominations in all six New England states
- Over 1,100 member churches in the Interdependent Church Network
- Training over twelve thousand Christians annually in conferences and seminars
- Member in good standing with the Evangelical Council for Financial Accountability since 1987
- Annual reports, ministry brochures, and audited financial statements available upon written request:

Vision New England
468 Great Road
Acton, MA 01720-4102
Tel: 978-929-9800
Fax: 978-929-9898
info@VisionNewEngland.org
Website:VisionNewEngland.com

Notes

Chapter 2: God's Empowering Presence

1. William Barclay, *The Letters to the Galatians and Ephesians, The Daily Study Bible Series* (Philadelphia: Westminster Press, 1976), 50.

Chapter 3: God-Exalting Worship

1. A. W. Tozer, *Whatever Happened to Worship?* (Camp Hill, Pa.: Christian Publications, 1985), 26.

Chapter 4: Spiritual Disciplines

1. Peter Marshall, *Mr. Jones, Meet the Master* (Grand Rapids: Revell, 1982), 147–58.

2. Reuben P. Job, *A Guide to Retreat for All God's Shepherds* (Nashville: Abingdon Press, 1994), 87.

3. Ibid., 90.

4. *"The Door* Interview: Dallas Willard," *The Door* (May/June 1993), 15.

5. Henri Nouwen, *Making All Things New* (San Francisco: HarperSanFrancisco, 1981), 71.

6. Janet Ruffing, "Resisting the Demon of Busyness," in *Spiritual Life* (Summer 1995), 81.

7. Nouwen, *Making All Things New,* 72–73.

8. Richard Foster, *Celebration of Discipline* (New York: Harper & Row, 1978), 86.

9. Nouwen, *Making All Things New,* 56–57.

10. Thomas à Kempis, *The Imitation of Christ* (New York: Pyramid Publishers, 1967), chap. 20.

11. Foster, *Celebration of Discipline,* 1.

Chapter 5: Learning and Growing in Community

1. Robert E. Coleman, *The Master Plan of Evangelism* (Grand Rapids: Revell, 1979), summary of eight main chapter headings.

2. Robert Fulghum, *All I Really Need to Know I Learned in Kindergarten* (New York: Ivy Books, 1988), 4–5.

Chapter 6: A Commitment to Loving and Caring Relationships

1. American Psychiatric Association, *Diagnostic and Statistical Manual of Mental Disorders,* 3d ed., rev. (Washington, D.C.: American Psychiatric Association, 1987), 349.

2. Donald Capps, *The Depleted Self: Sin in a Narcissistic Age* (Minneapolis: Fortress Press, 1993), 14–15.

3. Research conducted by New England Research Project, jointly sponsored by Vision New England, Burlington, Mass., and Gordon-Conwell Theological Seminary, South Hamilton, Mass. Full report of findings available: Vision New England, 279 Cambridge Street, Burlington, MA 01803.

4. Dolores Curran, *Traits of a Healthy Family* (Minneapolis: Winston Press, 1983), 31.

5. Norman Wright, *Communication: Key to Your Marriage* (Ventura, Calif.: Regal Books, 1985), 52.

6. John Powell, *Why Am I Afraid to Tell You Who I Am?*, rev. ed. (Allen, Tex.: Tabor Publishing, 1990).

7. Charles Swindoll, *Dropping Your Guard* (Waco, Tex.: Word, 1983), 103.

Chapter 7: Servant-Leadership Development

1. Michael Youssef, *The Leadership Style of Jesus* (Colorado Springs: Victor, 1986), 35–36, emphasis added.

2. Max De Pree, *Leadership Is an Art* (New York: Doubleday, 1989), 10.

3. Henri Nouwen, *In the Name of Jesus* (New York: Crossroad Publications, 1989), 61–62.

4. Ed Dayton and Ted Engstrom, "Followership," in *Christian Leadership Letter*, (September 1986).

5. Robert Clinton, *The Making of a Leader* (Colorado Springs: NavPress, 1988), 180.

6. J. Oswald Sanders, *Spiritual Leadership* (Chicago: Moody, 1980), 93.

7. Howard Hendricks and Bruce Cook, *Leading the Way* Workbook from video kit (Atlanta, Ga.: Walk Thru the Bible Ministries, 1987), 10.

8. John W. Gardner, *On Leadership* (New York: Free Press, 1990), summarized from 11–22.

9. Youseff, *Leadership Style of Jesus*, 163.

10. Nouwen, *In the Name of Jesus*, 71–73.

Chapter 8: An Outward Focus

1. Copyright 1998 by Barry Corey. All rights reserved. Used by permission.

2. Michael Green, *Evangelism through the Local Church* (Nashville: Oliver Nelson, 1990), 8–9.

3. Bill Hybels and Mark Mittelberg, *Becoming a Contagious Christian* (Grand Rapids: Zondervan, 1994), summarized from Participant's Guide, 13.

4. Green, *Evangelism through the Local Church*, 385.

5. For more information about the multiple ministries of Vision New England, send inquiries to: 279 Cambridge Street, Burlington, MA 01803.

Chapter 9: Wise Administraton and Accountability

1. Max De Pree, *Leadership Is an Art* (New York: Doubleday, 1989), 9.

2. Hannah Whitall Smith, *The Christian's Secret of a Happy Life*, rev. ed. (Springdale, Pa.: Whitaker House, 1983), 130.

Chapter 10: Networking with the Body of Christ

1. Tim Stafford, "God's Missionary to Us," *Christianity Today* (December 9, 1996), 29.

2. Ibid., 29–30.

3. Clive Calver and Rob Warner, *Together We Stand* (London: Hodder and Stoughton, 1996), 6, 7, 9.

4. Ibid., outline summarized from 51–58.

5. Ted Haggard, *Primary Purpose* (Orlando: Creation House, 1995), 176.

Chapter 11: Stewardship and Generosity

1. For more information about ECFA, write: P.O. Box 17456, Washington, D.C. 20041-0456. Paul D. Nelson, President.

2. Dan Shaughnessy, "With a Block and a Prayer," *Boston Globe Magazine* (September 15, 1996), 17.

3. George Beverly Shea, "I'd Rather Have Jesus," Chancel Music, Inc., 1966.

4. William Barclay, *The Gospel of Matthew*, vol. 2 The Daily Study Bible Series (Philadelphia: Westminster Press, 1975).

5. Shel Silverstein, *Where the Sidewalk Ends* (New York: HarperCollins, 1974), 35.

6. For more information about CSA, write: P.O. Box 07747, 3195 S. Superior Street, Milwaukee, WI 53207. Brian Kluth, President.

Selected Bibliography and Strategic Planning Resources

Prayer and Scripture

Blackaby, Henry T., and Claude V. King. *Experiencing God*. Nashville: Broadman and Holman, 1994.

Foster, Richard J. *Prayer: Finding the Heart's True Home*. San Francisco: HarperSanFrancisco, 1992.

Manning, Brennan. *Abba's Child: The Cry of the Heart for Intimate Belonging*. Colorado Springs: NavPress, 1994.

Nouwen, Henri J. M. *Making All Things New: An Invitation to the Spiritual Life*. San Francisco: HarperSanFrancisco, 1981.

God's Empowering Presence

Fee, Gordon D. *God's Empowering Presence: The Holy Spirit in the Letters of Paul*. Peabody, Mass.: Hendrickson, 1994.

Graham, Billy. *The Holy Spirit: Activating God's Power in Your Life*. Dallas: Word, 1978.

Nathan, Rich, and Ken Wilson. *Empowered Evangelicals: Bringing Together the Best of the Evangelical and Charismatic Worlds*. Ann Arbor: Vine Books, 1995.

Packer, J. I. *Keep in Step with the Spirit*. Grand Rapids: Revell, 1984.

Sproul, R. C. *The Mystery of the Holy Spirit*. Wheaton: Tyndale House, 1990.

Wagner, C. Peter. *Your Spiritual Gifts Can Help Your Church Grow: How to Find Your Gifts and Use Them to Bless Others*. 1979. Reprint, Ventura, Calif.: Regal, 1994.

God-Exalting Worship

Dawn, Marva J. *Reaching Out without Dumbing Down: A Theology of Worship for the Turn-of-the-Century Culture.* Grand Rapids: Eerdmans, 1995.

Garlington, Joseph L. *Worship: The Pattern of Things in Heaven.* Shippensburg, Pa.: Destiny Image Publishers, 1997.

Morgenthaler, Sally. *Worship Evangelism: Inviting Unbelievers into the Presence of God.* Grand Rapids: Zondervan, 1995.

Tozer, A. W. *Whatever Happened to Worship? A Call to True Worship.* Edited by Gerald B. Smith. Camp Hill, Pa.: Christian Publications, 1985.

Webber, Robert E. *Worship Is a Verb: Eight Principles for Transforming Worship.* 2d ed. Peabody, Mass.: Hendrickson Publishers, 1992.

Spiritual Disciplines

Foster, Richard J. *Celebration of Discipline: The Path to Spiritual Growth.* Rev. ed. San Francisco: HarperSanFrancisco, 1988.

Job, Reuben P., and Norman Shawchuck. *A Guide to Prayer for All God's People.* Nashville: Upper Room Books, 1990.

MacDonald, Gordon. *Restoring Your Spiritual Passion.* Nashville: Oliver Nelson, 1986.

Peace, Richard. *Spiritual Journaling: Recording Your Journey toward God.* Colorado Springs: NavPress, 1995.

———. *Spiritual Storytelling: Discovering and Sharing Your Spiritual Autobiography.* Colorado Springs: NavPress, 1996.

Thomas à Kempis. *The Imitation of Christ.* Edited by Paul M. Bechtel. Chicago: Moody, 1980.

Whitney, Donald S. *Spiritual Disciplines for the Christian Life.* Colorado Springs: NavPress, 1991.

Willard, Dallas. *The Spirit of the Disciplines: Understanding How God Changes Lives.* San Francisco: HarperSanFrancisco, 1988.

Learning and Growing in Community

Barker, Steve, Judy Johnson, Rob Malone, Ron Nicholas, and Doug Whallon, eds. *Good Things Come in Small Groups: The Dynamics of Good Group Life.* Downers Grove, Ill.: InterVarsity Press, 1985.

Clark, Robert E., Lin Johnson, and Allyn K. Sloat, eds. *Christian Education: Foundations for the Future.* Chicago: Moody, 1991.

Dawn, Marva J. *Is It a Lost Cause? Having the Heart of God for the Church's Children*. Grand Rapids: Eerdmans, 1997.

Finzel, Hans. *Unlocking the Scriptures: A Fresh, New Look at Inductive Bible Study*. Colorado Springs: Victor, 1986.

A Commitment to Loving and Caring Relationships

James, Fairfield. *When You Don't Agree: A Guide to Resolving Marriage and Family Conflicts*. Scottdale, Pa.: Herald Press, 1977.

Komp, Diane M. *A Window to Heaven: When Children See Life in Death*. Grand Rapids: Zondervan, 1992.

Smedes, Lewis B. *Forgive and Forget: Healing the Hurts We Don't Deserve*. New York: Harper & Row, 1984.

Tournier, Paul. *To Understand Each Other*. Translated by John S. Gilmor. Geneva: Editions Labor et Fides, 1962. Reprint, Atlanta: John Knox Press, 1976.

White, Jerry and Mary. *Friends and Friendship: The Secrets of Drawing Closer*. Colorado Springs: NavPress, 1982.

Servant-Leadership Development

Barna, George. *The Power of Vision*. Ventura, Calif.: Regal Books, 1992.

Clinton, Robert J. *The Making of a Leader: Recognizing the Lessons and Stages of Leadership Development*. Colorado Springs: NavPress, 1988.

Covey, Stephen R. *Principle-Centered Leadership*. New York: Summit Books, 1990.

De Pree, Max. *Leadership Is an Art*. New York: Doubleday, 1989.

Ford, Leighton. *Transforming Leadership: Jesus' Way of Creating Vision, Shaping Values and Empowering Change*. Downers Grove, Ill.: Inter-Varsity Press, 1991.

Greenleaf, Robert K. *Servant Leadership: A Journey into the Nature of Legitimate Power and Greatness*. New York: Paulist Press, 1977.

Katzenbach, Jon R., and Douglas K. Smith. *The Wisdom of Teams: Creating the High Performance Organization*. New York: Harper Business, 1993.

Nouwen, Henri J. M. *In the Name of Jesus: Reflections on Christian Leadership*. New York: Crossroad, 1989.

Sanders, Oswald J. *Spiritual Leadership*. Rev. ed. Chicago: Moody, 1980.

Youssef, Michael. *The Leadership Style of Jesus: How to Develop the Leadership Qualities of the Good Shepherd*. Colorado Springs: Victor Books, 1986.

An Outward Focus

Borthwick, Paul. *A Mind for Missions: 10 Ways to Build Your World Vision.* Colorado Springs: NavPress, 1987.

Green, Michael. *Evangelism through the Local Church: A Comprehensive Guide to All Aspects of Evangelism.* Nashville: Oliver Nelson, 1992.

Hybels, Bill, and Mark Mittelberg. *Becoming a Contagious Christian.* Grand Rapids: Zondervan, 1994.

Stott, John. *Being a Responsible Christian in a Non-Christian Society.* Vol. 1 of *Involvement.* Grand Rapids: Revell, 1984.

———. *Social and Sexual Relationships in the Modern World.* Vol. 2 of *Involvement.* Grand Rapids: Revell, 1984.

Telford, Tom, with Lois Shaw. *Missions in the 21st Century: Getting Your Church into the Game.* Wheaton, Ill.: Harold Shaw Publishers, 1998.

Wise Administration and Accountability

Campbell, Thomas C., and Gary B. Reierson. *The Gift of Administration: Theological Bases for Ministry.* Philadelphia: Westminster Press, 1981.

Thompson, Robert. R., and Gerald R. Thompson. *Organizing for Accountability: How to Avoid Crisis in Your Nonprofit Ministry.* Wheaton, Ill.: Harold Shaw Publishers, 1991.

Warren, Rick. *The Purpose Driven Church: Growth Without Compromising Your Message and Mission.* Grand Rapids: Zondervan, 1995.

Willow Creek Community Church. *Church Leaders Handbook.* 4th ed. Paul Braoudakis, ed. Barrington, Ill.: Willow Creek Association, 1997.

Networking with the Body of Christ

Bryant, David. *Stand in the Gap: How to Prepare for the Coming World Revival.* Ventura, Calif.: Regal, 1997.

Calver, Clive, and Rob Warner. *Together We Stand.* London: Hodder and Stoughton, 1996.

Haggard, Ted. *Primary Purpose: Making It Hard for People to Go to Hell from Your City.* Lake Mary, Fla.: Creation House, 1995.

Haggard, Ted, and Jack Hayford, eds. *Loving Your City into the Kingdom: City-Reaching Strategies for a 21st Century Revival.* Ventura, Calif.: Gospel Light, 1997.

Stewardship and Generosity

Blue, Ron. *Master Your Giving: Discovering the Freedom of Generous Living.* Grand Rapids: Zondervan, 1997.

Christian Stewardship Association, Milwaukee, WI. Brian Kluth, President.

Crown Ministries, 530 Crown Oak Center Drive, Longwood, FL, 32750-6758

Dayton, Howard. *Your Money Counts: The Biblical Guide to Earning, Spending, Saving, Investing, Giving, and Getting out of Debt.* Longwood, Fla.: Crown Ministries, 1996.

Evangelical Council for Financial Accountability, Washington, D.C. Paul D. Nelson, President.

Strategic Planning Resources

ASAE's *Long-Range Planning Information Background Kit.* Washington, D.C.: American Society of Association Executives, 1993. Write to ASAE, 1575 Eye Street, N.W., Washington, D.C. 20005.

Barry, Bryan W. *Strategic Planning Workbook for Nonprofit Organizations.* Rev. ed. Saint Paul, Minn.: Amherst H. Wilder Foundation, 1997.

Below, Patrick J., George L. Morrisey, and Betty L. Acomb. *The Executive Guide to Strategic Planning.* San Francisco: Jossey-Bass Publishers, 1987.

Drucker, Peter F. *The Five Most Important Questions You Will Ever Ask about Your Nonprofit Organization.* San Francisco: Jossey-Bass Publishers, 1993. Request both the Participant's Workbook and User Guide.

Oswald, Roy M., and Robert E. Friedrich. *Discerning Your Congregation's Future: A Strategic and Spiritual Approach.* Bethesda, Md.: Alban Institute, 1996.

Vision New England's *Guide to Effective Church Planning.* 468 Great Road, Acton, MA 01720. Attn: Church Leadership Services.

Rev. Stephen A. Macchia is founding president of Leadership Transformations, Inc. (LTI), a ministry serving the spiritual formation needs of leaders in churches and ministries nationwide. Until 2003 he served as president of Vision New England, the largest regional church renewal association in the country. He was part of the pastoral staff of Grace Chapel in Lexington, Massachusetts, and is on the executive committee of the National Association of Evangelicals (NAE).

Additional resources relating to the topic of this book may be found on Leadership Transformations' website at:
www.LeadershipTransformations.org or www.healthychurch.net
These resources include:

Ten Characteristics of a Healthy Church Brochure (available in English and Spanish)
Leadership Team Discussion Tool
Healthy Church Visitation Survey and Results Summary
Church Attitude Surveys and Executive Summaries
SMART Goals Worksheet
Weekly and Monthly Staff Report Forms
Annual Performance Review Forms
Guide to Effective Church Planning
Ministry Resource Catalog
Training Seminars
Annual Congress, Equip, and Leadership Conferences
Vision New England Staff and Ministry Services
Evangelistic Outreach Ministry Resources